Plots and Powers

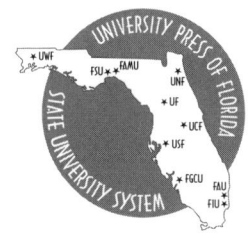

Florida A&M University, Tallahassee
Florida Atlantic University, Boca Raton
Florida Gulf Coast University, Ft. Myers
Florida International University, Miami
Florida State University, Tallahassee
University of Central Florida, Orlando
University of Florida, Gainesville
University of North Florida, Jacksonville
University of South Florida, Tampa
University of West Florida, Pensacola

Plots and Powers

Magical Structures in Medieval Narrative

Anne Wilson

University Press of Florida

Gainesville · Tallahassee · Tampa · Boca Raton
Pensacola · Orlando · Miami · Jacksonville · Ft. Myers

Copyright 2001 by Anne Wilson
Printed in the United States of America on acid-free paper
All rights reserved

06 05 04 03 02 01 6 5 4 3 2 1

Library of Congress Cataloging-in-Publication Data
Wilson, Anne, 1934–.
Plots and powers: magical structures in medieval narrative / Anne Wilson.
p. cm.
Includes bibliographical references and index.
ISBN 0-8130-2121-9 (alk. paper)
1. Literature, Medieval—History and criticism. 2. Magic in literature. I. Title.
PN682.M34 W55 2001
809'.9337—dc21   2001027594

The University Press of Florida is the scholarly publishing agency for
the State University System of Florida, comprising Florida A&M University,
Florida Atlantic University, Florida Gulf Coast University, Florida International
University, Florida State University, University of Central Florida, University
of Florida, University of North Florida, University of South Florida,
and University of West Florida.

University Press of Florida
15 Northwest 15th Street
Gainesville, FL 32611–2079
http://www.upf.com

To Nancy and Aidan Chambers, of the Thimble Press,
who rescued my project in its darkest hour.
Without their vision,
the developments of the final ten years
could never have happened.

Contents

List of Charts ix

Preface xi

Questions, Definitions, and Practice 1

Introductory Studies 33

   Part I
      Sir Degarré 34
      Bevis of Hampton 42
      Lanval 47
      The Story of Meriadoc 50

   Part II
      The Basket of Flowers 58
      The Wide, Wide World 61
      Rebecca 65

1. Emaré, Catskin, and Constance: Princesses in Exile and Accused Queens 70

2. The King Lear Stories and Cap o' Rushes 83

3. Cinderella and Other Sovereignty Tales 97

4. Cúroí's Castle and Its Tests 107

5. The Tristan Verse Romances and *The Pursuit of Diarmaid and Gráinne* 117

6. The Hamlet Stories 142

Appendix: Charts 3–21 151

Notes 211

Bibliography 223

Index of Texts 231

Index of the Methodology 233

Charts

Charts in the Text
1. The Horn Plot 18
2. The Ywain Plot 20
22. The Nine Moves of Saxo Grammaticus's Magical Plot 149

Charts in the Appendix
3. The Sovereignty Plot in *Degarré* 152
4. The Sovereignty Plot in *Bevis* 156
5. The Sovereignty Plot in *Lanval* 159
6. The Sovereignty Plot in *Meriadoc* 161
7. Purification in *The Basket of Flowers* 165
8. Purification in *Emaré* 168
9. Purification in *La Manekine* 170
10. Purification in "Penta the Handless" 172
11. The Purification Story in *Vita Offae Primi* 174
12. The "Peau d'Anon" Plot 176
13. The King Lear Judgment in Eight Texts Compared 178
14. *Roswall and Lillian* and "The Goose-Girl" Compared 182
15. The Porkington and Percy Versions of the Carl of Carlisle Tale 186
16. The Defense Structures in Eilhart's *Tristrant* 190
17. The Defense Structures in Beroul's *Tristran* 194
18. The Cambridge Fragment and *Tristrams saga* Compared 198
19. The Defended Narrative in *The Pursuit of Diarmaid and Gráinne* 202
20. Saxo Grammaticus's Hamlet Plot 204
21. The Plots of Saxo Grammaticus's Hamlet, *Bevis of Hampton*, and *Meriadoc* Compared 208

Preface

So little is understood about nonrational thought that we tend to lack even an awareness of its activity alongside other forms of thought. We know of it only in small glimpses, as neatly packaged theory, usually with a clinical or mystical bias. Literary people, in particular, have still to develop sufficient independent skills so that we can address nonrational thought wherever it appears in texts, just as we would any other kind of thought. This has been a great loss, because nonrational thought has been a wonderful creator of stories, stories having much to tell that we have not heard about elsewhere.

This book is about a number of remarkable narrative texts produced by a hitherto unrecognized system of irrational thinking. We tend to assume that the thought responsible for any narrative is of a kind familiar to us, and, where critics do wish to address the nonrational, the temptation is to conjecture on the basis of our present knowledge rather than study the living thought in the text.

Distinctive logical problems betray the presence of irrational thought, and we ourselves create these when, as critics, we approach texts with prior assumptions. The problems become manageable when we work out appropriate methods of study. The characters and adventures in these narratives are employed for unacknowledged ritual purposes, which have no resemblance to the roles they play in other fictions. Inconsistencies, contradictions, and incongruities arise when we attempt interpretations that assume a rational form of thought; they also arise when authors give us texts in which a ritual narrative of this kind has an overlay of characterization and moral themes.

Few consistent attempts have been made to address these logical problems, obvious and even famous though some of them are, and the difficulty presented by our not identifying the nature of the thought making use of the narrative components has held back our critical analysis. This book describes methods by which we can study these texts in a disciplined, illuminating way.

As the form of thought that has emerged employs magic, operating at a deep level in the texts, the account of my methods includes an explanation—in intellectually rigorous terms—of just what this means at every point. Magic is demystified and given the new, practical definitions that literary people need in order to be able to address this type of thinking when it is responsible for a narrative. When people think in magical terms they invest power in objects and processes, and magical texts contain highly organized structures in which audiences can invest power for particular purposes within the narrative experience.

Superficially, this book may look more like a medievalist study than a larger literary investigation, narrower in interest than it actually is. Medieval narrative texts have provided the best evidence for my subject, but modern works have also been involved. The present book is the final one of four pursuing this line of inquiry, the other three having been milestones along the way that could not give a complete explanation. The subject investigated could not be seen or understood with sufficient clarity until these final stages. The explanation I can now give takes a predominantly fresh set of texts for its demonstration of my methods of study, and it includes classifications, as far as these are possible, of the logical problems I have been concerned with and the nonrational structures I have found in this unusual group of narratives.

My subject may sound rather dry, but it is actually liberating to be able to explore these narratives in terms of the thought that has assembled them. My methods open doors onto an area that can be studied with precision, since the highly organized character of the thought structures under investigation provides some firm guidance. But this subject presents great challenges, and I have no idea how the field will emerge when it is studied more widely. It is fortunate that the thought structures, even where intricate, form clear pictures in the mind and can therefore be considered visually. Visual thinking, as opposed to verbal reasoning, has played an important part in discovery, because it provides a more flexible, fluid dimension to the process of reflection. An unknown type of thought has to be studied by means of building up a picture of its progress through the text, and this requires both close attention at the verbal level and a readiness to discern patterns and regularities, even where they are of an extraordinary kind, apparently making little sense.

It would not be helpful to describe my approach as psychoanalytic criticism, because psychoanalytic critical theory is concerned with the effects of unconscious activity in individual authors, as it is expressed in writing, and in the processes of writing and reading. By contrast, I have found myself concerned with unconscious activity as it takes place beyond the world of authors and their writing—indeed, as it takes place commonly, perhaps universally, in the human mind. Such shared unconscious activity may sometimes appear in a text, giving it widespread appeal and telling us nothing distinctive about the author. Moreover, my focus is primarily on the structure of this raw unconscious activity, rather than on motive or function. Psychoanalytic practice itself is concerned with the raw unconscious, of course—as a discipline that studies the spoken language of human subjects in free association, not as a discipline applied to literary problems in texts—and insofar as I can relate my approach to psychoanalysis, I can do so by saying that I have had to approach the unconscious in a text as if the text were a human subject, alert to how the unconscious might emerge in repetitions, patterns, and rituals. My task of resolving problems in texts has to be addressed by new methods worked out within the disciplines of strictly literary criticism. A familiarity with psychoanalysis helps the critic to work with unconscious thought forms, but its interpretative and therapeutic approaches can be a hindrance. Some critics have even claimed to have found therapeutic material in a medieval narrative text, such as a journey from an Oedipal situation to a status called psychological maturity. I find Oedipal situations too, but I am not concerned with therapeutic interpretations. Such approaches fail to address and illuminate the specific types of unconscious thought structures that are the subject of my work.

The greater part of this book is designed as an introduction, but there is also an introductory section entitled "Questions, Definitions, and Practice," devoted primarily to my definitions and classifications. The many kinds of logical problems I find in relevant texts are set out at the beginning (briefly) and end of the section, and most of the section's first part is concerned with explaining magic. Its second part begins with an explanation of how I have carried out my project, from the initial steps culminating in my first book, *Traditional Romance and Tale*, to the more important later stages, when I crept forward from one text to the next, tracing puzzling logical structures in each and struggling to grasp what these structures were doing there. This account has been asked for by people who want to know how my various publications relate to each other, especially since my views of certain works, particularly *Sir Gawain and the Green Knight,* have changed so radically. The account provides an alternative narrative explanation of my investigation, and it also records how an unusually original project came my way and was carried out.

The section titled "Introductory Studies" that follows uses a mixed group of texts, some of them modern, to demonstrate how I use my methods, concentrating particularly on the kinds of things I notice that lead me to identify a relevant text. Some of these studies explore textual situations that arise when there are two separate levels of thought behind the creation of a text: the presence of the nonrational thought is unacknowledged, and the logical problems created by two levels of thought running counter to each other assist the researcher. Charts are used as visual aids in the case of most studies throughout the book, to show the magical structures I see in each text. (Charts 1 and 2 appear in chapter 1; chart 22 is in chapter 6; and charts 3–21 will be found in the Appendix.)

In the chapters that follow, I show that the thought system I am concerned with does not inherently belong to a type of story, but to a particular text. Of the four Tristan verse romances I study, only two are magical texts; in the case of the other two, the same Tristan narrative has been used by "higher," rational levels of thought. I find the same phenomenon among the Accused Queen texts, where Chaucer's *Man of Law's Tale* is not a magical text, and the King Lear stories are not magical stories, while having an intriguing connection with the Cap o' Rushes tales.

The chapters bring together magical and nonmagical versions using similar narrative material wherever possible, to demonstrate how I distinguish between them. Most of these chapters also have the particular concern to demonstrate two types of plot I have come to know since the publication of my last book *The Magical Quest*. All together, I have now identified three types of magical plot. The first, and only one I knew for many years, is now called the sovereignty plot, and it appears in the present book among the introductory studies and in the Cinderella chapter. The second, the purification plot, appeared first in *The Magical Quest*, in my study of the Apollonius of Tyre texts, and it is exemplified here in my studies of the Accused Queen, Catskin, and Cap o' Rushes texts. The third, the defended plot (which I call the defended narrative), appeared first in *The Magical Quest*, in my study of *Sir Gawain and the Green Knight*, and here it is exemplified in my studies of the Carl of Carlisle and Tristan texts. Since it is a more difficult type of plot, I devote part of my introduction to a detailed explanation.

Shakespeare's *Hamlet* derives ultimately from the Hamlet narrative of Saxo Grammaticus, in his *History of the Danes*, and Saxo's story closely resembles two other medieval stories, *Bevis* and *Meriadoc*, which are included among the introductory studies. The final chapter demonstrates how these three stories relate to each other: all contain magical plots that are both similar and interestingly different. *The Story of Meriadoc*, an attractive and neglected romance, is introduced into Hamlet studies for the first time, and my methods make a fresh contribution to the unresolved debate over Saxo's puzzling text. This investigation of Saxo's narrative is followed by a brief discussion of the play, based on my full study published elsewhere. Shakespeare's play appears to be a remarkable example of the two-tier situation I find in some texts, where two levels of thought coexist, neither knowing about the other. Saxo's magical plot has been retained and overlaid by a great superstructure of themes created by "higher" rational and imaginative writing. Some of the famous problems in the play arise from this situation.

I want to acknowledge the following publishers for permission to reproduce material in this book. Parts of Mildred Leake Day's *The Story of Meriadoc, King of Cambria* were reproduced by permission of Taylor and Francis, Inc./Routledge, Inc; parts of Paul Schach's *The Saga of Tristram and Ísönd* were reproduced by permission of the University of Nebraska Press, copyright 1973; and parts of *Tristan* by Gottfried von Strassburg, translated by A. T. Hatto, copyright 1960 by A. T. Hatto were reproduced by permission of Penguin Books, Ltd.

I am indebted to many people who have helped me to work through to this explanation. Some have given me their attention during my experimental papers and talks at conferences and in English departments, and I must thank these fellow medievalists for their questions and patience. Others have answered questions of my own and given me guidance and encouragement when most needed. My greatest debt is to Professor Maldwyn Mills, professor of English at the University College of Wales, Aberystwyth, who read this book while it was in preparation and advised me over revisions needed and who also directed my attention to *Bevis of Hampton* and to the value of the exile-and-return plan for an understanding of Saxo Grammaticus's Hamlet story. Dr. Hilda Davidson assisted me, too, with my study of Saxo's Hamlet story, giving me her time in Cambridge and sharing with me her understanding of Saxo's characteristics as a writer. Dr. Mildred Leake Day introduced me to *Meriadoc*, and her interest in my endeavor gave me faith that it would at last be understood. When I came to revise my introductory material in 1999 and also reconsider my work in relation to other critical approaches, I was greatly helped by Dr. Frances Wilson at the University of Reading, and also by

John Cummins, who has given much thought to the possible significance of my material and advised me over draft after draft of my rewriting at this stage. As always, what has finally appeared in this book is entirely my own responsibility.

This book owes a debt of a different kind to Elisabeth J. Bik, medievalist and French specialist in Amsterdam, whose enthusiasm for the kind of research I was attempting put heart into me at difficult stages during the preparation of this book. I knew her for two years, between our meeting at the International Arthurian conference in Durham, England, in August 1990, and her death in August 1992. Elisabeth Bik combined imagination with meticulous scholarship to a rare extent, and she was a polymath, bringing to the scholastic scene, so often parochial, a sense of adventure and delight in the sharing of knowledge. My debt to her is not only for all these things: she also provided invaluable criticism while I was trying to find the clearest means of explaining my project, showing me gaps in my explanations and picking out helpful sentences.

A project like mine needs as much moral support as it can find, and here it owes much to my husband, Anthony Wilson, whose insight into what I was trying to do helped the project to take form and develop during many arduous years in the (inevitable) wilderness. He also advised me during my long search for a publisher, as also did Peter Stockham of the Staffs Bookshop in Lichfield, whose efforts led to success. I am grateful to the University Press of Florida for taking this unusual book on and to the readers for UPF, who gave the book careful attention. Sue Bowen gave me excellent professional help with the different stages at the computer, enabling me to submit a manuscript that had rocketed into the modern world from its original typewritten form of ten years ago. The project also owes its very survival to the vision of Nancy and Aidan Chambers of the Thimble Press, who published my second book and several articles and gave formative opportunities and criticism over many years; it is to them that I am dedicating this book.

Questions, Definitions, and Practice

When we study a narrative, we are fundamentally interested in why the characters and events, and all the other details, appear as they do. We are concerned with the thought that created the text, and in the case of a few remarkable narratives a form of thought unknown to us has been involved. It has eluded and teased us, because the methods we bring to our analysis have not been of a kind that could help us to learn about it.

The narrative texts in which I have found this unknown form of thought appear mainly within the genres of romance and folktale. When they appear elsewhere, it tends to be where a narrative has been borrowed, for example, by Shakespeare for a play. They have been the source of some of our most powerful and famous stories and also of some of our best-known literary puzzles.

In our approach to these texts, we need to be liberated from a dependence on the use of a ready-made meaning. We need to be able to use our full skills in textual analysis, tracing the processes of thought that have employed the materials to create the narrative. An essential part of this analysis is learning to notice and address any features that point to the presence of a thought process unacknowledged in the text and taking a course unrelated to either the rest of the text or to anything we might expect to find.

The features that point to the presence of this unacknowledged thought process arise from conflicts between different logical systems: the conflict between the unacknowledged, irrational process and the rational thought in the text and also between the irrational process and our expectations. Texts can contain separate, radically different levels of thought that do not know about each other, and critics tend to approach texts assuming the presence only of rational thought. When we approach an irrational narrative assuming a rational one, the elements can be forced into incorrect relationships with each other, presenting tensions, gaps, and illogicalities because their true relationships bear no resemblance to rational thought patterns. Nevertheless, we tend not to notice these problems or take them seriously; we do not think they signify more than the particular characteristics of certain genres, to which authors remain faithful. Characters behave quite out of character and make inexplicable decisions without there being any comment in the text, and elements contradict each other, again without causing the author concern; incongruities add to the mystery surrounding the narrative and, indeed, seem an essential part of it.

It has been the presence, in certain important works, of an additional level of thought, superimposed by the author on a borrowed story, that has enabled my investigation to proceed past these barriers. If the curious features were no more than a matter of custom belonging to a genre, suitable adjustments could be made without dishonoring an old story, so that the author's purposes and chosen plot created a harmonious whole. But these works revealed a situation where no adjustments were made and two levels of material coexisted, unaware of each other. In some, I found that the author had added moral themes to a narrative that undermined them, taking an opposing course. In others, there were rationalizations and developments that served only to throw up problems elsewhere in the text and emphasize the existence of a separate purpose in the plot. A typical example of the two-tier situation is the uneasy coexistence in a number of medieval texts of two particular themes: a deep irrational theme of the hero's treachery and theft and a lighter, courtly theme of his knightly misdemeanor. Sometimes two separate tiers of thought become inextricably entangled in a passage of writing, the conflict of purposes being so entirely unresolved that the passage makes no sense at all.

Thus it came about that a few texts established the presence of circumstances existing, in one form or another, in a larger number, mainly medieval though occasionally much more recent. Sometimes a text can be fruitfully studied using my methods even though it does not present the characteristic logical problems: it is when the irrational system of thought uses powerful strategies in the course of the narrative that it becomes most obtrusive.

We tend to think of the nonrational in a rational context, while we need also to be able to consider it as having its own processes, untamed by the rational and providing not just subject matter but the thought that has assembled the narrative material to create the text. Thinking is a kind of doing, a process with objectives, taking particular steps towards a conclusion, and it is as various an activity as are any other kinds of doing. Those forms of thought that I call irrational (or nonrational) are concerned with meeting the needs of the personal inner world, and these purposes have made them very different from our reasoning processes and our imaginative thought, where we consciously step into experience other than our own. Psychologists have studied aspects of the irrational, using their specialist skills and data, for their own purposes; while, as literary critics, we may find that we must address aspects of it too, using our specialist skills and the data in the texts, for our particular purposes.

The nonrational thought system with which I have been concerned is highly logical within its own terms and is characterized by clear laws that guide the critic into developing rigorous methods of approach. I have consequently been able to work out methods that create conditions allowing the text to tell me about a thought structure whose existence I cannot predict. A key feature of these methods is the adoption of a position in relation to the text that immediately reveals striking logical structures.

Anyone engaging in such work has to discard all allegiances beyond an allegiance to the text itself. I could not indulge in an allegiance even to my own developing methods: texts might or might not turn out to be relevant to my investigation, and the thought structures I found were peculiar to each individual text. During my journey into my subject, I had to discard my initial theories and adjust continually to changing and developing perspectives. But every critic is indebted to the work of others.

The student of relatively unsophisticated narrative inherits a variety of useful approaches to the text, and among these is the work of Vladimir Propp.[1] He was one of the Russian formalists who were first to see how Ferdinand de Saussure's theory of structural linguistics, delivered in lectures at the University of Geneva between 1906 and 1911, could be applied in disciplines beyond linguistics. Propp studied Russian folktales as structural units: he saw a grammar in the limited types of characters (hero, princess, king, rival or opponent, villain, and helper) and in such recurring actions as the hero's arrival, departure, set of adventures, victory, return home, and reward. This early form of structuralism liberates the critic into seeing patterns and regularities and can thus be a starting point for many kinds of approach to narrative. My own work has had to address structure at a much deeper level.

Could the deeper level be approached through the use of psychoanalytic criticism? I have certainly found psychoanalysis useful, for it has argued that unconscious systems of thought exist, and it has made us familiar with irrational fears and guilt, personal defense systems, Oedipal situations, and other features that I have had to consider in narrative texts. But I have had to go forward from this point, aware of how limited our knowledge still is and of how much a proper study of narrative texts could teach us if we put the consulting room behind us and learned how to address nonrational systems of thought in places where they have to be considered as normal human phenomena, not in need of therapy. Psychoanalysis has had much to say about Shakespeare's Hamlet and his delay, about his inability to act against Claudius because Claudius's crime and marriage seem to be an expression of his own unconscious Oedipal feelings.[2] However, Shakespeare's narrative sources have no theme of delay: Saxo Grammaticus has superimposed a revenge story on material that contains an unconscious plot with quite different concerns. Shakespeare inherited a version where two levels of thought conflict with each other, and the unconscious underlying framework does not provide the concerted advance towards revenge demanded by a true revenge story. So, I argue, Shakespeare found a delay and added, in his own overlay, the theme of lack of resolution.

The myth approach in literary criticism is, like the psychoanalytic approach, concerned with the motives that underlie human behavior. In his essay *Hamlet and Orestes*, Gilbert Murray sees Hamlet, together with the heroes of the Greek plays *Oedipus* and *Agamemnon*, as mythic in origin, in this case as sacrificial figures. In the time of Sophocles and Aeschylus, the sacrifices were no longer performed but were acted out symbolically on stage. Hamlet's role is to deliver the nation by avenging the king and offering up himself as scapegoat for the regicide; his delay arises from his reluctance to accept the role of cathartic agent.[3] Jessie L. Weston similarly finds the ritual of the Dead King restored to life behind the Fisher King in the grail texts; she holds that the grail story was once actually performed (120–21). I have also come to see a ritual character in unconscious narratives, but without using the myth approach and with very different results.

To turn to more widely accepted approaches, literary specialists agree that point of view is an essential aspect of form that must not be misread. A story is presented in a certain way by a narrator who is not the author: the narrator controls what will be told and how it will be perceived. Narratology is the criticism that has addressed these matters in detail, but they have also been a concern of the earlier formalistic approach that came to be called the New Criticism.[4] There is, however, no narrator in an unconscious story; there is no speaker doing something that we have to discover. Instead, there is an essential point of view within the story itself:

the characters seem to be like those of dreams, the products of a train of thought that places characters in various postures as part of its solipsistic concerns; these characters have not been given a point of view. The single point of view needs to be seen as functionally that of the hero or heroine, who is a member of the audience (unconsciously) identified with the narrative and its chief character.

The unconscious narrative has the appearance of a sequence of mental rituals. It is possible that the repeated telling of stories at a deep level of the mind is essential for emotional homeostasis. There is something suggestive of cybernetics, that there may be an automatic process performing a function in the mind almost structural in nature: such stories might be regarded as regular reruns of long-past mental stages or as housekeeping algorithms operating at the edge between things staying the same and things changing.[5]

While I cannot be fundamentally concerned with function, I think there is evidence that the ritual narrative structures I have identified use magic. In order to recognize and study the operation of magic at this deep level, it is essential to have a concept of magic as a system of thought, complete and self-sufficient. Magic makes use of the common stock of material for its own particular purposes, just like any other form of thought; and, in order to study the operation of this thought in a narrative text, we need to address all the details of the text in their relationships with each other, just as we generally do in literary criticism.

It is unfortunate that the word "magic" has to be used to describe the thought concerned, because this word has been so misused, and the subject it refers to is now so little understood outside specialist circles. The subject has been left without a name, while the word wanders about, referring to a great variety of things, and the reason for this has been our reluctance to address ourselves to a vulnerable activity essential to us throughout history. As no fresh term can be used to replace "magic," I shall use the word, providing accompanying definitions and explanations. In this section I shall also relate my particular area of study to the larger field of magic, and, as part of the process of placing my subject, I shall explain, as far as I can, how it relates to myth.

Although the current theories of magic do not include the kind of definitions that are needed by literary critics, I shall begin with these, making particular reference to the excellent attempt by Daniel Lawrence O'Keefe in his work *Stolen Lightning* to give us a general theory of magic, bringing together all the scattered fields of inquiry. While my study of narrative texts has presented somewhat different definitions, and magic altogether has diverse manifestations, O'Keefe's explanatory account and my own nowhere contradict each other: it is therefore possible to provide a quite brief general explanation of magic for those concerned with literature.

Enormous and various as the field of magic is, certain basic principles can nevertheless be identified at its heart, and it is worth risking oversimplification to give these here. The first principle is that magic always has the fundamental purpose of defense: it defends the individual self at the various levels of experience where this self is threatened—whether the self is threatened by situations within the mind or by situations in the external world. The second principle is that magic always aims to make or change something. And the third principle is that magic strengthens the power and control of the individual, fighting helplessness with action.[6]

In a sense, magic is a phenomenon that can make something out of nothing, a fact well known: magic is correctly thought of in terms of producing a rabbit out of a hat. It is also true that it often resorts to aids traditionally invested with power, such as the sacred symbols of religion, but it equally uses quite ordinary resources, invested with power for the occasion. One of our problems with understanding magic is that we cannot easily see what it is making. To use a simple example, we tend to dismiss the rainmaker's magic because it cannot make rain, while the magic is actually designed to create a sense of control, thus dispelling useless, frightening helplessness. The fact that the control is not true in one sense does not affect its having an important truth in another sense.[7]

Magic has vital functions in the mind, as I have just illustrated. Modern remedies still cannot address many of our fears or our irrational guilt, or render us other than ultimately helpless. In fact, history shows that it can be when society and religion reach heights of rationality and intellectualism that magic will erupt in the public scene. The Greek mystery religions and Hellenistic magical theologies—gnosticism and Neoplatonism—are a case in point, and so is the Renaissance resort to Hermeticism, Neoplatonism, astrology, and alchemy, to say nothing of the re-emergence of such cults and theosophies today.[8] It has been argued that the Eleusinian mystery cult met the needs of individuals who felt lost in their changing, urbanized society: the rites involved membership rituals like sacrifice and initiation (put, at Eleusis, to new, more individual uses), and there was an emphasis on purification, redemption, and personal happiness (O'Keefe 532). The magical theologies, meanwhile, provided a magical worldview and also such services as a divination system (527).

These important areas of magic have their interest for literary people, but we need to find a way *inside* the process, so that we can work at the correct, deep level in the mind. It is for this reason that I now turn to psychoanalysis, even though its theory is not directly connected with the concerns of magical narrative, dealing instead with a deeper level and very little convincing evidence. What it does offer is a useful model of unconscious activity that helps us approach the magical narrative: this is a model in which there is a profound, continual construction of a fragile sense of self out of identifications and love involvements and out of barely resolved conflict with the powerful forces of the passions and deeply instilled prohibitions.

In psychoanalysis, it has been argued that the building up of the ego and the defense of this ego's equilibrium and integrity could be regarded as magical processes. The ego is a fragile entity struggling to create some organization in the mind, and it is in dependent relation to the claims of two powerful forces. The first of these is the id, which has no structure at all except a few earthworks thrown up by the ego against the instincts. The second force is the superego, which acts as a shield against the id, strengthening the ego by helping it to transform unconscious drives into thought and action, but which—being a structure prohibiting the fulfillment of wishes—crushes initiative and punishes the ego, causing anxiety (O'Keefe 281–87).

The ego makes itself out of nothing, using other things: it makes itself out of its identifications (a process similar to Mead's mirroring of significant others), its love involvements, and its innumerable collected objects, which it transforms into symbols, tokens by which it can think.[9] Its coherence, meanwhile, depends upon further fabrication: its repression of the id and its transformation of drives into thought and action. This is a continuous, ongoing process, a constant creation of a coherence, which works moderately well, out of quite opposite ingredients—conflicting forces, largely unstructured. Illusion is an important part of the process: only those who make special efforts to do so will be aware of more in their minds than the limited, transformed material present in consciousness. And yet, the unconscious material in the id and the superego is still there and in operation, affecting circumstances not only within the mind but also beyond it.

Psychoanalysis describes unconscious defense mechanisms that are also useful to us. In her list of defense mechanisms, Anna Freud includes repression, projection, and denial; and she also includes "undoing" what has been done (making use of thought or behavior having the opposite meaning), "reversal into the opposite," and "turning against the self," procedures interesting in the light of some of my findings in narrative.[10]

Commenting on "undoing what has been done," Sigmund Freud writes that precautionary measures to prevent an occurrence are rational, while trying to get rid of something by "making it not to have happened" is irrational and in the nature of magic. He calls this technique "blowing away" and regards it as one belonging not only to neurosis but also to popular customs and religious ceremonies. In obsessional neurosis, one action is canceled out by a second, so that it is as though neither action has taken place, whereas in reality both have. Freud sees magic as a defense against psychic death, anxiety being basically a return to helplessness, and helplessness being ego death.[11]

Aspects of public magic that have relevance here are the use of symbolic performances (ritual) and of linguistic symbols (both incantations and single words). The core of an incantation is usually a simple statement of the end that is desired (O'Keefe 40–43). Public magic is rigidly scripted, as this provides certainty that the participants are agreed on what they are saying and doing: agreement is an essential factor in magic. The sources of the scripts are traditional material, mainly borrowings from religion and myth, which give them greater potency.[12] E. E. Evans-Pritchard and Keith Thomas have shown that magical structures have a self-confirming character: they are closed-circuit systems, resisting any onslaught of reason (Evans-Pritchard 475–78; Thomas 767–69).

In public magic, as in private, the magic sets out to be in the service of the individual, building up selfhood, meeting individual needs, and protecting the self against the forces of society.[13] It has been described as "energy struggling against a mould," destined to harden with time into a new mold, becoming alienated from the individual, so that fresh magical energy has to be found. O'Keefe comments, "Magic is man's intimate resource, his personal symbolic power, but ultimately all magic is objectified, belongs to someone else, and confronts us as Other" (201, 322–23). I have referred to the rites of initiation and sacrifice used by Greek mystery cults in new ways to meet people's needs, and these were much concerned with both the birth of the individual and membership. In sacrifice, an individual or congregation offers up a symbol of the personal self to a god that represents the social group. The magic lies in the acknowledgment of a debt, and an origin, and of a total dependence of the personal self on the group. In consequence, individual power is strengthened; the self is symbolically sacrificed and then received back with its charter and right-to-be "strengthened by this renewal at the communal fount."[14]

Magical narratives make provision for audiences to bring about in the mind an enhanced sense of self and to dispel irrational guilt and fear.

They also provide for a sense of safety, enabling audiences to undergo frightening experience of an irrational, inner kind. The world of the magical narrative is primitive, largely unconscious and alien to the rational mind, and its thought patterns are entirely unlike any we expect in narrative. Its sole concern is the feelings of the inner world, and we have to be careful not to slip into thinking of magical narrative as operating on the same level as the concerns of rational thought. Audiences would join in the magical process by personally investing power in the magical structures they found provided in the narrative. The critic, meanwhile, will find a narrative that is very highly organized, there being tighter relationships than is usual between the details, and in a strictly linear sequence. The positions of the details in the text are of great importance.

Every magical narrative is unique, in terms of structure and the problems it presents to the critic. There can be no mechanistic approach, but magic is so highly organized that the study of each text provides a useful model for the study of some that follow. An important point is that a magical text can never be identified by the narrative material it uses: any system of thought can use narrative elements such as magic potions and spells. Moreover, the thought system of magic does not inherently belong to a type of story, but to a particular text. The Tristan verse romances appear very alike, since they all use a similar story, but I find the versions of Eilhart and Beroul magical, while those of Gottfried and *Tristrams saga ok Ísöndar* are not. This means that the roles played by the elements of the Tristan story in the versions of Eilhart and Beroul are astonishingly different from the roles they play in Gottfried and the saga. Magic, for example, is not concerned with character and adventure in any of the usual fictional senses: it uses characters and events to create a sequence of rituals in which the characters are figures, usually without a point of view.

Magic creates a narrative that is a sequence of mental rituals. By this I mean that audiences are offered narrative material organized for a magical engagement, which they may or may not use magically. If they use it magically, they will take part by total identification, engaging in an inner, private performance (this engagement usually at a deeper level than the conscious) and investing power in the devices provided by the narrative. The point of view of this participant using the narrative is the point of view I adopt for analysis. It is the only point of view in the narrative, for there is no distance between the participant and the narrative. I call it the point of view of the hero or heroine, which again refers to the participant (identified with the chief character) rather than to the chief character, who is a figure in the rituals. Much of the magical organization consists in the strategic arrangement of characters and events in repeated ways, performing and unperforming actions, setting up protective structures around actions and using narrative material to make ritual statements. In texts where there is also substantial material created at another level of thought, the effects are remarkable. The separate levels ignore each other and conflict with each other in ways suggesting the author's unawareness of the magical level. Authors add characterization, motivations, and moral themes to a narrative where the characters have no point of view and make no decisions, their function being that they are moved from one ritual position to another. Yet, because the essential factor in the narrative is not the narrative material used but the kind of thought making use of it, the author must be the author of that process, whether he or she introduced it or found it in the sources and re-created it. The author could not have used a system of thought unless his or her own mind had been involved.

So far, I have defined magic as a system of thought and as concerned with inner feelings without reference to the laws of the world beyond the mind; I have also described it as creating highly organized structures, such as rituals, in which participants invest power. Fundamentally, magic is concerned to create a sense of power and control in the mind, with the serious purpose to bring about a desired state of mind. Very far from having trivial aims, it is humankind's ultimate remedy for helplessness and is used a great deal to dispel fear and defend us. The magical process begins with an investment of power in the thing to be employed as an aid—and this investment accompanied by a belief that it will work. The power, meanwhile, is for the benefit of the person making the investment: the entire operation of the magic is in the thought of the user. While magic often makes use of materials already designed for it—and an Anglo-Saxon charm is a useful example here—the magic is the user's own active, creative investment of power, made on the spot, for the immediate use of the power. In fact, magic can make use of all kinds of things and just anything; in narrative, it frequently uses story materials that have not been used magically elsewhere.

Since the actual magical activity takes place in the thought of the participant using the text, the critic can only study narrative structures and consider whether—and how—they might invite an investment of power. We have to be able to think of magic as thought—as active and creative—pursuing a purpose, finding means, investing power in things, believing in the power, and making use of it. Such thought would have created the narrative in the detail in which we find it in the text, and such thought would be engaged in by the participant choosing to make use of the rituals.

Some of the fundamental principles I give here are demonstrated by the Anglo-Saxon metrical charm *Wið Færstice* [Against a sudden pain]. In a study of two Anglo-Saxon charms, L.M.C. Weston shows both the operation of magic in a charm and the kind of difficulty thoughtful critics can have with magical material.[15] Close textual analysis, which can only be touched on here, is used to trace how each charm verbally accomplishes a gathering together of power and then the release of this power. The process is one of preparing the healer for the healing of the patient, who has already arrived for the consultation; it is to empower the healer and effect an entrance into the healing state. Our modern interpretation that the effect would be on the patient, and that there would be healing by the power of suggestion or by the enhancement of positive thinking, is quite incorrect.

L.M.C. Weston's analysis of *Wið Færstice* demonstrates how the power is built up in the first part of the charm and how it is expended in the second part. The elements making clear the precise function of the charm are the diction in the first part and the striking changes in the forms of the verbs throughout the charm. In the first part, there are narrative lines referring to a battle in the past against supernatural foes, in which the healer played an active part. The past tense and stylized, elevated diction distance the curative ritual from the normal present: the healer, speaking the words over an herbal potion and knife (according to the accompanying instructions), becomes a warrior in combat against supernatural foes. He or she is connected with the mythical, and this is by no means the self-mystification that one critic has suggested. The lines of the charm switch back and forth strategically between this ur-battle and imperative injunctions to the agent of pain (addressed as a spear):

Hlude wæran hy, la, hlude,   ða hy ofer þone hlæw ridan,
wæran anmode,   ða hy ofer land ridan.
Scyld ðu ðe nu,   þu ðysne nið   genesan mote.
Ut, lytel spere,   gif her inne sie!
Stod under linde,   under leohtum scylde,
þær ða mihtigan wif   hyra mægen beræddon
and hy gyllende   garas sændan;
ic him oðerne   eft wille sændan,
fleogende flane   forane togeanes.
Ut, lytel spere,   gif hit her inne sy!

Sæt smið,   sloh seax lytel,
* * * iserna,   wundrum swiðe.
Ut, lytel spere,   gif her inne sy!
Syx smiðas sætan,   wælspera worhtan.
Ut, spere,   næs in, spere!
Gif her inne sy   isernes dæl,
hægtessan geweorc,   hit sceal gemyltan.

[Loud were they, lo! loud, when they rode over the hill, / Resolute were they when they rode over the land. / Defend yourself now, so that you may escape from this violence! / Out, little spear, if herein you be! / I stood under the targe, beneath a light shield, / Where the mighty women deliberated on their strength / And screaming spears sent. / I another will send them back / A flying arrow in their faces. / Out, little spear, if herein it be! / The smith sat, forged his little knife, / * * * by an iron hammer beaten out severely, / Out, little spear, if herein you be! / Six smiths sat, making war-spears. / Out, spear, not in, spear! / If herein be any iron, / Work of witches, it shall melt.] (My translation)

In the second half of the charm, the predominant tense shifts to the present, as the charm moves from the evocation of power to its immediate use. In lines using heavy and close repetition, the healer chants that in whichever part of the body the patient has been shot (is in pain), the remedy will now help.

Gif ðu wære on fell scoten   oððe wære on flæsc scoten
oððe wære on blod scoten
oððe wære on lið scoten,   næfre ne sy ðin lif atæsed;
Gif hit wære esa gescot,   oððe hit wære ylfa gescot
oððe hit wære hægtessan gescot,   nu ic wille ðin helpan.
Þis ðe to bote esa gescotes,   ðis ðe to bote ylfa gescotes,
ðis ðe to bote hægtessan gescotes;   ic ðin wille helpan.
Fleoh þær * * * on fyrgenheafde.
Hal westu,   helpe ðin drihten!

[Whether you were shot in the skin, or were shot in the flesh, / Or were shot in the blood, / Or were shot in the limb, never shall your life be harmed! / Whether it were the shot of gods, or it were the shot of elves, / or it were the shot of witches, now I will help you. / This is your remedy for the shot of gods, this is your remedy for the shot of elves, / this is your remedy for the shot of witches: I will help you. / Flee * * * to the mountain-head; / be whole! May the lord help you!]

The healer must then plunge his knife into the potion (which is made up of certain herbs boiled in butter). The chief function of the close repetition in this second part is that it binds anatomy and remedy in the cure.

Previous critics have not addressed this charm as magic. Howell Chickering has suggested that all such charms are dramatic verbal performances "in which the very act of saying creates its own magic" and that we should therefore direct our attention to the rhetorical nature of the charms, to the "goal-directedness of magical gesture, the way it is organized toward a specific result," and not to "its verbal beauty or argumentative organization." While this critic expresses interest in the function of *Wið Færstice,* he finds in this charm a loose oral rhetoric that is concerned with the psychological or psychosomatic effect on the listening patient. As L.M.C. Weston comments, the magical nature of the charm becomes buried, and, as a magician, this critic's healer is a fraud. Meanwhile, another critic's healer is simply a poet: Weston comments that this critic makes an excellent case for the charm's unity and skill, but restricts the influence of magical function to allusions and to determining a bipartite structure of attack and exorcism. Effect is neglected, and thus the poem has been divorced from its existence as a charm.

In the charm we can observe a practical, functional process of thought generating curative power in the mind, and I would add to L.M.C. Weston's comments that, essentially, the healer invests power in the various elements of the charm, powerful though this scripted incantation, with its use of the mythical, must already be felt to be; the healer becomes a partner in the investment. This is a place, too, to emphasize the importance of belief: magic is effective action within the context of belief. Its sphere of effectiveness may be the mind alone, but the mind is a very important place.

The fundamental principles of magic were first brought to my attention by the dreams of the child Martin.[16] In the dreams of Martin, I saw that the prime origin of magic is in the individual mind, not in material handed on by society, and I saw just how it was used to give the user control in the face of helplessness. But, chiefly, I began my journey towards understanding magic as a form of thought. In the dreams, fear conjured up events, over which Martin sought to exert control: in one dream, he chose to use a magic word to reverse his having been beheaded, and in another he used two devices, a primitive identification ritual and a form of imitative magic, to make himself the strongest in the world and give himself impregnable defenses. In the case of the identification ritual, this seven-year-old child touched a king's blood to make himself the strongest in the world: no one had told him that the human race has long invested blood with special power, or that identification rituals of the kind he used in touching the king's blood have been practiced over thousands of years (in one or other symbolic form). The ritual was his own invention: he brought his urgent desire about through using a ritual that sprang to his need from the depths of his mind.

> We got a spear off one of the men [attacking us] and we killed a king who was so powerful that when you touched his blood you would be the strongest in the world; so we touched his blood and so we were the strongest in the world. (Martin, recorded on the morning after his dream)

Martin's strange magic word EMIN is worth more consideration than I have hitherto given it, and I shall quote the relevant part of the dream once again here.

> The girl peeped through a small little door and called us all to come because a man wanted our heads. The boys went into a house and I followed them in. I saw a pair of shoes and a pair of hands and a head. In his hands was an axe, and above the axe, on the wall, was written EM and two letters after that; I called the word EMIN. The man made us vanish and then he took us all and put us on two blocks with our necks over the gap between them. He chopped off our heads, and then he made us come back to life again without any heads. He put our heads back on us and stood us up. There was a line round our necks, but the axe had no blood on it. We walked down the corridor very slowly so that our heads wouldn't fall off. When we were quite far I remembered the magic word EMIN, so I said EMIN to make our heads come back to life again. Then our heads were fixed on again so that we could run back to the place where Daddy had a new car. And then we went home with Daddy. (Martin, recorded on the morning after his dream)

I have two guesses as to the origin of the word EMIN, and they both point to the word's expressing the dreamer himself: his second name was "Emmet" and EM also spells "me" backwards. It is possible that the dreamer conjured up himself in this powerful form so that he could restore himself. The imitative magic used by Martin is also interesting to consider. It was a strong pressing movement made with arms folded, during the construction of a fortress to protect Martin from the enemies attacking him. As each wall and the roof was made, this magical gesture was used. The dreamer acted out this part of his dream as he related it, explaining with great seriousness why he used the pressing movement. It made the construction stronger, and it seems—on analysis—that a feeling of strength was created and invested in the building. I call the pressing movement imitative magic, because, like some forms of magic used in rainmaking, it appears to use a symbolic enactment of what is desired, an enactment invested with a power believed to be transferred. But, in a dream, all that takes place seems at the time to be action while it is really thought, and its subject matter is feelings. Martin was essentially conjuring up the desired feeling, and that was all that was necessary in his dream. He turned to a ritual that expressed his own strength and told himself it had special power; this special power could then be expressed in the fortress.

The relationship apparent in *Wið Færstice* between magic and the mythical may exemplify the most frequent kind of relationship between magic and myth. Mythical material—because of the regard in which it has generally been held—has been liable to be selected by magic as a source of power. We might find a similar use of the mythical in narrative texts. I do not regard myths as being themselves magical by definition. I have not made a systematic investigation anywhere in this field—one reason for this being that I need a wealth of full-length texts, neither abbreviated nor modified for other uses—but I believe that it might prove useful to consider myths in terms of their thought, in a way not unlike my consideration of magic as thought. By doing so, we would see the mythic process as using narrative material like other forms of thought—for its specific (mythic) purposes. Our own, modern myths must be a chief source of information for the nature of myth, both those in the form of literary texts (such as—possibly—*Dr. Jekyll and Mr. Hyde* and *The Lord of the Rings*) and those that are extraliterary and current in society. My impression of myths is that they are narratives by which we live: as C. S. Lewis says, they are stories where we feel, not "Will the hero escape?" but "I shall never escape this." Their usefulness to us is evidently of various kinds; some myths, for example, connect us with the transcendent, while others have been shown by Lévi-Strauss to neutralize the contradictions of existence, allowing people to live with basic dilemmas. Monolithic theories of myth have been attempted, but the category called "myth" includes too wide a range of material for such treatment.[17]

Lévi-Strauss's structuralist work is one of the best-known attempts to study myth. Lévi-Strauss based his analysis on the conviction that, behind all the surface varieties among the myths thrown up by different cultures, there existed deep regularities and patterns, and he argues that we should look beyond the manifest content to the structures of symbolic opposition (which are resolved in the myths). While his work does show that underlying relationships, rather than overt subjects, may be the significant factor in some myths, his methods are somewhat mechanistic compared with mine, which must begin with the individual study of complete texts and proceed by means of the questions they raise. Lévi-Strauss begins with presuppositions about the human mind—that it has consistent structures, such as the polarization of experience, which determine the forms of myths—and the first step in his method is to break down each story into the shortest sentences possible. Anatoly Liberman, in his comparison of the work of Vladimir Propp and Lévi-Strauss, argues that Propp's results are reproducible by anyone, while the relationships seen by Lévi-Strauss are of a kind seen by a poet rather than a scholar. For example, Lévi-Strauss, in his analysis of the Oedipus myth, says that a close relationship exists between a riddle and incest, for the riddle unites two irreconcilable terms, and incest unites two irreconcilable people. Liberman comments,

> The important element is not the creed but the value of the results obtained with its help. Nothing in structuralism guarantees that its practitioners will not produce nonsense. Between the adoption of some principle and the practical results lies method. Only those problems are solved correctly that are solved in a correct way. Many philosophers have thought so ("the way to the truth itself must be of the truth"). If the truth is simply guessed, it is nonverifiable.[18]

This is a principle by which I myself have tried to work.

The account I give of my project in this next part serves also as an introduction to the structures I have found in narrative texts, and it is followed by further attention to definitions in relation to these structures and to my questions.

My research project began in 1971, with some questions I was asking concerning illogicalities I saw in the Middle English texts before me. These questions were not themselves of a kind that could guide my project very far: I needed questions that focused my attention on the dissensions in the text, while, instead, my questions tended to be more general queries relating to illogicalities in the stories. But learning how to ask the most useful questions had to come later, when the project was more advanced, and, meanwhile, my first questions had their usefulness, because they firmly directed my attention to the thought in the texts, suggesting the presence of an unexpected type. Particularly useful was my concern with the illogical decisions frequently made by the characters: I was caught by the contrast between the apparent pointlessness of these decisions and their determined reappearances, and I suspected a hidden activity.

My first attempts to address my questions drew particularly on depth psychology and the study of dreams. While these fields were too distant from my subject and used disciplines inappropriate to literary criticism, this period was far from time wasted. In particular, a remarkable book *L'Imagerie Mentale* by two Swiss psychotherapists, Roger Frétigny and André Virel, gave me a concept of narration taking place at a deep level in the mind. These therapists used the guided daydream with the aim of changing a state of mind, and their patients employed imagery of great power. The study of dreams such as those of Martin also helped to give me this concept. But there was no way forward until I had found appropriate methods for textual study. In September 1972, I took my first step in this direction, once again assisted by my study of dreams.

I decided to try out the notion of there only being a single point of view in the narratives I was investigating. The characters in these narratives seemed to me to be—like those in dreams—the products of a train of thought that placed characters in various postures as part of its solipsistic concerns; such characters would not have been given a point of view. I saw this single point of view as being functionally that of the chief character, with whom members of the audience identified. Later, I was to modify my idea of this point of view a little, when I came to see the narrative as a sequence of rituals used by audiences (in which the chief character was a figure), but experimentation with the notion as it stood had instant, remarkable effects. Using the single point of view directed me to look at the detail in the narrative from a point of view quite different from any of my previous approaches, and, in the case of *King Horn,* above all, an apparently uncouth narrative, often making little sense at all, immediately assembled into a conspicuous structure.[19] This structure was extremely odd, but its organized, step-by-step arrangement could not be dismissed.

The structure was a sequence of strategic arrangements of character and event, all closely related to each other; I saw that characters and events were being repeated in an organized way, there being various kinds of replay of central material, forming a progression, and ending in a successful outcome. While this structure was clearest in *King Horn,* I thought I could see it in other narratives too, and thus the structure I saw in *King Horn* came to serve as a model for further exploration. I show this model

Chart 1. The Horn Plot

1	2
Horn's king father is killed by pirates	Horn is a thrall at King Aylmer's court
Horn is exiled with Fikenild	He is loved by the king's daughter Rymenild
	Fikenild tells the king that Horn will kill the king and marry Rymenild
	Horn is exiled
STEP 1 TO KINGDOM	STEP 2

3	4
Horn is Goodmind at King Thurston's court	Horn returns to King Aylmer's court bolder, wins Rymenild from her suitor and is betrothed
He saves the king from an invader and refuses the reward of the king's daughter and kingdom	He declares his innocence and his plans to win his father's kingdom
FIRST EXORCISM OF FIKENILD'S ACCUSATION (STEP 3)	STEP 4

5	6
Horn recovers his father's kingdom and becomes king	*Horn returns to King Aylmer's court, where Fikenild is threatening the king and seizing Rymenild*
	Horn defeats Fikenild
	He marries Rymenild
STEP 5	SECOND EXORCISM OF FIKENILD'S ACCUSATION

in chart 1, presenting the plot as I would now describe it. In fact, my view of this particular narrative has altered little over the years. What did alter, as I studied more and more texts, was my idea of this model's usefulness, for I discovered important variations and, eventually, two radically different types of plot, which could, moreover, teach me much more than could the King Horn plot. Nevertheless, it was the King Horn plot that gave me my first breakthrough and was to help me do essential exploratory work over the next dozen years.

The squares in the chart represent the "moves," as I called the steps in the structure (a word taken from Vladimir Propp, but describing a quite different, much more frequent, kind of repetition).[20] The detail given in italics is where, as I later came to argue, magic is intensively used in order to deal with fear and guilt. In the early stages I saw only that Horn was being "Goodmind" in his third move (or "Cutbeard") and that, in that changed mood, he saw the "aspect of himself which [wished] his father dead" as a terrifying giant and destroyed it; later, in the sixth move, he was to destroy that "still lurking feeling" again (Wilson, *Traditional Romance and Tale* 61–62). The developments in my understanding of this plot—in particular, my leaving my view of it as dream for a view of it as ritual—came with my examination of much more detailed, informative narrative texts; here it is important only to point out how very highly organized my first model is.

The relationships between the details are what is significant; there is no particular significance in the number of moves (or size of the squares). It can be seen that the action in the first move in italics (move 3) reverses the accusation in the preceding move. Fikenild's accusation (that Horn will kill the king and marry the king's daughter) is reversed in the following move, where Horn saves a king from an invader and turns down the offer of the princess (using the name Goodmind while doing so). There is also a strategic relationship between the two moves in italics (moves 3 and 6). In the first, surrogates are used, while in the second move we find a parallel action using the exact situation: the accusation is reversed using Thurston, and finally it is reversed again using the accuser Fikenild himself and the exact king and princess of the second move (Aylmer and Rymenild). Thus we have a step-by-step relationship between the moves in italics over and above the step-by-step progress to the kingdom that can be seen in the plot. After Horn has played Goodmind, he returns to King Aylmer bolder, speaking of his innocence and plans, and he is betrothed to Rymenild. Then he becomes king, and finally he plays the Goodmind role in the exact place and removes the accuser with the accusation.

Relationships like this cannot be seen to be significant until it is found that they reappear in other plots. The example I give in chart 2 (the Ywain plot) is—typically—different, and yet the same relationships reappear. I do not mean by this that such relationships reappear in this way in all the plots I am concerned with: I have chosen the plot of "The Lady of the Fountain" (as it appears in Chrétien de Troyes's *Yvain*) because it empha-

Chart 2. The Ywain Plot

1	2
At Arthur's court Calogrenant tells of his journey to the Fountain dominion and his fight with its lord Arthur is pleased by this adventure THE MAGIC FORMULA FOR GAINING A DOMINION IS PREPARED	Ywain secretly undertakes the adventure He kills the Fountain lord and marries the widow Arthur's approval is won THE MAGIC FORMULA IS SUCCESSFULLY USED
3	4
The Fountain lady denounces Ywain as a thief and traitor *In the wilderness* *Healed by the lady of Noroison* *Ywain stops Count Alier's thefts from her dominion and then refuses her offer of marriage* PENANCE FOLLOWED BY EXORCISM OF THE ACCUSATION OF THEFT	*Ywain returns to the Fountain and clears Lunete (his assistant in winning his dominion) of the charge of treason* EXORCISM OF THE CHARGE OF TREASON

sizes my point.[21] The plots in general are all highly individual, employing a great variety of devices.

Here it can be seen again that the action in the first move in italics (move 3) reverses the accusation relating to the action in the preceding move. The Fountain lady's denunciation (that Ywain is a thief and a traitor), and Ywain's action in taking the dominion and its lady, are reversed in move 3, where Ywain saves another lady from someone else (Count Alier) who is engaged in stealing *her* dominion, and he then turns down her offer of it, in marriage. There is also the same strategic relationship between the two moves in italics that I find in the Horn plot, in spite of the division of the charges between the moves, one dealing with the theft and the other with the treachery. In the first move, surrogates are used, while in the second we find the use of the exact situation. The theft in the denunciation is reversed using the lady of Noroison and Count Alier, in the first move, and in the second the treachery is removed using the exact place (the Fountain) and the assistant, Lunete.

The various authors who use this plot present the Fountain lady's denunciation as arising from Ywain's failure to return to the lady by the agreed time, and Chrétien de Troyes and Hartmann von Aue have obscured it further, Chrétien by turning it into a courtly play on the idea of the thief who has stolen his lady's heart without caring for it, and Hartmann by developing it in terms of the point of view of the women characters (the lady's vulnerable position and Lunete's concern for her). These textual situations are typical of the kind of conflicts to be found between the thought in the plot and the thought in the author's additional material: the authors have added courtly treatment and other developments of the material, providing a reason for the denunciation that is at odds with the plot's reason, and also providing a point of view for characters who are no more than figures in the plot, playing roles that cannot be given rational motivation. If I made a chart that included the additional material of Chrétien and Hartmann, this material would appear as an overlay precariously balanced on top of a plot that had an alien life of its own: the roots of its thought do not reach far into the plot, and its developments and rationalizations do not always connect up well with each other. It was an essential part of my work to learn how to examine systematically, in the small details of the text, all the areas of conflict between the different levels of thought.

But such advances in my work had to take their time, and the problems presented by texts like those using "The Lady of the Fountain" were too formidable for me in the early stages. On the one hand, the plot of "The Lady of the Fountain," with its use of Calogrenant's tale (in moves 1 and 2), was too difficult until I had moved on to an understanding of the thought in the texts as magic and had experience of magic's selection and use of narrative material. On the other hand, I could not address the problems caused by the overlay until I was sufficiently advanced in my understanding of the plot. However, what I could do was work with a model that was a much finer instrument than I realized, and, from the outset, I added further disciplines: that I must account for every detail and regard as important the order in which the detail appeared in the text. These initial methods made a sound beginning, and, as I slowly learned with their help, I modified them and added further disciplines.

My being able to work with a useful model was owing to the highly organized nature of the narrative structures I had stumbled upon, structures much more organized (rather than less organized, as might have turned out) than I originally thought. In fact, in the early stages, I did not see myself as working with a model at all. But my model, with its essential features of the point of view and the move structure, and further disciplines gradually to be discovered, enabled me to study many relevant texts, exploring how the details related to each other and what the emerging structures in each text were doing. I was released, to some extent, from the intrusion of what I knew already, so that I could address the unknown and take the unexpected and apparently absurd as I found it and learn from it. While the model was entirely wrong for many texts—I needed the two further models I acquired between 1986 and 1987—and it was also not of a kind that could help me to grasp fully the operation of magic in narrative, I was able to make advances, and these owed much to the research situations I selected. Realizing that I needed a superabundance of information, I chose more detailed texts and texts where two levels of thought conflicted with each other, and later I worked on groups of texts using the same story material. I also concentrated on texts where there was an intensive use of magic; only recently have I been able to spend time profitably on texts making a lighter use.

I worked with the first model for some years, and as my concept of the kind of plot I was investigating became more defined, I could form a more accurate idea of how widespread it would turn out to be. It turned out to be chiefly confined to the genres of romance and folktale, and within those genres, proving less common than I had originally expected. During these years I identified the cleansing ritual punishment, narrative exorcism (removing the idea that the hero's or heroine's wishes and actions are evil), the use of the verbal formula (the spell), and another kind of magic formula made up of fragments of narrative taken from tradition.

It was the texts of "The Lady of the Fountain" that introduced me to the second kind of formula, made up of narrative fragments. This was one of the rare occasions when recourse to information beyond the texts proved helpful. I found Calogrenant's tale to be a strategic assembly of sundry sources of power, the selected items forming an adventure designed to propel the hero to the acquisition of a dominion. Among its ingredients was reassurance, the chief reassurance being that the king approved of it (after hearing Calogrenant's account of it, in which Calogrenant was defeated). In order to study this adventure as magic, handicapped as I was by not having the information supplied by a move structure within the tale, I needed to discover the properties of the story elements, and a particularly useful text for this purpose was the Irish *In Gilla decair*, where several of the elements appeared, including those relating to the Fountain itself. It was a case of having to discover the essential features of the elements, the features magic would be using in the various "Lady of the Fountain" texts, and the Irish text helped me to make a decision about these. Analysis depending so much on interpretation could only be tentative, but my exploration of Calogrenant's tale confronted me sharply with the activity of magic as thought, selecting and using materials just like any other form of thought. The tale had ceased to be a fixed, inscrutable entity, its meaning belonging to the past, and instead stood revealed to me as alive in the text in every detail, used by living thought for an immediate purpose.[22]

I now saw magical plots as purposeful in every detail, while, nevertheless, of their very nature ambiguous in meaning. Even in cases where a wealth of highly organized detail gave me every assistance, I found it impossible to pin down meaning. Magical plots were emerging as vehicles capable of catering to a range of purposes, even of contradictory kinds, to meet the various needs of audiences. In view of the long popularity of many of the texts concerned, it was hardly surprising that they would turn out to have this usefulness. I increasingly felt that I was giving undue attention to meaning, but some attention to it was necessary as part of my study of function; such attention was, wherever possible, dependent on what emerged from an analysis of the magical structure concerned.

With so many difficulties on so many fronts, progress could only be slow with the first model, but, after the publication of my study *Magical Thought in Creative Writing* in 1983, I took the step of extending my field beyond my English specialty to study texts in other languages, and my progress accelerated. I was more able to approach my subject through the study of groups of related texts, and the Perceval and Ywain groups of texts proved especially valuable experience. I also found that great individual texts like the *Perceval* and *Yvain* of Chrétien de Troyes helped me to refine my methods, and they provided admirable examples of texts where an author has superimposed substantial material on an old story. The most important reason, however, was that my extended researches led to my identifying two new types of magical plot, the purification plot and the defended narrative. It was my study of the Latin Historia texts of the Apollonius of Tyre story that led to my identifying the purification plot, and all that I learned from these texts and Chrétien's *Yvain* led to my identifying the defended narrative in *Sir Gawain and the Green Knight*. I had needed a firmer concept of magic as a system of thought, selecting its narrative materials. Both these new types of plot opened new doors: I was able to study many more texts, and I was also given the opportunity to study texts that were more intensively magical than those using the King Horn type of plot. Some purification plots are exclusively concerned with exorcism and ritual punishment, while the prime concern of the defended narrative is to protect the hero or heroine entering the story. But I must add here that the three models I had now acquired have turned out to represent three extreme types: texts often show characteristics of more than one of these models, many of them, for example, making use of protective devices at particular stages of the plot.

My studies of the Perceval and Ywain romances, *Sir Gawain and the Green Knight,* and the Apollonius texts were published in *The Magical Quest* in 1988, when I still did not have a sufficient view over my new subject to provide a useful theory for it. My work with the use of the two new models was only just beginning, and this work was to take me, in a very few years, to the production of the theory I offer in this present book. The chapters of this book are chiefly studies made with the help of the new models, and the assembly of Accused Queen texts in chapter 1 presents perhaps my best case for the purification plot. The roles of purification in magical narrative are better discussed in the studies than they can be here, so this introduction will now concentrate on the defended narrative, which needs a full explanation at this point. Studies using the first model—which I now call the sovereignty plot—appear among the introductory studies and in chapter 3.

While my identification of the purification plot was a direct step forward from the sovereignty plot—there simply being a greater preponderance of devices for dealing with irrational guilt and fear—my identification of the defended narrative was a more difficult step forward: its structure was of an entirely different kind. I needed to have not only a full grasp of magic as thought selecting its materials but also a concept of the use of defenses in narrative, and this concept was a development from my reading of Leo Bersani's essay on *Wuthering Heights* a few years earlier.[23] Bersani was not concerned with magic, but his argument for a narrative structure that legitimized a forbidden adventure led me to wonder whether there could be such a structure created by magic. Magical plots were concerned with forbidden experience—not with experience socially forbidden, as Bersani meant, but with experience felt to be forbidden, too forbidden to be acknowledged at a deep level of the mind. When I came to identify the defended narrative, I found it to be a narrative that could remove fear by providing devices invested with the power to keep the participant safe. The resulting structures were much more difficult to see than those of the sovereignty and purification plots, particularly as the move structure, which provided so much guidance in the slippery world of the irrational, became upstaged and of little help, the important magical structures being safeguards built up around the adventure. In view of the difficulties, the defended narrative must have its own particular introduction here.

First of all, I argue that a defended narrative selects for its safeguards narrative material that lends itself to such use, while essentially it is the kind of material that could be found used for quite different, nonmagical purposes in other texts. Among the roles that magic might give it is the establishment of some kind of permission or sanction for the adventure, or the creation of a framework ensuring from the outset a safe adventure and safe retreat from it at the end. It might also be used to create final rituals concerned with the bringing about of forgiveness and the resolution of guilt. The defenses thus created tend to be a heavy accumulation of rituals at each end of the adventure and enveloping it; they are highly organized and may even have their own step-by-step structure.

I first identified the defended narrative in the text of *Sir Gawain and the Green Knight*, where I argue that Gawain's adventure is defended by two enveloping bargains, set up beforehand and honored at the appointed times: the hero would have a measure of control, the power to ensure his reprieve. The questions about this text that caught my attention most were those relating to the confession at the Green Chapel. Why were there two confessions within a few hours of each other, the first before a priest and the second before the secular Green Knight, and why, when the priest had absolved Gawain to the extent that he was clean enough for the Day of Judgment, did Gawain find himself unbearably guilty the following morning? Why, too, did he confess to covetousness and treachery? His confession to cowardice and lack of fidelity would seem a full confession. There is a suggestion of a serious crime in conflict with the *Gawain*-poet's theme of a knight's misdemeanor, a conflict typical of texts containing both a magical plot and chivalric material. I argue that covetousness and treachery are the two sins to which the hero must confess, and the Green Knight is the very character who must hear this confession and grant absolution, thus completing the safeguards the narrative provides for the adventure with the lady.[24]

When I came to my study of the Tristan verse romances, I had the advantage of studying five texts side by side, three of them containing magically defended narratives and two not. In the nonmagical texts, those of Gottfried and *Tristrams saga ok Ísöndar,* the ritual structures I found in the other texts were simply not there, and, without these structures, the authors were free to develop the characters and their motivation and strategies and to add their themes, without there being conflict with a magical plot lurking underneath. Although my full discussion of this group of romances forms part of this present book, I shall summarize some of my findings here, for my explanation of the defended narrative. Before I go further, I must say that the defended narrative I find in the texts does not include the exile, after the parting of the lovers. Many texts I find magical contain additional adventures that have nothing to do with the magical structures.

In Eilhart's *Tristrant* (the only text I shall refer to here), I find the narrative's opening defenses massive, the chief of them being in the scenes in Ireland (from the slaying of the dragon up to the departure from Ireland). Following this is the use of the potion, and, at the end of the adventure, the closing structures are the separating sword episode and the use of the king's confessor, the hermit Ugrim, for the safe return of the queen. Since this is a defended narrative, the safe return of the queen is crucial. The defense provided by the potion, with its essential limited period, surrounds the adventure itself: the potion is overwhelming for its limited period and then (strategically) ceases to be so. Meanwhile, for the safe return of the queen, what is needed is the king's conviction of her innocence and an advocate of great power, and these needs are met by the ritual in which the king sees the lovers asleep with the sword between them and by the use of the king's confessor Ugrim as advocate.

In Gottfried's version, the hermit Ugrim has been discarded, and the separating sword episode and the potion have been transformed to play courtly roles (the potion having unlimited duration); but most interesting of all is the contrast between the scenes in Ireland in the magical and nonmagical versions. It is a contrast demonstrating some of the qualities of the thought I have been investigating. In Gottfried, the scenes in Ireland concern a rational set of arrangements whereby Tristan and the royal women find good reasons for protecting each other, and the king is persuaded, in a sensible discussion, that a reconciliation with Tristan is to their advantage. In Eilhart, by contrast, the detail of the text forms a sequence of ritual procedures for making safe an adventure with a forbidden woman. I shall give the steps of this sequence briefly and then explain how I think they make sense within the terms of the thought system concerned.

First of all, I argue, we must avoid rationalizing the problems and instead address the details in the text just as they are. Tristrant first wins the princess, since she is promised to the dragon slayer. Then he wins her acceptance of him, enemy though he is (having killed her kinsman Morolt), because he is preferable to the false steward (who is pretending to have killed the dragon), and she has to marry one or the other. Then, through Isalde's step-by-step negotiations, the king's forgiveness is obtained. First, Isalde makes known to the king that she knows the real dragon slayer and says this dragon slayer deserves the king's favor. The king says, "Whatever he may have done to me will be forgiven because of this." Isalde replies, "Kiss me, father, for the warrior, and make a complete and lasting peace with him," and the king says he fully pardons him from this day. The next step is that Isalde leads Tristrant forward to the king before a gathering of their people. The king asks who Tristrant is, and Isalde replies that he must kiss Tristrant first. The king kisses him and grants a firm pardon to him and all his family. Then Isalde tells the king who Tristrant is, and the king confirms that, because he has already been pardoned, all remains forgiven. This is followed by the false steward's declaration that he has not slain the dragon and that Tristrant should have the princess. Tristrant reminds the king of the reward of the lady, and the king does not refuse him. Then he tells the king that he wishes to give the lady to King Mark. The king is glad, and he places Isalde in his charge, on Tristrant's oath that he will consider her fully with honor and bring her to his uncle.

The king looks like a puppet, granting forgiveness without the full facts before him, and I argue that that is precisely his function. Tristrant, meanwhile, wins the princess, gains the king's agreement to this, and then gives her to his uncle—although, in this text, Mark does not want a queen at all—and I argue that this all makes excellent sense. The king's next act, on hearing Tristrant declare his generous gift, is to put him on oath that he will treat Isalde honorably as his uncle's bride. Again, I argue that—in the thought system I am concerned with—there is no incongruity in the juxtaposition of the gift and the oath in the text. King Mark does not want a queen for the reason that he wants Tristrant to be his heir. But Mark does not actually have a point of view: he is one of the figures playing the king, and, in the narrative's opening defenses, the hero (identified with the figure Tristrant) establishes himself as the loved son of the king and his champion against enemies. In view of the adventure to be defended, the idea of being the king's enemy has to be removed, and the figures Morolt and the false steward are used to expel the idea of the hero's being an invader threatening the king's sovereignty and also a thief (as the steward is called in the text). This is done by the ritual arrangement of characters, Tristrant defeating these characters. Far from seeing the contradictory details as canceling each other out, I think we have to see them as a piling on of positives, so to speak: the more there are, the stronger the defenses. The hero is the loved son and champion of the king; he steals nothing from him and acknowledges his right. He has a sense of the king's forgiveness and also of his permission to take the lady. Meanwhile, he has won the lady: she is his and yet essentially she belongs to the king and must be safely returned to him. The gift of Isalde to the king and the oath that she will be treated accordingly are important parallel rituals defending the adventure.

The apparently incongruous juxtaposition of the gift and the oath in Eilhart's text and the strangeness of Tristrant's decision to give the princess he has won to his uncle, are two typical kinds of logical problem I find in magical texts. Such problems as these can easily be set aside or rationalized by readers and critics, while puzzles relating to larger incidents with more appeal (such as the limited duration of the love potion) hold the stage. Little attention is given in this introduction to the kind of indications I look for before deciding a text might be relevant, because this matter is dealt with in all the necessary detail in the introductory studies to follow. But a few general points can be made here. While the presence of a magical plot throws up particular types of problem, the problems I notice vary greatly from text to text. The indications can vary even in the case of texts using the same plot—which is a reason why it is useful to study such related texts side by side wherever possible. The treatment of an author or storyteller will sometimes point up or obscure magical detail, and various treatments in various texts reveal or obscure in different places and different fashions. Meanwhile, some texts show very few indications. One has to grasp the whole thing before one can work effectively in this area: one knows what to look for by knowing well the thought concerned.

All magical texts have important purposes that are never acknowledged, and often this is how one can spot a magical text. Magical plots have urgent feelings to satisfy or dispel, in situations that seem extraordinary to the rational mind but are nonetheless real in their own area of experience. The thought concerned belongs to a world consisting of the protagonist and parental figures, and is therefore haunted by prohibitions: the desire for sovereignty (which is to be understood in the widest sense) is haunted by a sense of treachery, and sexual love by ideas of theft and incest. This world is the source of the desires, guilt, and fear in the magical plot, and there can be no true connection between this material and the additional material of an author, beyond some indirect emotional links. Magic, too, has no true connection with thought at any other level, and it can go about its business beyond the control of the author as a conscious artist. A situation in the text that catches my attention is where there is a suggestion that the chief character has committed a serious crime, while this is not given the treatment or comment that it needs; instead, I may find that some minor or courtly misdemeanor has taken a prominent position, while the magical theme of the serious crime lurks beneath, and this can give rise to some interesting situations. Particularly informative are the occasional attempts of authors to cope with some of the problems, finding unsatisfactory solutions instead of addressing the problems directly, and similar attempts on the part of translators are equally interesting. There is a small example in a translation of Eilhart's *Tristrant,* where Tristrant's oath that he will consider Isalde with honor, as his uncle's bride ("mit êren wol bedêchte"), is rendered to mean that he will take care of her; the magical import so problematic to the rational mind thus disappears.[25]

While it is impractical to attempt categories for the logical problems, the textual situations that can cause such problems can be usefully set out here. First, there is the presence of two levels of thought in the text, operating in ignorance of each other and producing, for example, Gawain's knightly misdemeanor side by side with his serious crime. Then there is the commonest source of logical problems, because it affects every magical text: the adoption of an incorrect approach—an approach, that is, which may seem to be correct, but from which we cannot see how the text is coherent at the most basic level. Such an approach produces (and may find a solution for) the contradictory situation of Gawain's two confessions. Contradictions of this kind disappear when the correct approach is adopted. The problems of this second category can be made more obtrusive by the author's additional, rationalizing work, which may be present in texts even where there is no extensive second level. It is this work that produces the curious contradictions in the description of the hanging of the children in *The Story of Meriadoc:* the author develops the ritual scene at a "higher" level of thought, providing characterization and technical strategies that can only be quite unconnected with the ritual and leave us with an entirely confused passage of writing. Wherever a magical plot is present it is dominant. It is often the only level of thought in the text, and where there is an added level, that level has dependent status, even in cases where it is of great importance. The author's additional work can, in fact, range from quite thin, patchy development of material in the plot to a massive superstructure of themes. A magical plot will never yield to the "higher" purposes of an author; its own purposes come first, and the other level is left with any problems this causes. To prevail, the "higher" purposes must remove the magic altogether.

But there is also a borderland to my subject, where I find texts that can be fruitfully approached using my methods, even though they do not provide very marked opportunities for a magical engagement. These are narratives that do not contain much guilt or fear: magical structures are most powerful when they seek to bring about objectives in the face of such forces as irrational guilt and fear. The greater the anxiety, the more likely we are to find logical problems in the text concerned, because the magical devices employed make greater efforts and their oddness becomes more visible. However, relevant texts presenting few or none of the characteristic problems can still have plots of great power. *The Basket of Flowers*, included in my introductory studies, has a powerful plot and a formidable but simple objective: to remove a sense of sin and bring about a sense of perfect goodness. Borderland texts are discussed in my chapter on the Cinderella stories.

The problems created by there being two separate levels of material are discussed in my studies of *Lanval, Meriadoc, The Wide, Wide World,* and *Rebecca* (in my introductory studies) and of Saxo Grammaticus's Hamlet story. The problems created by Saxo's treatment of the Hamlet story as a revenge story are particularly interesting. Saxo's overlay treats Amleth's meetings with his foster sister and mother as tests, and yet the reasons Saxo supplies for the testing of Amleth through these meetings are worse than unconvincing: they show unresolved conflict between two separate purposes and do not logically add up at all. The episodes are really about something entirely different, and it is an impossible task to present them as tests. It is an equally impossible task to achieve moral consistency in a text bringing together moral themes and a magical plot: magic has purposes quite at odds with the moral concerns of an author. Chrétien fails to achieve moral consistency in his treatment of the Fountain adventure in *Yvain*, where he is making use of a borrowed magical story, and Susan Warner (writing as Elizabeth Wetherell) fails to do so in *The Wide, Wide World*, where she has created her own magical plot.

Inconsistencies and illogicalities relating to the characters are among the most important indications of a magical text, and yet there are difficulties here because the strange behavior of a character can have a variety of narrative causes. Among the examples that appear in the studies to follow it can be seen that problems are created by both the two levels and the incorrect point of view. In *Meriadoc,* the magical plot strategically turns the emperor into a traitor in the final move, a situation that appears to be the emperor's decision when we consider it as if it were an event in the usual fictional sense, and such a decision appears unwise to an incredible extent in its context. It is also made yet more incomprehensible by the additional work of the author, who supplies a motive for the decision and one so ill-chosen that it increases the illogicality rather than successfully rationalizing it. Turning the emperor into a traitor is a key magical device to exorcise the hero's sense of his own treachery, and it is the kind of important stratagem likely to appear odd on the surface of the text. Many magical characters "change character" in this way, when the plot moves them into fresh strategic positions, sometimes in a yet more startling fashion. In the Apollonius of Tyre texts, the princess Lucina is strongly characterized as determined to marry Apollonius and to travel with him, and yet she does not take obvious steps to return to him when she then finds herself in Ephesus. All these details about her need to be seen as magical strategies: the plot requires Lucina's determination to marry Apollonius, and her determination to travel with him, and, following that, her sojourn in Ephesus, in ritual separation from him.[26] My chief guide when considering such problems has always to be what emerges under analysis. A magical plot (unless it is a defended narrative) advances in steps, magic being used to enable each step forward, so, as I examine the relationships between the details in a text, this is one of the features I look for.

The work requires a full grasp of the level of the thought itself; it is all too easy to consider this thought as if it were of the same kind as thought forms we know. For example, it might be argued that the magic love potion is even more of a defense in the nonmagical Tristan version of Gottfried, where its unlimited powers could be held to excuse absolutely everything that the lovers do after leaving Ireland. But that kind of defense is an excuse in the face of society's censure, and the word "magic" in relation to this potion is a descriptive term conveying that it has particular powers used by the characters in this story. In Eilhart's magical version, magic is more than a descriptive term: the magical plot I see would have been used as magic by real people because it worked for them. It is an essential feature that there is a magical plot rather than just a "magic potion" used by Gottfried's rational thought—which could not devise real magic. The critic's task is to address a thought system that is as distant from the conscious, rational mind as this and to think through how the narrative concerned could be used by participants to meet real needs. It is useless simply to look for features on the surface of the text, whether they be potions, patterns, or problems, without addressing the thought responsible for the entire narrative and identifying its level.

I have been asked what literary specialists should make of all this: should they feel differently about Shakespeare, Chrétien de Troyes, and other major writers who have sometimes used magical plots? The problem here, I think, is that we have not come to terms with the nonrational as a fact of human life. Those with great intellectual and artistic gifts share a common humanity with us all, and their not being (apparently) aware of their use of a magical plot does not shock me. Meanwhile, the texts concerned can be among their greatest: magical plots have exceptional power and can coexist in harmony with other thought in a text. The irrational has its own important places in human life, and, while we cannot be aware of its activity all of the time, the rational thinking we prize so much cannot be truly effective unless it becomes able to take into account the larger human reality of the passions and their forms of thought.

Introductory Studies

Many narrative texts superficially resemble texts I identify as magical. Some have an episodic form, for example, or fantastic, apparently magical subject matter; some relate a "family drama" of some kind or a story in which identification is an important feature. So how can we avoid confusion?

That question is a chief subject of this book, and one of the ways in which I address it is to place magical and nonmagical texts side by side wherever possible. But these introductory studies will concentrate on the kinds of things I notice that lead me to identify a magical text and how I go about analysis. The texts involved have not been chosen because they represent particular types of magical text: they are, in fact, all included here as interesting texts that are best studied in this isolated fashion, and, as such an assembly, they illustrate perfectly how different I find each magical narrative, how my questions vary from text to text, and how misleading any mechanistic approach would be. Beyond the taking up of the single point of view (which is common to all magical plots), the critic has no methods that could be called a straightforward rule.

A magical text has, strictly, to be a text that can be shown to provide opportunities for magical use, and I have had to concentrate on texts where I find marked magical structures inviting an investment of power. But magic is a form of thought, and thought is free. Such texts will not always have been used magically, and, conversely, the magical use of texts, of the narrative type and otherwise, is probably a more widespread phenomenon than can be shown by the examination of a few texts containing marked magical structures. It is important to bear these matters in mind when considering the magical use of narrative. Meanwhile, I can have no panoramic view of my subject as a result of a slow, intensive investigation of a comparatively few texts, so my introductory studies do not reflect such a view. The seven studies are divided into medieval texts in the first part and nineteenth and twentieth century texts in the second part only to assist the reader. As a medievalist, I have worked chiefly with medieval texts, but, perhaps, had I been a modernist, I would never have embarked on my investigation. Magical narrative is likely to be commonest in popular tradition and least common where authors invent their own plots. Medieval and Renaissance authors made ready use of traditional stories, thus sometimes encountering magic, and this may be why they have given us a number of magical texts. Magic creates compelling stories, and it has the power to take hold of an author's mind.

A magical text can never be "spotted" from a synopsis—the full text has to be considered over a period of time—and therefore it is hardly a good introduction that I provide synopses here. But I cannot avoid including synopses, or failing to include the full text, and, meanwhile, I can put the synopses to good use in the creation of charts showing the magical structures I have identified. The charts are visual aids provided wherever helpful throughout this book: they show the moves or other structures I see and point up in italics the parts of the narrative where I find magic intensively used. (A magical plot is magical throughout, of course, since magic is the very thought behind it, but its use of magic becomes more intensive at particular stages.) Everywhere in the book, line and page numbers refer to editions and translations given in my notes and bibliography.

Part I

Sir Degarré

Sir Degarré is a Middle English romance preserved in a number of manuscripts, the earliest (the Auchinleck) belonging to the early fourteenth century, and also in printed texts. My study has concentrated on an edition based on the Auchinleck text and, additionally, on the late version preserved in Bishop Percy's Folio Manuscript and known as "Sir Degree."[1] Chart 3 (in the appendix) follows the Auchinleck version and supplies the ending, lost in Auchinleck, from other texts.

Critics have noted the assembly of familiar motifs in the romance, one observing that, "though there are a few loose ends, the patchwork is cunningly done" (Pearsall 23) and another noting the presence of the possessive father somewhat like the father in *Emaré,* and of the ravishing knight, the exposed infant, and the father-son combat (Donovan 141). Critics have also commented on the reappearance of the innocent or fool setting out on his adventures with no knowledge of chivalry and only a club or staff as a weapon. In making the same observations, I myself wonder whether there is anything interesting about the thought in the text, selecting these story elements.

Some critics have also noted the Oedipal and family drama character of the material used in the text. The material has something of the mythic in its appearance, too, recalling the myth of the birth of the hero and initiation into manhood. I shall give some attention here to the criticism relating to the Oedipal and family drama aspects, since this will answer questions as to how my approach is distinguished from such criticism.

Lee C. Ramsey sees the romance as a relatively open one about family connections, strongly suggesting comparison with the Oedipus legend (*Chivalric Romances*). The main purpose of the early part of the narrative is to set up a situation in which Degarré can fight fathers and marry his mother without seriously violating the social and religious laws of the time. There is the "specific idea that one must marry one's mother before finding a lover and fight with one's father before the sword (sexual potency) can become whole" (161), and the romance writer makes the marriage with the mother possible, at the point where Degarré wins her, by having him forget about the glove test until after the ceremony. The underlying problem appears to be fear that family relationships "may become too close to be socially and psychologically acceptable" (161), and the "intricate and contrived family connections" of the romance "are a way of achieving the appearance of closeness combined with safeguards against the dangers of full emotional involvement" (162).

Julie Burton includes *Sir Degarré* in an essay on narratives dealing with separation of family members and their eventual reunion, seeing in them a pattern using one of three tale types (the Calumniated Wife, the Man Tried by Fate, and the hero's exile and return) (176–97). *Sir Degarré* uses the sequence of the hero's exile and return. The pattern itself is concerned with a family group during a period of transition: it spans the time from infancy to adulthood, when the children are ready to become parents themselves and the sequence can begin again, one step further on. The main characters face problems representative of what every parent or child faces, and this "representative nature allows the Pattern to serve as a medium to convey the idea that life proceeds from generation to generation by a sequence of cyclical renewal" (179–80). The children's maturity is symbolized by the family reunion, where parent and child relate as adult to adult. An important part of Degarré's maturation is his learning how to distinguish the maternal and sexual roles in women; at first, he confuses both roles in all women. In her discussion, Julie Burton addresses the two apparently incompatible functions of the gloves, as a recognition test for the mother and as a marriage test for the prospective wife. She comments that the lines suggest the danger of future incest between mother and son as well as the mother's reluctance to lose her son's love to another woman. Degarré's confusion about his mother is traced through his reflections on the function of the gloves. When with the hermit, swearing to seek his kindred, he is clear that the gloves will identify his mother:

> That bi þe gloven he sscholde i-wite
> Wich were his moder.... (ll. 312–13)

Then, after he has married her, he refers to the gloves as a marriage test, recalling that the holy man

> Bad he scholde no womman take
> For faired ne for riches sake
> But ȝhe miȝte þis gloves two
> Liȝtliche on hire hondes do. (ll. 641–44)

When he tells the bride's father his problem, his words bring together the two views of the purpose of the gloves:

> "I schal never, for no spousing,
> Þerwhiles I live, wiþ wimman dele,
> Widue ne wif ne dammeisele,
> But ȝhe þis gloves mai take and fonde
> And liȝtlich drawen upon hire honde." (ll. 658–62)

Julie Burton thinks that the addition of "mai take and fonde" and the use of "dele" rather than "take" (l. 641) make an essential difference, because Degarré is now simply saying that he will not consider marrying the woman who will not try on the gloves; he may be implying that he will not marry the woman who can wear them. His confusion over whether his mother should play a maternal or sexual role towards him ends when his bride is identified as his mother.

Derek Brewer sees the romance as a series of fantasies based on our innermost experiences, the chief contestants being the protagonist and his parents (*Symbolic Stories*). The main theme is that of the emerging male protagonist: the fight with the dragon signifies his coming of age; he then has to switch his affections for his mother to someone of his own age; finally, he needs to be accepted by his father as fully grown before he can settle down with a wife. The image of the gloves fulfills in part a function like that of Cinderella's slipper, of identifying the beloved, but it is ambivalent since the beloved is identified in order to show that she is unavailable. In the river castle, Degarré is treated maternally, being put to sleep and tucked up in bed, and this paralyzes him sexually, but he then defeats another father-figure rival (the suitor seeking to seize the river castle lady) and is thus "paradoxically" able to think of the lady of the castle less in terms of a mother image. In this way he wins her, and he leaves her because he is not quite "ripe," not all his inhibitions having been shed. He then fights a further father-figure and identifies him as the real father, and thus identifies himself. The father's pointless sword is a phallic emblem, still incomplete, and Degarré's proof that he can use it, in the battle with his father, makes the sword complete. "His masculine character is now fully integrated" (70).

All these approaches are primarily concerned with interpretation, and use is made of ideas already current concerning the nonrational areas of human experience. Each critic also sees a development in the narrative in terms of the protagonist's psychological maturation, which implies the work of rational, as opposed to nonrational, thought somewhere behind the text. Nonrational thought in the text would not be concerned with emotional maturation, but with achieving its own objects in its own way. Psychoanalysis, of course, is essentially the bringing of rational and didactic forms of thought to the irrational, and it joins forces with our interest in personal and social development. Many narratives share this interest, but the form of thought I have found in some texts does not.

My approach cannot be primarily interpretative—for example, saying that the sword symbolizes sexual potency—because I have to investigate a form of thought using the sword and other narrative material, and this involves tracing it through the text, beginning with the problems of logicality that have drawn my attention to the text in the first place and including intensive study of the relationships between the details. If my methods are relevant to the text, meaning gradually emerges, and this meaning is of a kind that cannot be predicted from current knowledge.

The two apparently incompatible functions of the gloves draw my attention to the Degarré texts in the first place. The mother's initial instructions are as follows:

"Takeþ him þis ilke gloven two,
And biddeþ him, whar-evere
    he go,
Þat he ne lovie no woman in
    londe
But þis gloves willen on hire
    honde—
For siker on honde nelle þai nere
But on his moder þat him bere."

(Auchinleck ll. 213–18)

with itt shee giues a payre of gloues,
& bade the child wed no wiffe in
    Lande
without those gloues wold on her
    hand;
& then the gloues wold serue no
    where,
sauing the mother *tha*t did him
    beare.

(Percy ll. 166–70)

The Percy version, which shows many alterations in the narrative, preserves the ambiguity here. In more considerable texts than these, which contain the author's added developments and themes, I would expect to find more illogicalities and conflict in the text to assist me, but the Degarré texts provide help of another kind, in containing a narrative with a number of episodes (potential moves). If I find that these episodes relate to each other in certain highly organized, step-by-step ways, I can establish the presence of a magical plot and learn a great deal about it from the move structure.

If we have a magical plot before us, the mother's instructions accompanying the gloves will be quite logical and purposeful as they stand within the laws of the plot; it is only when we seek to rationalize them that we see an inextricable confusion of two functions. The instructions say that Degarré must not marry any woman except one whom the gloves fit and that the gloves will only fit his mother. In a magical plot, Degarré will make use of these instructions, following them to the letter: in swearing to the hermit that he will seek his mother, who is to be identified by the gloves; in not accepting the grateful earl's offer of all he has because the gloves fit no woman there; and then in marrying his mother upon winning her from the king, and using the gloves to identify her as his mother before incest is committed.

Bearing these matters in mind, I consider the plot as a whole, using my various models, and find that the particular arrangement of the episodes, with their repetitions of detail, suggests a sovereignty plot, even though—as is so often the case—the structure I see is unlike any I have seen before. Sovereignty would be achieved when Degarré wins his mother and sealed when he marries the lady of the river castle. The plot would be unusual in that it uses the exact location of Degarré's birth and the character designated as his mother (the initial situation of move 1) for the winning of sovereignty, rather than a substitute place, as in *King Horn* and "The Lady of the Fountain." A substitute would be used after the exact location, in the following move at the river castle. The use of such a direct method as the exact location and characters for the winning of sovereignty would explain the extent of the magical devices apparent in this plot, particularly in the use of the gloves and the moves both preceding and following the move where sovereignty is won. Devices would be needed to protect the hero from his fears and sense of guilt, and perhaps even to purify him, in greater abundance than in the case of most sovereignty plots. My other models would therefore be of some use in considering this narrative, provided they were used with caution: many narratives show characteristics of more than one model.

The gloves and their accompanying instructions should provide useful guidance in discovering how this plot would work as magic. In the move (as I shall call it) with the earl, Degarré fights to save the earl from an enemy who will kill him (the dragon), and the grateful earl offers him all that he has, but Degarré has set out to find his kindred, and he uses the gloves to demonstrate this; they are the reason why he turns down this sovereignty. As a son seeking his mother and renouncing sovereignty for this purpose, he passes into the move where he is to defeat the king and marry the queen-figure, the only woman he may marry since she is the only woman the gloves fit. The trying on of the gloves after, rather than before, the wedding allows them to fulfill their combined role as the mother's permission for the marriage and the firm proof of her identity as forbidden. In fitting her, they prove the achievement of sovereignty, and, from henceforth, they defend the hero against the fear of incest, the forbidden woman now being identified. Passing into the move at the river castle, taking with him the pointless sword, the hero's concern is now chiefly with the father; the lady herself will be a repeat character, standing in for the forbidden woman whom the gloves fit, while the hero completes the business of the plot.

I use the word "hero," rather than the name Degarré, when I am considering how the narrative might be used magically by anyone identifying with it. This person becomes the hero, while Degarré is, like the other characters, a figure in the rituals. I should add here that those identifying can use the narrative for a range of purposes, and thus the sovereignty achieved will have a range of meanings.

In the structure I see, the move with the earl transports the hero to the crucial sovereignty move on the wings of a demonstration of opposite feelings from those that must haunt the sovereignty move. He has saved the earl from his enemy, renounced the reward of the earl's property, and left to seek his mother. The inclusion of a lady in the earl's property is implied in the Auchinleck text and stated as the earl's daughter in the Percy text.

The apparently ambiguous gloves emerge, in this move and the following one, as unambiguous in their role, while being adaptable according to their context. They assist the hero in making his combined statement that he is not seeking sovereignty but only his mother, in the move with the earl, this leading to the next move where they provide proof of identity, serving the sovereignty of that move, and also protection against incest, serving that move and the one to follow at the river castle.

It is now time to look at the magical structure as a whole. In the early part of the plot, Degarré is separated from the king through the device of his conception by a fairy knight in a forest, and he is then separated from his home by his upbringing with a hermit and that holy man's sister. Such family separations are necessary in a plot using the family characters for the sovereignty move, and the use of the holy man associates the hero with goodness, this being a source of power. The hero leaves this holy position to fulfill his vow to seek his kindred, a purpose upheld by the "Goodmind" move that follows, and then the dangerous sovereignty move is undertaken. The sovereignty move itself provides safeguards, these being chiefly the use of the gloves, but also the king's initiation of the combat.

The last two moves, at the river castle and with the fairy father, are chiefly concerned with the king-figure, Degarré having left his mother to seek his father, but it is interesting to consider the role of the river lady. Degarré is wedded but not bedded with his mother, moving on, instead, to be bedded with the river lady. Having fallen in love with the lady, he takes himself up to her chamber and falls asleep on her bed to the sound of the harp. The lady covers him warmly and gets into bed beside him (in the Percy text, she gets into another bed). The next morning, she reproaches him for sleeping instead of paying attention to her women.

He fel adoun on slepe stille.	& through the notes of the harp shrill
So he slep al þat niȝt;	he layd him downe and slept his ffill.
Þe levedi wreiȝ him warm apliȝt	*that* ffaire Lady *that* ilke night shee bade couer the gentle Knight;
And a pilewer under his heved dede,	& rich clothes on him they cast, & shee went to another bed att Last.
And ȝede to bedde in þat stede.	& soe on the morrow when itt was day,
Amorewe whan hit was dai liȝt	the Lady rose, the sooth to say,
Sche was uppe and redi diȝt.	& into the chamber they way can take.
Faire sche awaked him þo:	
"Aris!" sche seide. "Graiþ þe and go!"	shee sayd, "Sir K*nigh*t, arise and wake!"
And saide þus in here game,	& then shee sayd all in game,
"Þou art worþ to suffri schame	"you are worthye ffor to haue blame!
Þat al niȝt as a best sleptest	ffor like a beast all night you did sleepe;
And non of mine maidenes ne keptest."	& of my mayds you tooke no keepe."
(Auchinleck ll. 852–64)	(Percy ll. 703–16)

Degarré is tucked up in bed, already asleep, as a child is by his mother, and he spends the night with the lady as a child would, fast asleep. He left the previous move as his mother's son, not as her lover, and the chastity of the relationship is here stated, both in the bedding and in the lady's words next morning, saying that he has only slept, having nothing to do with a woman. The alteration in the Percy text, where the lady goes to another bed, merely weakens the ritual. The move then proceeds to a ritual removing the idea that the queen-figure has been seized. Degarré becomes the lady's champion, defeating the suitor who is trying to seize her, and it is for this act that he wins "the lady and the land" for the final time. But further work has to be done before the marriage can take place.

The removal of the idea of seizure has been carried out using only a surrogate, and, in the final move, the idea of theft is removed from the exact situation. On leaving the lady, Degarré meets the fairy knight (designated his father in the texts), who accuses him of poaching in his territory.

"Belami, wat dost þou here In mi forest to chase mi dere?"	& he sayd, "villaine! what doest thou here within my fforrest to sloe my deere?"
(Auchinleck ll. 1013–14)	(Percy ll. 835–36)

Combat follows until the knight recognizes the pointless sword, provided for his son by himself in the first place, as a recognition token, and given to Degarré by his mother when he leaves her to search for his father (instead of going to bed with her). As such, the sword is a powerful magical aid to being recognized as a son rather than a thief; the tip of the sword provides final proof, like the fitting of the gloves. The marriage of Degarré's parents is then the final, essential ritual that frees the hero to take his sovereignty. Degarré's marriage to the lady of the river castle in the sight of his parents, the king, and the whole court follows, ending the narrative.

It is, in every sense, difficult to prove that magic is responsible for a narrative text, but I think I have proved it here. There are no shortcuts to such a conclusion beyond the limited help provided by my models. A narrative of similar appearance can be the product of a quite different form of thought. I hope my analysis goes further than prove to demonstrate why we must find ways of directly addressing nonrational thought in narrative. Among the essential disciplines is the avoidance of analogy with other narratives and also of the importation of meanings: only the texts under investigation can provide information about the thought that has assembled them. In the case of the nonrational area I have been investigating, I regard each new, relevant text as the authority, rather than the models that I bring to bear; my models are subject to continual alteration and development as each new text provides fresh information.

Bevis of Hampton

The story of Bevis of Hampton was enormously popular in Western literature. The original Anglo-Norman romance of about 1200 A.D. proliferated into Continental French, Welsh, Middle English, Norse, and Irish versions, and the Continental French romance had its own descendants, being turned into a French prose romance in the fifteenth century, a Dutch prose version printed in 1502, and a series of Italian versions. There was also a Yiddish version, composed in 1501 and frequently reprinted, which served as the source for a Rumanian translation in 1881, and a Russian version appeared in the sixteenth century. In *King Lear,* Poor Tom quotes a couplet from the romance.[2] Printed copies of it in verse and prose were in constant popular demand in England until the nineteenth century, when it became a tale for children.

My study has concentrated on the Middle English texts of the romance, the oldest of which is the Auchinleck manuscript of the early fourteenth century.[3] These texts, in manuscripts and old prints, cover several centuries and vary considerably at the verbal level, but they nevertheless follow the original Anglo-Norman narrative quite closely (apart from several added battles that came with the English translation).[4]

The narrative of *Bevis* has similarities with *King Horn* and more striking similarities with the Hamlet story of Saxo Grammaticus with which I deal in my final chapter. In this brief study, I shall concentrate on a comparison between two different approaches to the structure of the Bevis plot, my own and the exile-and-return plan argued by Maldwyn Mills.[5] Professor Mills finds in the texts of *King Horn* and *Bevis* clear demonstrations of the symmetrical exile-and-return narrative structure, and he also uses the approach to give a liberating view of Saxo's Hamlet story, while I find *Bevis* such a clear example of a magical plot (see chart 4 in the appendix) that it shows how my models can, in the case of relevant texts, help us see further significant patterns within the exile-and-return plan.

Maldwyn Mills demonstrates that the six episodes of the King Horn narrative (which I chart in my "Questions, Definitions, and Practice" as six magical moves) have a symmetrical exile-and-return structure in the case of the first five, while the sixth episode might be seen to be added to the fourth, as a necessary complement to it. The episodes are designated A, B, or C, according to the geographical location of the events and the particular characters belonging to that location. A refers to Horn's home country, B to the court of the princess he loves, and C to Ireland. Hence, the structure of *King Horn* can be described as A^1, B^1, C, B^2, A^2, B^3. The final B may seem to complicate the symmetry, but B^3 can be seen to put right an injustice perpetrated in B^1 (Fikenild's accusation), for Horn kills Fikenild for the very treachery Horn was accused of, and B^3 also has a close relationship with B^2, since in both Horn breaks up a wedding feast, the second time conclusively.

The less tightly structured romance of *Bevis* shows a duplication such as we find in B^3, but it takes the form of a sequence of episodes rather than a single episode. This duplication, which begins with the killing of the king's son by Bevis's horse Arundel, can be described as a second move in the sense that Vladimir Propp understands a move, where a fresh misfortune begins a new story. The designations A, B, and C, meanwhile, may signify only the presence of the same dominant characters rather than the same geographical location. A signifies Southampton, B the loved princess Josian, and C events elsewhere. The following analysis is again that of Maldwyn Mills.

First move

A^1 Bevis is sold into slavery after the murder of his father by his mother's lover, the emperor of Germany.

B^1 At the Armenian court he accepts the love of the princess Josian and defeats her father's enemy Brademond, but is sent to the latter to be killed after he has been accused to the king of seducing Josian.

C^1 In Damascus, Brademond throws him into a dungeon. Josian is told that Bevis has married the king of England's daughter.

B^2 Josian is married to Yvor of Mombraunt, but with the help of magic preserves her virginity.

C^2 After seven years' imprisonment, Bevis escapes and comes to Jerusalem, where the patriarch exhorts him to marry only a virgin.

B^3 He comes to Mombraunt disguised as a palmer and escapes with Josian. He takes the giant Ascopart into his service and they come to Cologne, where Josian is baptized and left in Ascopart's care.

A^2 Bevis returns to Southampton to claim his heritage.

B^4 Josian is forced into marriage with earl Miles, but strangles him on their wedding night. Sentenced to be burnt, she is rescued by Bevis and Ascopart.

A^3 Bevis defeats the emperor of Germany and has him executed (his mother, grief-stricken, then falls to her death). He is married to Josian, and succeeds to his father's earldom.

Second move

A^1 Bevis's horse accidentally kills the king's son, and Bevis goes into exile with Josian, Terri, and Ascopart.

B^1 Ascopart changes sides once again and carries off Josian after she has given birth to Guy and Miles; Bevis and Terri find foster parents for these.

C Bevis wins the hand of a princess in a tournament, but is allowed seven years' grace to find his wife before consummating the marriage.

B^2 Saber kills Ascopart, and he and Josian seek Bevis for seven years. When they are reunited, the princess marries Terri.

A^2 Bevis returns to England and then to Armenia, where in due course he and Josian die together.

A^1 in the first and second moves show very different reasons for Bevis's exile. Meanwhile, Ascopart is helper in the first move and agent of the enemy in the second.

Charles W. Dunn writes, "Basically, the plot of *King Horn* is very similar to that of *Bevis of Hampton* and other expulsion-and-return tales of the Apollonius type" (20). In all the texts mentioned here I find eminent examples of the magical plot, and perhaps the reason is not far to seek. Expulsion and return (from A back to A) are typical features of the magical plot and so are strategic transfers to and from surrogate locations (forming Maldwyn Mills's ABA, BCB). There being a complementary relationship between B^2 and B^3 in *King Horn* is a situation also found in magical plots, although, in the magical plot I discern in *King Horn,* there is a closer relationship of this kind between C and B^3—that is, between the surrogate situation and the exact situation.

In the case of the King Horn plot, the magical moves I suggest coincide exactly with the exile-and-return divisions ABCBAB.

Move 1 (Mills's A^1) Horn's father is killed and Horn transfers to a new court.

Move 2 (Mills's B^1) At the new court, Horn accepts the princess's love. An accusation that he will kill the king and marry the princess leads to the next move.

Move 3 (Mills's C) Horn transfers to a surrogate situation where the accusation is reversed: Horn saving the king from an invader and refusing the princess.

Move 4 (Mills's B²) Horn returns to the first princess, where a step forward can be taken as a result of move 3, and he is betrothed to her.

Move 5 (Mills's A²) Horn's home situation can now be readjusted, as a result of moves 3 and 4. He becomes king.

Move 6 (Mills's B³) Horn returns to the princess, and there is a final removal of the accusation by means of a reversal, using the accuser himself and the exact location and characters. Horn marries the princess.

Where *Bevis* is concerned, however, these divisions do not coincide. I find moves 2 and 3, and part of move 4, where Maldwyn Mills finds B¹, for example. B¹ is indicated by the events at the Armenian court relating to Josian, while moves 2, 3, and 4 are three replays of the narrative material relating to marriage with a lady representing sovereignty, material introduced in the first move. The contrasting treatments of the subject and the changes made in the characters employed are strategic. In move 1, Bevis's mother marries her husband's murderer, and Bevis opposes this. In move 2, a king offers his heir to Bevis and she is refused (but she falls in love with him). In move 3 Bevis saves the king from an invader wishing to seize the princess and then agrees to accept her love for him. In move 4, the accusation of the two knights presents the idea that Bevis has traitorously seduced the princess, and this idea is dealt with by the punishment of seven years' imprisonment.

Each move is a step forward in the arrangements. The princess is turned into a king's queen in move 5, while strategically remaining a virgin. Bevis, meanwhile, leaves prison and receives the injunction of the patriarch that he must marry only a pure virgin. As a result of the arrangements in move 5, the hero is in a position, in move 6, to "take" the queen. At this point, the expedition to avenge the murdered father is undertaken, to be interrupted, in move 8, by a seizure of the queen that establishes that she will kill anyone who wrongfully takes her in marriage. In move 9, Bevis avenges and succeeds his father, and he marries the queen. But the business of the plot is still not finished. Ritual family separation follows, in move 10, to remove fears relating to the queen. Bevis is temporally married to a princess who remains virgin. The final move opens, after this seven-year period, with the resumption of the marriage with the queen and an alliance with her father against her king husband. Bevis later kills her husband, becoming king in his place.

This archetypal sovereignty plot, with its chesslike moves forward to take queen and king, only makes sense to us when we grasp the primitive character of the thought process and the consequent guilt and fear attached to the procedures. Our difficulties in following the thought are alleviated by the tightly knit laws by which it works: the contrasting replays take the process forward step by step, concurrently removing the attendant guilt and fear. Among the magical devices used are reversal, ritual punishment and ritual separation (both using the number seven), and the authority of the patriarch of Jerusalem; the themes of the virginity of the queen (when she ceases to be a princess) and of her power to resist capture are also magical devices for protecting the hero (participant). Of course, the unconsummated state of Josian's marriages is essential if she is to remarry, but, in the separate logic of the magical plot, the queen is taboo, and the prohibition surrounding her has to be warded off, the need for this increased by her being made a mother. This problem governs the whole plot, moves being used to demonstrate loyalty to kings and reluctance over queen-figures. Throughout, the Bevis plot's purifying arrangements resemble those of the Apollonius texts.

The exile-and-return approach, like the work of Vladimir Propp, offers the critic a liberating means of studying the larger patterns of certain narratives. We can then go on to study further patterns in the text and address what lies behind them. The larger patterns observed continue to guide us: for example, the second (Propp) move of *Bevis* indicates a renewed ABCBA narrative at a point where we would expect the story to end, and our attention is concentrated on the structure and detail of this apparent afterthought. In the case of the magical plot I find in *Bevis*, the BCB arrangement points to the strategic use of "the other woman" in C (for ritual separation, I believe). But BCB does not point to the important final step within it of killing the queen's king and taking over his kingdom, a step showing this (Propp) second move to be an integral part of the earlier narrative.

I would not expect to find every exile-and-return narrative magical: *Guy of Warwick* is illuminated by the exile-and-return approach, while not being relevant to my investigation.[6] So what initial indications suggest the relevance of *Bevis*? First of all, there is the accusation, so common a feature of magical plots and occurring in a context raising the kind of questions that I also find an indication. Following the accusation of the two knights, King Ermin changes character sharply in believing two such whisperers rather than confront his erstwhile trusted liege man, and his desire that Bevis should marry Josian has entirely disappeared, in spite of his invaluable service. Bevis's behavior is also incongruous and inexplicable: his becoming the king's unquestioning, unarmed messenger, and his cruel response to Terri in telling him Bevis has been hanged, point to a magical purpose for the accusation.⁷ Bevis's response to Terri will be a statement parallel to that of the seven years in a dungeon, announcing to the world that due punishment has been carried out.

Another initial indication is the family separation following childbirth, again occurring in a context raising the kind of questions that suggest a magical plot. The giant Ascopart changes sides, returning to King Yvor, *after* the marriage rather than at the more obvious time, *before* it, and he had a good opportunity to return Josian to Yvor when left alone with her at Cologne, before her marriage to Bevis. This kind of timing problem is a typical sign of the presence of a hidden, magical agenda.

Lanval

Lanval is one of the Breton lays of Marie de France, and it belongs to the late twelfth century.⁸ My study will also refer to Thomas Chestre's early-fifteenth-century English version, known as *Sir Launfal,* which has as its sources two works close to Marie's lay, and which—in spite of additions and alterations—I find to have essentially the same magical plot.⁹ The plot given in chart 5 is that of Marie's lay.

Alfred Ewert comments that "Marie has very skilfully adapted the injunction to secrecy, which is a commonplace of fairy tales, to the contemporary theory of love [courtly love], one of whose chief tenets was the obligation on the lover to observe the utmost discretion" (*Marie de France* 173). While this may be true, it is the lack of relationship between Lanval's boast of his lover and the suggestion in the text that he has committed a serious crime that draws my attention to a division—rather than unity—in the text. This division is the chief subject of my investigation: there is little else to guide me, since, if the Lanval plot is magical, it will have only two moves, therefore providing me with minimal assistance from one of my main sources of information. The division, however, guides me in my tracing of two levels of thought in the text.

Taking a close look at the words spoken by Lanval, the queen, the king, and the fairy mistress, in both the French and English versions, I can trace two entirely separate themes that are placed in the text significantly: the theme of the sexual advances to the queen and the theme of the boast. The distinction between them is made clear by the fact that the king's anger and the trial both look quite different in light of Lanval's boast from how they look in light of Lanval's alleged sexual advances to the queen. If we can take our attention away for a moment from the courtly aspects of the French text, we can see that the king's anger makes much more sense in view of the alleged sexual advances to his queen, and yet the trial is presented as being concerned with the boast.

In the French version, the theme of the sexual advances is the subject of the first words spoken by the queen, the king, and Lanval, and it is also the subject of express words of vindication spoken by the fairy mistress. The theme of Lanval's boast of his fairy mistress and the insult felt by the queen take second place in the speeches. The theme of the boast takes first place at the trial, for the trial requires Lanval only to prove this boast: however, the fairy mistress takes the trouble to say to the king, "You should know that the queen was wrong, as he never sought her love."

Lanval's immediate response to the queen, when she offers him her love, is to say he will not betray the king; his boast comes only when the queen says he prefers young men and that the king may have lost salvation through having Lanval near him (vv. 269–302). Strong motivation is provided for his boast. The queen then tells the king that Lanval has requested her love and, upon her refusal, boasted of a beloved whose poorest servant is worthier than her (vv. 316–24). The king says to Lanval:

"Vassal, vus me avez mut mesfait!
Trop començastes vilein plait
De mei hunir e aviler
E la reïne lendengier.
Vanté vus estes de folie:
Trop par est noble vostre amie,
Quant plus est bele sa meschine
E plus vaillanz que la reïne." (vv. 363–70)

["Vassal, you have wronged me greatly! You were extremely ill-advised to shame and vilify me, and to slander the queen. You boasted out of folly, for your beloved must be very noble for her handmaiden to be more beautiful and more worthy than the queen." (77)]

Lanval denies having shamed the king and maintains that he has not sought the queen's love; then he acknowledges his boast of his lady (vv. 371–77). The fairy mistress says to the king:

"Reis, j'ai amé un tuen vassal:
Veez le ci! ceo est Lanval!
Acheisuné fu en ta curt—
Ne vuil mie que a mal li turt—
De ceo qu'il dist; ceo sachez tu
Que la reïne ad tort eü:

Unques nul jur ne la requist.
De la vantance kë il fist,
Si par me peot estre aquitez,
Par voz baruns seit delivrez!" (vv. 615–24)

["King, I have loved one of your vassals, Lanval, whom you see there. Because of what he said, he was accused in your court, and I do not wish him to come to any harm. You should know that the queen was wrong, as he never sought her love. As regards the boast he made, if he can be acquitted by me, let your barons release him!" (81)]

In the English version, *Sir Launfal,* the presentation of the two themes in the characters' speeches and at the trial is the same, except in the case of one notable speech: that of the king to Launfal. The king sends for Launfal so that he can be hanged and drawn (ll. 724–26), and, when Launfal is before him, he says:

"File atainte traitoure,
   Why madest thou swiche yelping?

That thy lemanes lothlokest maide
Was fairer than my wif thou seide.
   That was a foul lesinge!
And thou besoftest here before than
That she shold be thy leman—
   That was misproud likinge!" (ll. 761–68)

Here, the theme of the boast ("yelping") is placed before that of the sexual advances ("you besought her before then to be your lover"). If the themes were placed the other way around, the speech would make more sense. Stronger language is used in this version, references being made to treachery and a traitor's death, and these emphasize the presence of a situation typical of texts using a magical plot: accusations of treachery appear without there seeming to be any good reason why they should be there. We have what might seem to be a reason—that the king has believed the queen's lie about Launfal—but the theme of the boast occupies places in the text where the theme of the sexual advances should be.

   If there is a magical theme of sexual advances to the queen, this will be a theme of treachery, and it will be invisible from points of view concerned with the theme of the boast. Making use of my model of the sovereignty plot, I see two moves in which the accepted advances of a queen-figure are followed by the rejected advances of a queen-figure. These queens have no point of view, and they are figures standing in for each other. The first bestows sovereignty, while the second is wife to the essential king, both king and queen being needed for rituals to remove a sense of treachery over the taking of sovereignty. The second queen's accusation that Lanval has made the advances is the accusation initiating the rituals, having the same function as the accusations in *King Horn* and "The Lady of the Fountain." The plot uses a trial, in which the theme of the boast appears alone in the accusation, and the arrival of the fairy mistress seems to be the reason why Lanval is found not guilty. But, in the magical plot, it is the words the lady speaks to the king that will be operative.

Does the theme of the boast have a role as disguise? It has the effect of disguise, but its presence in the texts will be due to Marie's desire for an additional, courtly theme in her otherwise somewhat obscure material. I think Ewert is probably right that she seized an opportunity presented by an injunction to secrecy in the sources. It is difficult to tell where an apparent disguise is intended to be disguise. Disguise can be a feature of magical texts, but magic itself has no interest in disguise (having no interest in external censure), and its structures are so hidden from the conscious mind that they have little need for it; authors would not usually see that there was anything to disguise. Marie re-creates a hero plot (as opposed to a heroine plot) in all its slightly obtrusive magical detail—this demanding an involvement—while she also converts the material into a fine, courtly lay.

The Story of Meriadoc

J. D. Bruce comments on the two Latin prose romances, *The Story of Meriadoc, King of Cambria* and *The Rise of Gawain*, that the author is "intoxicated with the exuberance of his own rhetoric" and quite unaware that the main interest of his compositions is their preservation of romance material that otherwise would have perished (2:34). For my investigation, one of these romances is of great interest, as a relevant text composed by an ambitious author, and therefore presenting some informative problems and useful questions. *Historia Meriadoci Regis Cambrie* is of uncertain date—somewhere between the later twelfth century and the early fourteenth century. Its story materials have been explored for their relationships to materials found elsewhere,[10] while I am interested in what these materials are used for in the text before me.

The questions the text raises have to do chiefly with the decisions made by the characters, giving me an opportunity to discuss how I choose my questions in a context where events tend always to be unusual. The questions are as follows:

1. As Mildred Leake Day points out, it would be easy to dispatch two children, and yet an "elaborate routine" resembling "a ritual sacrifice" is chosen (*Story of Meriadoc* xxvii); we might contrast this with the proposed drowning of Havelok. I also find curious contradictions relating to the hanging.

> Griffinus quoque, videns suos nepotes suis provolutos vestigiis, ad misericordiam flectitur, eosque ab intentata cede absolvit. Verumptamen proprie saluti consulens sciensque quod, si salvi evasissent, semper quoquomodo debitas a se penas exigerent, iussit eos ad silvam que Arglud nuncupatur deduci atque laqueo suspendi. Ita tamen ut fragiliori fune, que citius rumpi posset, sibi colla necterentur, fidei sacramento ab xii viris hoc nefas executuris accepto, ut numquam inde discederent, donec rupta corda cecidissent.
>
> Acceptis igitur infantulis, tortores forestam Arglud pecierunt. At ubi ad silvas ventum est, ceperunt mutuo de eorum conqueri exicio, dicentes nefarium esse tam crudeli morte perire quos nihil constabat deliquisse. Motique pietate sic eos statuerunt suspendere, ut et funis cito rumperetur et salvi evadere potuissent. In quodam autem saltu ipsius nemoris annosa quercus a diluvii exstabat tempore. . . . Super huius ramum roboris pueros, coniunctis adinvicem vultibus, mutuis inherentes amplexibus, debili fasce illaquearunt, ut, sicut dixi, rupto fune cicius caderent illesisque gutturibus indempnes manerent; citius namque deficiunt qui nexi guttura laqueo suspenduntur. Suspensos autem pueros ipsi econtra, ut sibi imperatum fuerat, observantes residebant. (28, 30)

[Griffin, too, seeing his niece and nephew throw themselves at his feet, was moved to pity and freed them from the intended slaughter. But, nevertheless the truth was that when he considered his own safety, knowing that if they escaped unharmed they would unceasingly demand in every possible way the debt he owed in judgement, he ordered them taken to the forest called Arglud and hanged by a noose in such a way that their necks would be tied by a quite thin rope that could be broken quickly. He received the oath of loyalty from twelve men who would carry out this monstrous thing, never leaving that place till at length the ropes broke and they had slaughtered the children.

With the little children in hand, the executioners made for the forest of Arglud. But when they had come to the forest, they began to deplore the necessity of the death of the children, saying to one another that it was evil to execute those known to have never committed a crime. Moved to pity, they decided to hang them in such a way that the rope would break quickly and they would be able to escape safe and sound. In a certain grove of the same forest an aged oak had stood since the Flood. . . . Upon a branch of this oak they hanged the children together with weak binding. They were turned face to face, clinging together with arms entwined, so that, as I have said, when the rope broke quickly, they would fall with throats uninjured, remaining unhurt. (For those who are hanged with a noose around the neck die quickly.) The men stood opposite, observing the hanging children as they had been ordered. (29, 31)]

However, when Ivor, having dispatched the executioners, lifts the children down, they have been suspended for nearly half a day. I have sometimes found that a passage of narrative does not "add up" because it is really about something else never directly referred to in the text and has been presented to us by the author in an unsuccessfully rationalized form. A quicker dispatch for the children than this hanging in the forest would meet both Griffin's pity and his interests more appropriately. The executioners' methods, meanwhile, do not meet either their pity or their oath of loyalty, so why do they not come to some other decision? There is also a curious confusion over the hanging: Griffin orders the use of a thin rope quickly broken while also ordering the men never ("numquam") to leave until at length ("donec") the ropes break and the children are dead, and the executioners decide on a particular way of hanging that will cause the rope to break quickly enough for the children to survive; then, when the children survive their being suspended for half a day, there is no comment in the text. If a magical plot were present, the prolonged suspension would be an important ritual, and the characters presented as responsible for it would have no point of view; their pity might turn out to have a magical function, or alternatively to be part of the author's developments.

2. As Mildred Leake Day observes, the emperor's daughter has a "strangely ambiguous position" (*Story of Meriadoc* xxxv–xxxvi). Although she is a prisoner abducted by force, her abductor treats her like a daughter, and even as his lady. She tells Meriadoc that the sovereignty of all Gundebald's kingdom lies under her command ("'Tocius enim sui regni principatus meis subiacet iussionibus,'" 168, 170). Her situation is full of contradictions. The king yields to her will in all things ("'Ipsemet rex mee voluntati in omnibus obsequitur,'" 170), not wishing to do anything opposite to what he knows is her intention, and yet she remains his prisoner and his people suffer his "'malicious customs and insupportable tyranny'" (171; "'morum perversitatem et importabilem tirannidem,'" 170, 172), as she herself describes them. Since she is a captive, her allegiance must be in doubt, and the king is at war with her father over her abduction, and yet she administers the city in his absence and also houses his arms. If these characters were figures in a magical plot, the ambiguity and contradictions would disappear. It would be important that the emperor's daughter was a prisoner abducted by force and also that she had the position of a queen; it would be important too that Gundebald yielded to her will in all things while, at the same time, ruling the kingdom in ways she condemned.

3. In the last part of the narrative, the emperor suffers the invasion of the king of Gaul, and he chooses this moment to wish to subdue his invaluable soldier Meriadoc to his own power. Since Meriadoc has made known to him in writing everything he has accomplished, the emperor will know that it is worth using Meriadoc's services one more time to defeat his new enemy. Instead, he chooses to sell his daughter—rescued for him by Meriadoc—in exchange for peace with this enemy. The author presents the situation and the emperor's reasoning as follows:

> Dum autem Meriadocus in hiis esset occupatus negociis, ingens bellum inter imperatorem et regem Gallie exoritur, quo imperatorem valde comprimi et coartari contigit. Rex quippe Gallie ex inproviso super eum ducens exercitum, longe lateque eius depeculiatus provincias, quasdam quoque preclaras urbes et municipia expugnavit, cives captivavit, reliqua omnia ferro et flamma pessumdans. Tres eciam ipsius duces cum maxima multitudine sibi occurrentes prostravit omnemque eorum usque ad internicionem fudit exercitum. Imminente igitur sibi rege et

assidua infestacione incumbente, compulsus est imperator cum eo pacem firmare talique condicione inire concordiam, ut filiam suam quam Gundebaldo Meriadocus eripuerat maritali lege coniungeret, concessis ei omnibus que de suo imperio armis optinuerat. Iam quippe ei Meriadocus universa a se gesta scripto innotuerat. Cavit autem diligentissime imperator ne quod cum rege Gallie super filie sue desponsacione convenerat, ullo modo Meriadoco patefieret; unde et ad huius rei noticiam non nisi consiliarios suos quemquam admiserat. Noverat enim probitatem Meriadoci et quantum in re militari valeret quantumque iam sibi ex duobus regnis que adquisi[v]erat robur accrevisset. Studuit itaque eum fraude circumvenire, qua filiam suam de manibus eius auferre ipsumque sui potestati posset subigere. (188, 190)

[However, while Meriadoc was occupied in these affairs of state, bitter war arose between the Emperor and the King of Gaul, who was pressing the forces of the Emperor and driving them back. The King of Gaul, leading his army against him in a surprise move, had pillaged the length and breadth of his provinces, raided some of his most splendid cities and castles, taking the people captive and razing the countryside by sword and fire. He had conquered three of the Emperor's dukes who had mounted a counter-attack with a great number of men, and he routed the entire army almost to destruction. With the unremitting and continuously hostile attacks falling upon him, the Emperor was forced to negotiate peace with the King, and the conditions to initiate a concord were such that he would unite his daughter (the young woman Meriadoc had rescued from Gundebald) with the King he had taken from the Empire by force of arms. This was done even though Meriadoc had made known to him in writing everything that he had accomplished. For this reason the Emperor was extremely careful lest what he had agreed concerning his daughter's betrothal to the King of Gaul be revealed to Meriadoc in any way; he further allowed no notice at all of this treaty to be sent to any of his counselors. For he knew the prowess of Meriadoc and the extent of his brilliance in military strategy, and how much already his authority had grown as a result of the two kingdoms he had won for him. The Emperor undertook therefore to trap him by treachery so that he could regain his daughter from his hands and be able to subdue the man himself to his own power. (189, 191)]

This is the kind of narrative situation that appears when the material is really about something else not acknowledged in the text, and when both what it is really about and how the author wishes to treat the material are important in the text. The author develops the subject of the emperor's disasters in war with his characteristic exuberant rhetoric, emphasizing the emperor's necessity in an attempt to give his decisions an urgent motive, and the result is that the military events relate the more unhappily with the emperor's preoccupations. Such an emperor should be the less able to think of anything else but the immediate need to remove the king of Gaul and the immediate usefulness of Meriadoc; Meriadoc's military power must, in the short term, be preferable to the peace arranged with the king of Gaul. In a magical plot, the emperor would be a figure in the rituals, without a point of view, rather than a character who could see that Meriadoc had a power more beneficial to emperors than that of the king of Gaul. As this figure, he would be given roles that play an important part in the text, roles invisible from the points of view adopted by critics, but by no means subordinate or easily altered by authors developing the material. As a general rule, the author's additional work is subordinate, and the text before us exemplifies a typical situation where the author's additional work is functionally little more than a decoration of the magical narrative. This becomes apparent in the kind of contradictions I have found: they are all between details operative in the magical plot and therefore of a kind that disappears when the correct point of view is adopted; some are made more obtrusive by the author's additional, rationalizing work, while none are caused by the separate operation of two levels of thought ignorant of each other in the creation of a two-tier structure.

Distinguishing between the different kinds of contradiction is a matter for the critic's subsequent analysis of the text. One learns to recognize various types of problems at the question stage, but there are no short-cuts. My questions illustrate my priority at the outset: to look for indications of important purposes in the text that are not acknowledged. These purposes give rise to problems of logicality, because the thought concerned operates quite differently from thought systems we are familiar with and also—which can be a great help to the critic—quite differently from any additional thought system that may be present in the text.

As a magical text, this text would have a sovereignty plot, but, when I apply my model (see chart 6), I find that the episodes in their sequence do not give the assistance I find in the case of the *King Horn* and *Sir Degarré* texts. Many romance plots consist of a sequence of fantastic episodes without being magical,[11] and my task is always to discover the nature of the connections between the episodes. The sequence in the earlier part of the narrative appears less highly organized than I would expect in a sovereignty plot, lacking the step-by-step structure I find in the Degarré plot, and yet the final episode, with the king of Gaul, looks decidedly like a magical change of direction in order to remove an irrational sense of treachery—one using the intriguing method of turning the emperor into the traitor. My questions draw my attention particularly to this final episode and to the early event of the hanging, which has the appearance of a ritual punishment, or of a ritual declaration of innocence. For Meriadoc's initial appearance to be that of an innocent victim in the case of a usurpation suggests the presence of heavy defenses, which, in turn, might explain the lack of the step-by-step structure in the plot. Upon close examination of the early episodes and the last, I now argue a case for the unusual structure of the defended sovereignty plot—a structure with something more of a move sequence than is present in the defended narrative of my model, but a move sequence only clearly visible in the latter part.

A defended narrative usually provides heavy defenses at both the beginning and end of the narrative, so, having decided that the hanging suggests the presence of characteristics of this kind of narrative, I look to see if there are more defenses following the hanging, and I find many more. The initial episode recounts a usurpation of Meriadoc's father's throne from which Meriadoc is distanced in a sequence of events. First, he is a victim, being hanged and then spending five years in exile in the forest. Both the hanging and the exile with the good father (Ivor) will have additional purifying functions. Then the usurping character is punished and Meriadoc made king in his stead with the approval of the kings who have carried out the punishment. This episode is followed by the episode with the Black, Red, and White Knights, where Meriadoc is Arthur's champion against three knights in succession who all claim land from the king as lawfully theirs. Having won the land for the king, Meriadoc receives it from him as a reward and gives it to the claimant in the presence of the king. The ritual procedure of winning land for the king and then giving it to the rightful claimant is enacted three times over. "The hero" is champion of the landowners, claiming nothing for himself, while, conversely, the claimants also represent the hero (they have sworn an oath of fealty and obedience to Meriadoc), receiving their land from the king by means of an honorable transaction. These details are their properties as they become Meriadoc's sworn companions in the progress towards sovereignty. This progress takes place while in the service of the emperor, in his war to recover his daughter abducted by King Gundebald—by these means taking place under cover of being an opposite action to that of taking sovereignty.

Thus heavily safeguarded against the idea of usurpation, the adventures to follow show no highly organized progression, although they do have magical relationships with each other. There are the two castles of fear, the first undertaken after Meriadoc, pursuing the emperor's enemy, has recovered stolen goods, and the second followed by Meriadoc's destruction of two "vile thieves" who have killed a lady's husband. I examine the events in their context, but, without a strong move structure, I can do little to establish their function. Reclining alone at the high table with the great lady of the first castle, Meriadoc is overcome with fear and flees, while, at the second castle, in a quite opposite mood, he enters and snatches the food and drink he wants from the lady of the castle, as she sits at table. This lady of the castle is reduced in size, while Meriadoc succeeds through his "pertinacity" (144) in taking the food he wants and getting away with his thefts.

In the next part of the narrative, preparations are made for the sovereignty move. Meriadoc wins a kingdom for the emperor and sends him word of his success. The delighted emperor replies that what he has acquired and what he will acquire will be his: if he were able to rescue his daughter, she will be given to him, together with riches and glory. The emperor's daughter, meanwhile, hearing of Meriadoc's daring, sends for him to come and rescue her. So with the sanction of both emperor and daughter, Meriadoc sets off with the Black, Red, and White Knights for Gundebald's kingdom. Gundebald is killed and the emperor's daughter won through the lady's work rather than through Meriadoc's. Afterwards, the kingdom is repeatedly declared to be Meriadoc's while Meriadoc declares that he is under the orders of the emperor: the lords reply that he owes nothing to the emperor ("se nichil imperatori debere," 186), and that they will place him in authority as if he were the king.

Many a story would end here: it would not include protests such as Meriadoc's as to whether the kingdom was won or not, and it would not give us the turn of events that follow. What would the hero gain from the arrangements of the final move? I think the answer is that he wins sovereignty all over again, using means that simultaneously remove a sense of treachery. The emperor is turned into the traitor, and his accusations against Meriadoc become accusations spoken by a traitor. Meriadoc can kill him as one who repaid his services with treachery. The king of Gaul, meanwhile, plays the role of invader, taking land and daughter, and he assumes the authority of the emperor, bestowing land and daughter on Meriadoc.

Part II

The Basket of Flowers

Das Blumenkörbchen,[12] by Christoph von Schmid, a Bavarian pastor, fascinated readers from its publication in 1823, and, in its American adaptation *The Basket of Flowers,*[13] became the archetype of the Sunday-school book, still popular in African missions in 1972 (Bratton 66–67). It is seen as a moralized romance, Anne Renier commenting that its plot of false accusation and final vindication gives scope for "the dramatic rendering of the triumph of the virtuous and the downfall of the wicked, very satisfying to the sense of fairness usually possessed by children" (6). J. S. Bratton describes the plot as "a doubled account of a heroine's descent from Eden, the idyllic garden, to the world of pain and loss, followed by her restoration.... Her true identity, her innocence, is carried through the story to be rediscovered at the end of two tokens: the ring, symbol of the dark forces that oppose her, and the basket of flowers, symbol of love and duty. By her retention of the basket through all her trials the defense of her threatened virgin innocence is figured forth" (68).

It is undoubtedly the plot that has gripped audiences (see chart 7), and this will have been in part for the reasons given by Renier and Bratton. Among the materials making up this plot is the motif of the magpie's theft and the false accusation, a popular theme of the time.[14] What interests me in the text is the use of the double accusations, the first initiating a sequence of punishments and the second a sequence of justifications. The second accusation, in particular—repeating as it does the same features of the stolen object, the strangely powerful accuser, and the insufficiently motivated hatred—is suggestive of a magical mechanism, ushering in rituals for vindication. This accusation on the part of the daughter-in-law appears somewhat awkward and superfluous, for, if it were simply omitted, Jacob's death would be the crisis facing Marie in exile when Amalia came to stay in the neighborhood and heard about her. However, magic would employ the second accusation as a device to parallel that of the first accusation, initiating the contrasting sequence of rituals for vindication.

Another feature that catches my attention is the basket of flowers itself, linked as it is with the flowers of the garden and all that they represent, including the virtues required in Marie. This basket is first presented as a birthday gift to the young countess Amalia, with Amalia's name and coat of arms on it, and then it is thrown at Marie by the waiting-maid, as Marie and her father leave Eichburg. Thus accompanying Marie in exile, this embodiment of goodness becomes the instrument setting in motion, and continuing indefinitely, the public declaration of Marie's goodness. Marie's gift to Amalia, with her name and coat of arms, looks forward to the role it is to play as a recognition token on the grave. And its being an assembly of virtues in a conveyance, traveling through the story with Marie, and of crucial assistance to her, suggests its having the role of a talisman, empowering the heroine in a purification process.

The inconsistencies in character shown by the bailiff and count's family cannot indicate a magical plot on their own, because inattention to such matters may have other narrative reasons, but the contrasts between harshness and generosity would have functions in the case of a magical plot. The harshness would play a role in certain rituals, while the generosity would have a role in others. Altogether, the presentation of the accusations and vindications in the narrative brings various details into remarkable relationships with each other, but features of this kind make a more satisfactory study in richer, more detailed texts, where the exigencies of a magical plot interfere with the themes and characterizations belonging to other levels of the narrative.

It can be argued that there is a magical plot present in *The Basket of Flowers* and, therefore, potentially a much closer relationship between audience and narrative than that suggested by Renier and Bratton. There can be more here than satisfaction over the triumph of the virtuous and downfall of the wicked and more than the endurance and restoration of a condemned heroine whose "true identity" is innocence. Critics often distance a narrative from readers inappropriately—as if, in this case, the loss of Eden and struggle to return to it were not an urgent, even terrifying, problem for humanity, not least in the evangelical nineteenth century, when impossible standards were imposed, and in the mind of a child, always vulnerable to the condemnation of adults.

My chart of the plot (based on Christoph von Schmid's original text) shows the three moves I see in it. In the first, Marie is placed in the garden and given a saintly father, who shows her perfection in the flowers and expresses the imperative to be pure of all wickedness. The magic is entirely concerned to bring about this perfection for the heroine, so this is a purification plot. In the second move, the flowers acquire a means of transport so that they form a talisman, and, as a gift to Amalia, they are prepared for their role as recognition token. The thieving magpie motif is then employed to initiate the rituals of punishment and penance—an essential stage in the expulsion of a sense of sin. There is an idea of temptation in the detail relating to Marie's acceptance of Amalia's dress and the theft of the ring, which indicates the presence of this particular fear in the plot, also to be removed. Innocence can be damaged by one word or thought, Jacob tells Marie, and the aim of the plot is to acquire a sense of unassailable virtue. It is typical of purification plots that the final punishment is death, in some way altered to exile. During Marie'e exile, the garden of flowers is re-created out of a neglected garden, and the virtues shown to thrive among thorns. The events of this second move are made use of by the vindication rituals of the final move.

The final move begins with the second accusation, immediately followed by the vindications relating to the first accusation. The count's family arrive at Marie's place of exile, where Marie is once again accused and exiled and Amalia discovers the truth about Marie. Having been shown the grave as something beautiful, with its basket of flowers, she seeks out the forester's daughter and the priest to hear Marie's story. Then she and Marie meet at the grave. The rest of the move is a piling-on of public declarations of Marie's innocence and goodness: the local people's praise of Jacob and Marie, confirmed by the priest; the observed scene of the loving daughter at the grave of the saintly man, together with the basket of flowers and the rose tree; the proof of Marie's innocence with regard to the ring; the horror over the injustice and the requests for forgiveness; the punishment of the wicked accusers; the present of the ring and of Jacob's cottage and garden; the welcome back to Eichburg from exile; the entry into the families of the count and bailiff; the countess's eulogy to the bailiff, praising Marie's consummate virtues learned in the school of suffering (including her humility, modesty, and innocence); and, finally, the priest's recital of the story of the basket of flowers to attentive visitors at Jacob's monument. This accumulation of magical devices is a typical feature: where we might think that one or two would be enough, many more are used.

In medieval texts, it is usually easy to tell where moves begin and end. A change of location is combined with the fresh magical step in many cases, and there are strategic transfers to and from surrogate locations; a new move may also be made clear by an obvious repetition of character or rearrangement of events. In the few modern texts I have studied, discerning the moves has not always been so easy. The ritual arrangements and rearrangements of magic are, however, quite clear in *The Basket of*

Flowers, leaving me only to wonder whether there are two moves or three. Finally I have decided that the vision of goodness in Jacob's garden at Eichburg has the force of a move on its own: it is the vision to be achieved and problem to be resolved, and its powerful ingredients are employed by the rituals to follow. The second and third moves each begin with an accusation and have the contrasting content of punishment and justification.

I use the word "heroine," rather than the name "Marie," when I am considering how the narrative might be used magically by anyone identifying with it, and male participants would be included here. "Heroine" refers to the sex of the chief character, the sex of the participant being irrelevant for a study of the text. It would, of course, be interesting to know a great deal about audience response that the texts cannot tell us.

The Basket of Flowers makes an interesting contrast with the Religious Tract Society's *Our Sister May or Number One* (London, n.d.), a story concerned in practical detail with the hard work of moral improvement. "Our Sister May" learns to think of herself as "number two" (11) and thus transforms a life full of "Neglected Duties" (13) into a "useful" life (128). In such a moral climate, Christoph von Schmid's story of false accusations and justification might seem surprising material for Sunday schools, but the invisible purification purpose would supply an urgently needed service. Magic does not concentrate on sin (except where it is assigned to disowned characters, such as Marie's accusers, for strategic purposes) and it bypasses the hard work. Instead, it offers ritual means of removing a sense of sin and acquiring a feeling of one's own goodness. In this concern to alter personal, subjective feelings, a further distinction between magical and moral can be seen. The magical purpose is entirely private. The public declarations of innocence and goodness, in the final move of *The Basket of Flowers,* are themselves — at the magical level — private ritual strategies for bringing the innocence and goodness about in the mind. Furthermore, as such, they are the product of a continuing struggle with sin, rather than a recognition of a "true identity" of innocence.

The Wide, Wide World

Susan Warner's *The Wide, Wide World* (published in 1850 under the name of Elizabeth Wetherell)[15] is an evangelical romance, for most of its great length unified as the story of an American childhood, in which an orphaned girl endures personal loss and is brought up and educated by a variety of people. Hardships are viewed as part of her religious and personal development. There is much pious discourse, and more attractive to the modern reader is the detail as to how a New England farmhouse was run in the mid-nineteenth century, from the production of the butter, the pork and hams, the candles and the catnip tea, to the making of a "bee," when the help of neighbors was needed for the preparation of the apples and the sausage meat. Ellen Montgomery has to be separated from her loving mother in New York, at the beginning of the story, when her mother falls ill and her parents go to France, eventually to die. She goes to her stern aunt in rural New England, and chief among the many contrasting people she knows are the parson's daughter Alice Humphreys and her brother John, both young adults. They play an important part in her emotional life and in her religious and general education, and, after her aunt marries and Alice falls mortally ill, Ellen takes Alice's place at the parsonage. It is at this point, in the last pages of the book, that unexpected and puzzling events take place.

Up to this point, one would not suspect the presence of a magical plot. There are contrasting episodes, with the loving mother, with the stern aunt, and with the deeply religious Alice, but such contrasts are not in themselves an indication, and the novel has powerful themes of another kind. Where I find an indication of a move structure is where Ellen transfers to Scotland, to undergo experiences that play no satisfactory part in these themes.

Letters are discovered expressing the wish of Ellen's dead parents that she go to Scotland, to her mother's relatives there. These letters had been unknown to Ellen because of peculiarities in her aunt's convincingly drawn character. Ellen does not wish to leave the parsonage family (now consisting of father and son), who have "adopted" her, but she decides it is her duty to carry out her parents' wishes. Her life in Scotland is a sharp change of direction in the narrative. Hitherto, it has been the Christian and American story of a girl winning through trials to an honored position in two families (at the farm and the parsonage). In Scotland, she finds a family who imperiously take her over and cut her off from her past. She is ordered to call her Scottish uncle, Mr. Lindsay, "father" and to change her name to his, and she is forbidden to refer to John Humphreys as her brother, which she has been doing since she and Alice began to call each other "sister." Any reference to America or religion is unwelcome: the Americans are regarded as a "parcel of rebels," disloyal to Britain, while religion is just "these notions" ("'Where did you get these notions?'"). This new family imposes its will on Ellen to the extent of making the child drink wine against her conscience; if her will ever runs counter to theirs, she finds it impossible to maintain her ground. Meanwhile, there is a remarkable reiteration of the uncle's insistence that he is her father and she his daughter.

> "You are my own child now, you are my little daughter, do you know that, Ellen? I am your father henceforth; you belong to me entirely, and I belong to you; my own little daughter!" (417)

On another occasion, her uncle makes her call him father, and she obeys trembling, "for it seemed to her that it was to set her hand and seal to the deed of gift her father and mother had made. But there was no retreat; it was spoken; and Mr. Lindsay folding her close in his arms kissed her again and again."

> "Never let me hear you call me anything else, Ellen. You are mine now—my own child—my own little daughter. You shall do just what pleases me in everything, and let bygones be bygones."

> "I have done it now!" thought Ellen. . . . "I have called him my father, I am bound to obey him after this. I wonder what in the world they will make me do next." (429)

She wonders what she would do if they wanted her to do something wrong.

Such scenes continue and the only event they lead to is the arrival of John Humphreys. Ellen introduces him to "her father" and, after a frosty beginning, Mr. Lindsay decides to introduce John to Mrs. Lindsay. John is warmly received as a guest. When Ellen tells John of her new family's having been opposed to both America and himself, he replies, "'What will they say to you then, Ellie, if you leave them to give yourself to me?'" The novel ends with this prospect in view and with the comment that four years of Scottish discipline "beautify [Ellen's] Christian character."

However, one cannot feel conviction that the four years are added to the narrative for that purpose, a purpose which would make the last episode part of the whole. They do not come across as a new trial to test or develop Ellen's Christian character: Ellen has to act against the principles she learned in New England in order to obey her Scottish relatives. These people are, in the context of this novel, moral inferiors with whom Ellen must mark time until she comes of age. J. S. Bratton takes a feminist view of the reiteration of Ellen's being a possession, and comments, "we are fobbed off with talk of discipline which did her no harm, and her duty to this seemingly quite spurious family to await the solution of the law"

(Ellen's coming of age) (155). My own approach is to look at the scenes and see what they actually do in the text. What they do is separate Ellen from her adopted family, the Humphreys at the parsonage, prior to the introduction of the idea of Ellen's marrying John. The Humphreys are not her family any more, for the Scottish household is emphatically her family, by her parents' wish and their own insistence. Had Ellen known her parents' wish, she would have gone to Scotland much earlier. The Scottish family also has other functions. Ellen's being entirely under their will, even where she must obey them against her principles, will be important, deviation as it is in this text, and its function is likely to be that the heroine—and here I mean the participant in the magical plot rather than Ellen the character—is freed from the dictates of her own conscience. This will be a useful arrangement in a move designed to remove a sense that what is desired (John) is wrong. The spiritual inferiority of the Scottish family, which again does not "fit" in the novel, will have a role in this arrangement and perhaps, too, in establishing a sense of the heroine's goodness.

Why, one might ask, does the novel have to go to these lengths to remove a fear of incest: why not distance the Humphreys family earlier by not having Alice, John, and Ellen adopt each other as siblings? I think the answer must be that John's being a brother is important, and a magical plot must give full expression to all that is important, no matter what problems it may cause. Meanwhile, magic has no concern with how the resulting material may look to the rational mind.

This text illustrates well how the devices for removing fear and guilt can remain obtrusive in texts well developed at other levels of thought. The devices of the magical process always require full expression in the text, and the process may demand ritual material and spoken statements that appear startling in the larger context of the work concerned. Hence the reiteration of the uncle's insistence that Ellen is his daughter—the kind of material that can be impossible to rationalize and which Susan Warner leaves without satisfactory development.

If the Scottish episode is a move, then there must be a complete move structure. I see four moves—in New York, with Ellen's parents; at the New England farm with the stern aunt; at the parsonage, when Ellen takes Alice's place; and, finally, in Scotland. The first three moves, with their contrasting parent-figures (including Alice and John Humphreys), are upstaged by the author's developments, most notably by her development of the characters at the aunt's farm. This is, in any case, a plot needing no exorcisms—the removal of the idea that the heroine's desires are evil—before the end; only at the end does the plot reach the point where marital plans are to be expressed. Alice and John Humphreys, in what might be called the sovereignty move, are religious figures, not well-drawn. John is presented as a godlike, perfect character, always Ellen's teacher. While, at other levels, the novel is concerned with growth towards Christian perfection, the magical plot seems to be concerned with accomplishing this magically, by alliance with perfection, and, at this deep level, a fatherly, elder brother-figure, son of the parsonage and ordained himself, represents this crowning condition. However, his ingredients make necessary a final move for exorcisms.

Rebecca

Magical stories, in general, have liberating effects, releasing audiences from irrational tensions deep in the mind. That they do this in a thoroughly irrational way is most striking—even though more difficult to show conclusively—in a popular modern text like *Rebecca,* where the plot is the invention of Daphne du Maurier herself.

In *Rebecca,* I find an idiosyncratic plot, which is nevertheless typical of magical narrative in its concern to remove an irrational fear so that something desired can be achieved and enjoyed. It is not entirely unlike the Accused Queen purification plots, which have a similar concern to remove irrational feelings haunting marriage, feelings arising from the connections there can be between sexual relationships and primal relationships. However, the plot of *Rebecca* is not a purification plot, removing ideas of incest; it has no theme of incest or of irrational guilt. In *Rebecca,* the conflict I find addressed is another aspect of the primal triangle haunting marriage: the heroine is a child, not a wife, and cannot change this position until she has dealt with the figures placed in the other two corners. The husband's parental dominance has to be removed and his former marriage expunged. The plot is quite close to that of *Jane Eyre,* except that *Jane Eyre* has an accompanying concern to remove the idea of incest.[16] Neither plot conforms to the model of the sovereignty plot, in which the heroine emerges in glory, because its victory depends on reduced circumstances and is marriage without fear rather than queenhood. Like Mr. Rochester, Mr. de Winter is reduced in power and removed from the setting of his former marriage, becoming dependent on the heroine. There are some modern features here that are interesting as the objective of magic.

I find the text of *Rebecca* very much the creation of two levels of thought. To the upper level belongs Daphne du Maurier's exploration of the pain of lack of confidence and also what she herself described as a study in jealousy.[17] The magical plot below can have no direct connection with such concerns, since it cannot study emotions, laboring instead to bring about those it wants and dispel those unwanted. The removal of the source of jealousy could be its concern here (it expunges Rebecca), but its concerns are really much larger and centered on the heroine's feelings about herself, rather than a third party.

In spite of the lack of connection between the two levels, this text is a good example of how a novel using realism can be harmoniously based on a magical plot. An imaginative exploration of the second wife's experience coexists with a magical operation reducing Rebecca to dust and Manderley to ashes, ruthless hidden solutions that have nothing to do with imaginative exploration. But, since a magical plot's operations take precedence over the upper level, the measures it employs must sometimes disturb the upper material too much. The style of characterization typical of romance tends to give us characters like Mr. de Winter, Mrs. Danvers, and Rebecca: they do not have to be the productions of magic, and, in fact, the taming of fierce men is a common theme in romance. Nevertheless, there is an uneasy relationship between the Mr. de Winter of the first part of the novel and the Mr. de Winter of the second, when an unfeeling man suddenly becomes a tender one. If he has loved his second wife for her unsophistication, why has he humiliated her for it, even in front of the servants (over the broken cupid)? His father-to-silly-child manner in the first part does not square with the husband of the second part, needing the love of an equal. Rebecca, meanwhile, is too "evil, vicious and rotten" (chap. 21) to have any reality, and one wonders why an object of jealousy has no redeeming feature? It is too suggestive of the single point of view. The study in jealousy cannot go deep in a scenario where it turns out that Rebecca was never loved by Mr. de Winter, and, instead, the novel can be seen to be expunging this first wife. The splendid romance character of Mrs. Danvers presents no particular problems. She represents the first Mrs. de Winter, living on in the house dead: she has "a skull's face, parchment-white, set on a skeleton's frame," and her hand is "deathly cold" as it lies in the second wife's "like a lifeless thing" (chap. 7). But I think that the characteristics of all three of these characters are functions of the magical plot I find in the text. The plot requires Mr. de Winter to appear in the contradictory ways he does, and it requires the reduction of the first Mrs. de Winter, first into a jealous servant, and next into a devil hated by her husband.

For my clues as to the nature of the plot, I do not look at the characters first, but at the sequence of events. The plot does not have a move structure clearly indicated by changes in location, but a step-by-step progression can nevertheless be traced. The text is also quite explicit as to the nature of the final happiness (given at the beginning of the novel) and the nature of the suffering: any magical step-by-step progression would lead from marriage with the master of Manderley, haunted by the continued presence of the "true" wife, to marriage without Manderley.

> The house was a sepulchre, our fear and suffering lay buried in the ruins. There would be no resurrection.
>
> I should think of it as it might have been, could I have lived there without fear.
>
> It is when I remember these things that I turn with relief to the prospect from our balcony.... At the moment it inspires me, if not with love, at least with confidence. And confidence is a quality I prize. ... I suppose it is his dependence upon me that has made me bold at last.
>
> Well, it is over now, finished and done with. I ride no more tormented, and both of us are free.... Manderley is no more. It lies like an empty shell. (chaps. 1–2)

The first stage of the process removing Rebecca opens with the arrival at Manderley, where Rebecca is dead and refusing to be so, haunting the house as a formidable housekeeper devoted to her memory; her possessions and lifestyle are everywhere in evidence. Mrs. Danvers says to the heroine, "'You'll never get the better of her. She's still mistress here, even if she is dead. She's the real Mrs. de Winter, not you'" (chap. 18). When the heroine breaks the cupid, she hides the pieces at the back of a drawer, and Mr. de Winter, learning of this, comments to the housekeeper,

> "Is not that the sort of thing the between-maid is supposed to do, Mrs. Danvers?"
>
> "The between-maid at Manderley would never be allowed to touch the valuable things in the morning-room, sir," said Mrs. Danvers.
>
> "No, I can't see you letting her," said Maxim. (chap. 12)

Clearly, a new move is needed, and it is entered abruptly on the morning after the ball, at the moment when Mrs. Danvers is persuading the heroine to commit suicide, telling her she will never replace Rebecca. There is an explosion made by the rocket of a ship gone ashore in the bay, and this heralds the next stage in the removal of Rebecca.

The heroine is "waiting for something to happen" and has "a latent sense of excitement"; it is as though she has "entered into a new phase of [her] life and nothing would be quite the same again." The finding of Rebecca's significantly named boat "Je Reviens" is what happens. Rebecca is now resurrected as a skeleton, with Maxim as her killer; he and the heroine are also transformed into equals and lovers. Maxim tells the heroine that Rebecca was entirely evil, and she repeats to herself over and over again, "Maxim did not love Rebecca. He had never loved her, never, never." Her heart, "for all its anxiety and doubt, was light and free." She knew then that she was no longer afraid of Rebecca: now that she knew her to have been "evil and vicious and rotten" she did not hate her any more. Rebecca could not hurt her. The effect of Maxim's new status as a murderer is that he is now vulnerable, and the heroine says, "I was free now to be with Maxim. . . . I would never be a child again. . . . We would face this trouble together. . . . I was not young any more. . . . I was not afraid. . . . Rebecca had not won. Rebecca had lost." She can take on more authority, being severe with Mrs. Danvers: "'I am Mrs. de Winter now, you know.'" It seemed to her that Rebecca had no reality any more. "She had crumbled away when they had found her on the cabin floor. It was not Rebecca who was lying in that coffin in the crypt, it was dust. Only dust" (chaps. 20–23).

A very thorough inquest arrives at a verdict of suicide, and Rebecca is buried. The magical process I see is, however, far from complete. Why should the devices leaving Rebecca dust, Maxim having never loved her and her killing safe from the law, not be sufficient? But it is typical of magic that the devices are piled on long after we might feel no more are needed, and the final devices can seem among the strangest. In the last part of the novel, Favell's attempt at blackmail initiates a curious pair of themes that do not have sufficient relationship with each other. In one, there is Favell's accusation of murder, which, while true, comes from a disreputable person whose witnesses do not support him. In the other, there is the untrue but very powerful verdict of suicide, which is supported by the doctor's later evidence that there was a motive for it— Rebecca's mortal illness. In spite of this, we are told that local gossip will need to be quelled, as if there were grounds for a build-up of suspicion. These two themes are tensely followed up until they disappear in the burning down of Manderley, presumably by Favell. This final event is the strangest of all.

While the burning down of Manderley is a curious ending to the novel, its power and importance are conveyed at the very beginning ("Last night I dreamt I went to Manderley again. . . . The house was a sepulchre, our fear and suffering lay buried in the ruins"). There is a striking similarity with the destruction of Mr. Rochester's house by fire in *Jane Eyre,* and I find that the burning down of Manderley plays the same magical roles: the elimination of the setting haunted by ideas relating to the primal triangle and the reduction of the husband's power. The destruction of Manderley is decisive for the plot, but it is likely that the two parallel themes of the continuing suspicion and the mounting support for Maxim's innocence play magical roles, as well as roles in the upper level of the novel. The heroine needs to secure both Maxim's freedom and his continuing vulnerability (under suspicion), which has a role in the altered balance of power.

Magic is ever-inventive, ready to make use of materials that have not been used magically before, while I also find the same narrative material turning up again and again for the same purposes. The burning down of the house haunted by the heroine's fears seems to be Charlotte Brontë's invention, and it may well be that Daphne du Maurier borrowed it from *Jane Eyre,* as a deep rather than conscious borrowing. Such borrowing will be a time-honored process. But every magical plot is different—a fresh challenge for the critic—and the plot of *Rebecca* is structurally without much resemblance to *Jane Eyre.* It is also less remarkable: as I find is usually the case, the greater writer has produced a greater text at all levels.[18]

I

Emaré, Catskin, and Constance

Princesses in Exile and Accused Queens

In this chapter, I shall discuss seven interconnected narratives, making the Middle English romance *Emaré* the central text. Most of these belong to the large group known as the Constance cycle, or as the story of the Calumniated Wife; Chaucer's *Man of Law's Tale* is a famous example. One other narrative, belonging to a different group—the Catskin group—but otherwise close to *Emaré*, is also given detailed consideration.

Six of these narratives, I shall argue, have magical plots concerned with purification, by which I mean that each plot is a sequence of rituals designed to dispel fear or guilt. In the case of the seventh narrative, Chaucer's *Man of Law's Tale*, I shall show that, although the material used is much the same, the plot is not magical. Each narrative will be discussed in turn, and for five of them I present a chart showing how I think the plot works (see Appendix); those details particularly concerned with purification are given in italics. As each narrative enters the discussion, further information is added.

Following my discussion of *Emaré*, a tail-rhyme romance belonging to about 1400 A.D., I turn to Beaumanoir's thirteenth-century romance *La Manekine*, and two much later texts close to it, the Italian tale of "Penta the Handless" in Basile's *Pentamerone*, and the Grimm story of the handless maiden, "Das Mädchen ohne Hände." The La Manekine group makes striking use of ritual punishment, and so, in a different fashion, does the version of the story from Matthew Paris's Latin *Life of Offa I*, which follows. This raises new questions, and, beyond this, the texts demonstrate the range of materials employed by magic. They also show how the rituals of the Accused Queen plot persist in material apparently much altered. Some of the plots apparently cater for both heroine and hero participation, which is an unusual feature. I then leave the Constance group to introduce the Catskin group of tales, considering, as my chief example, the French folktale "La Peau d'Anon." These tales use quite different material, while having very similar underlying magical purposes to those of *Emaré*. Finally, I use the opportunity offered by Chaucer's *Man of Law's Tale* to consider the difference between Constance stories with and without a magical plot. Full details of the Constance cycle are to be found in studies by Elizabeth Archibald and Margaret Schlauch.[1]

There are close links between this chapter and the two to follow, since the stories discussed are all, in some way, related to each other. In the chapter on the King Lear stories and the Cap o' Rushes tales, I consider the curious relationship between a literary tradition of nonmagical stories (about King Lear) and an oral tradition of magical tales (about Cap o' Rushes). The magical stories are concerned with purification, and one English tale exemplifies this type of magical plot so well that it is quoted in full. I am given an opportunity to discuss a range of factors connected with my wider subject: above all, how magical and nonmagical plots using similar material differ; what happens when magical stories are transformed into nonmagical stories; and how a magical source can affect nonmagical offspring.

In the third chapter, I consider the Cinderella story in relation to the Catskin and Cap o' Rushes tales, since these three groups have been linked by folklore analysts. The Scottish tale "Rashin Coatie" is quoted in full to exemplify the Cinderella narrative. I find the Cinderella plot to be of the sovereignty type and therefore radically different from the plots of the Catskin and Cap o' Rushes tales, and I go on to consider in relation to the Cinderella group two narratives similar to it that have a much greater need for magic—those of "The Goose-Girl" and *Roswall and Lillian*. This investigation gives opportunities to consider the contrast between narratives dealing with guilt and fear and those not doing so; the Cinderella texts exemplify a borderland area between magical and nonmagical. Finally, H. C. Andersen's *The Ugly Duckling* is briefly discussed as a comparable nonmagical story.

Emaré

Edith Rickert comments that *Emaré* is peculiar for the large number of repetitions that it contains, and Maldwyn Mills points out how symmetrical the plot is, Emaré moving forward from her first situation to her third and then retracing her steps, resolving her second situation and finally her first.[2] Maldwyn Mills also comments that, where we would expect sharp differentiation of treatment in the case of the monstrous father and Prince

Charming husband, we find very similar motifs applied to each character so that they "seem curiously alike" (xiv). Orders coming from each of these characters cast Emaré adrift at sea (although one of them is not personally responsible for these orders), and each character laments when it is too late; each sets out for Rome to receive a penance (although one of them is not guilty), and each is reunited there with Emaré, through the help of her young son. The "effect of such insistent repetition is to emphasize a similarity of function at the expense of individuality," Professor Mills observes, but he finds the patterning of the events "curiously reassuring" (xiv–xv): everything that goes wrong for Emaré in the first part of the story finds its "benevolent mirror-image" (xv) in the second part. The most striking repetition is found in the descriptions of the two voyages of exile, which contain what is essentially the same stanza, as Mills points out, and I have quoted these stanzas, together with the repetitions relating to Segramour's role at the end of the story, in my chart of the plot. The robe also excites comment. Rickert finds the description of the robe so out of scale with this brief romance that she thinks it may have been borrowed more or less verbatim from a longer narrative work (38). But Mills points out that the description is telling us about famous lovers adorning the cloth, and the cloth comes into the story just after we are told the widowed emperor greatly enjoys "playnge" (l.78); on the two occasions when Emaré wears the cloth as her robe, the man who sees her in it immediately expresses his determination to marry her. All these features make it likely that a chief function of the robe is to stand for the sexual attraction of the lady (197–98). Mills also comments on the contrast between Emaré wearing her robe and Emaré without it. In herself, she is pathetic, meek, self-effacing, long-suffering, and prepared to live quietly until such time as her husband finds her, while, wearing her robe, she "has all the seductive beauty of the fairy; dazzling, but also possibly dangerous" (xxv).

Maldwyn Mills sees resemblances between the Apollonius of Tyre story and *Emaré*, not only in the sea journeys and family separations and in the chief character's being cast by the sea onto a strange shore (there to make a royal marriage), but also in the recognition scenes, where there is a "sense of strangeness and the opening up of long perspectives of time" (xxiii). In my study of the Apollonius of Tyre texts, I have found that the plot used is concerned with purification—its rituals making striking use of family separations and the penitential sea voyage and also of recognition scenes in which rituals take the magical process through its final steps to the resumption of the relationships.[3] The same features are clearly present in *Emaré,* and, as it happens, both plots are also concerned with fear of incest. Both plots are, moreover, exceptionally strange, with little attempt at rationalization. In *Emaré,* a man leading the most public of lives intends to marry his daughter; he sets her adrift on the sea when she refuses, and he allows the jewels on the robe—one of them, he knows, richer than any jewel in Christendom—to go with her. The queen mother, meanwhile, in the next part of the story, engages in deceptions that will be discovered as soon as the king returns home. But when we view these plots as magical, they make excellent magical sense as a sequence of rituals to remove the idea of incest from marriage or the fear of it elsewhere. Each plot begins with the idea of incest, and then the rituals begin—an attempt at marriage being undertaken as part of this process, and the process finally bringing about the resumption of the marriage. The birth of a child is the point at which the married couple separate in each plot, but, in each case, too, becoming married, followed by becoming king or queen, are changes of status suggesting the usurpation of a parent's position and therefore requiring purification.

I shall now examine the purification purposes of *Emaré* (see chart 8), leaving out the role of Emaré's precious robe, which indicates other aspects of the plot and therefore needs a separate examination. The use of the same stanza (with small differences) in the narration of each sea voyage focuses attention on the ritual nature of these voyages. Giving ritual importance to the details of the stanza (as opposed to the kind of importance we might otherwise give to tail-rhyme lines), we can see that the number seven is used when we are told the duration of the voyage, and that the voyage is God's will, that Emaré suffers mentally and physically, and that her arrival in Galicia is through the grace of God. Since she is fleeing damnation ("'Yyf hyt betydde that ye me wedde / And we shulde play togedur in bedde, / Bothe we were forlorne!'" ll. 253–55), the references to God will be far from idle, in any case. On her arrival, she adopts the name Outcast, and she works as a servant. It is the robe that brings about the marriage with the king, while the ideas that Emaré is an evil spirit and her baby is a devil revert to the idea of damnation. The second voyage of exile is undertaken, with its exact repetition of penance, and Emaré transfers herself to Rome, the capital of penances, where the number seven is again used to give the duration of her exile there. The reconciliation scenes take place among characters who are all in the same place for the purpose of penance. Why is the child used to bring these about? His excellence counteracts the devil he was reputed to be, and the king's recognition of his excellence is the first step in the rituals. The king then desires his own son, and, next, he desires the very boy in his presence. After this, Segramour tells him that they are kin, and he takes him to Emaré. There is repetition of the statement that she is now Emaré and that she had changed her name to Egaré (Outcast): she speaks the words first, in her instructions to her son, and he repeats them to the king; he then speaks them again to the emperor. It is clearly a ritual statement that the heroine's penitential exile has come to a successful conclusion. It has purified her marriage so that it can be resumed. Meanwhile, the reconciliation with the father also plays a part in sealing the purification of the marriage: the emperor is now an old man, we are told, and he has repented his sin, becoming a good man, delighted with his daughter's marriage and son.

What is the role of the robe? The cloth is Saracen in origin, and it took seven years in the making. The lovers embroidered on it are Ydoine and Amadas, Tristan and Isolde, and Floris and Blancheflor. There is no development of the very different stories of these lovers, and it seems that their names alone are important, conjuring up the power of love. The description of the enormous number of precious stones on the cloth leads one to wonder how such a garment could be worn by a woman wandering alone without her meeting with effects more likely than her being an object of awe. But it is clear that the monetary value of the precious stones has no part in the story, and other questions challenge the critic. The cloth is closely connected with Emaré's father and his incestuous love. The long description of it comes between the account of the emperor's playful widowerhood and that of his incestuous desire for his daughter. He has the robe made for her out of the cloth, and when she puts it on, he tells her his plan to marry her. But this scene is paralleled by the scene in Galicia where the king sees Emaré serving in the robe and becomes determined to marry her (before the emperor, she seems no earthly woman, and, before the king, she seems no earthly thing). If the heroine is seeking to remove her fear of incest, why does she take this robe with her into exile? It contrasts strongly, in any case, with her penance. One answer is that the heroine evidently needs the robe to bring about her marriage to the king, a marriage essential to the plot's purification rituals. The robe gives her the power to win a king, while this aspiration is shadowed by her fear of incest. This would be a reason why the robe is first attached to her father, creating her need to detach her aspirations from him before she can acquire her king, and finally live with him without fear. A heroine engaged in such a purpose will take her robe with her, even as she undertakes her penance. The queen mother's comment that this is an evil spirit in the splendid garment expresses the sense of danger and damnation lurking about the heroine's sexual aspirations. The robe plays no part in the scenes in Rome, and yet it expressly accompanies her on her second penitential voyage, frightening the merchant who rescues her. The robe bestows upon the heroine a sense of her value and her splendor, and she takes these feelings with her into exile, where they have roles to play. She is also engaged in removing what is dangerous in all the robe represents, so it must be present as her rituals are performed.

It is clear from the space given to the description of the robe in the text (ll. 82–177)—nearly a tenth of the text's length—that this talisman, bestowing upon the heroine the power to win a king, must be at least as important in the plot as the purification rituals. The heroine has a desire and she needs to purify it: the dual function of the plot is to bring about the desire and to supply the necessary purification, and the extent of the purification necessary gives the plot its distinctive appearance.

La Manekine

As Hermann Suchier comments, Beaumanoir has developed a simple story into a work of 8,590 lines.[4] Such a prolix work, with long-winded development of the detail, is not likely to show any of the concentrated ritual use of language and verse that I have found in *Emaré*. But the ritual actions in each of these narratives are very similar, for all their apparent differences. Emaré's magical robe is absent in *La Manekine*, and this draws my attention to the absence in this plot of the especially heroine aspects present in *Emaré*. I believe the plot of *La Manekine* to be intensively concerned with purification (see chart 9), and it seems to be both a hero and a heroine plot. While the daughter undergoes most of the purification rituals, these rituals also work from the point of view of the king character: it is possible to use the plot through identification with the kings, with effects similar to those in the Apollonius of Tyre plot, where the female characters undergo much of the ritual activity. Like the Apollonius story, the plot of *La Manekine* was a favorite in popular literature throughout Europe and beyond, and perhaps the reason can now become clear.[5]

The plot makes use of ritual punishment, as well as of penitential exile at sea, family separations, prayer to God and the Virgin Mary, and the ritual change of name. The orders for the burning of the daughter have a punitive force and also a purifying force. Most significantly, the daughter is without a hand from the point in the plot where incest is suggested and until after her father has confessed to the pope. The name she adopts in exile is not Outcast, as in *Emaré,* but one which apparently refers to her mutilated condition. In Jean Wauquelin's fifteenth-century prose version of "La Manekine," we are told that the name is connected with Latin "mancus" and "manca," "manca" meaning a woman with only one hand.[6] Hermann Suchier thinks that Beaumanoir also linked "manekine" with "manca" and comments himself that "manekine" is more likely to be linked with "mannequin": "Dans les mystères, à l'exécution des tortures, on substituait à celui qui jouait un saint une poupée habillée comme le personnage et qu'on appelait un mannequin" (xxxiv n.).

The Roman host (the senator) plays a large part in the rituals of the first recognition scene in this plot. He is a widowed father, in whose house La Manekine is treated with honor for seven years, so he is an agent with magical power in the role of bringing the couple together. He tells the king the story of La Manekine's second exile, an act affirming that the rituals have been performed. The nuptial ring and the child (admired by the king, not a monster) are also agents in the rituals, both of them saying that the marriage is good and should be resumed. The power of all these agents derives from the performance of the purification rituals—the punishments, penances, prayers, and separations, culminating in the seven-year sojourn in a pure household (the senator's). Christian magic plays a role beyond the prayers in the plot: it is crucial in the rituals for the second recognition scene, where the power of the pope is employed, both for the father's confession and as the presiding presence at the reunion of father and daughter. It is also employed for the bringing about of the final sign of divine forgiveness—in the restoration of La Manekine's hand.

The story of La Manekine reappears in later collections of folktales, of which I shall mention two at this point: the Italian tale in Basile's *Pentamerone,* "La Penta manomozza" (Penta the handless), and the Grimm tale "Das Mädchen ohne Hände" (The girl with no hands). Both these versions have suffered alterations to the beginning of the story, but, in the case of "Penta the Handless," this is only that the daughter has become a sister. I am including a chart of the plot of "Penta the Handless" (chart 10), because it shows how the rituals of the story persist in material apparently much altered. The incidents relating to Nuccia (who plays the part usually played by the queen mother) appear inexplicable as *her* activities, but the interception of the letters is a useful mechanism for the presentation of the next departure into exile (which has its reasons elsewhere), and the various versions are little concerned with the motives of the interceptor, who is only an agent in the rituals.⁷ The essential part of this interception is the accusation, so familiar a feature of magical narrative.

All editions of the Grimm tale "The Girl with No Hands" have an apparently radically altered beginning. It seems that, after they had published their first edition, the Grimm brothers came across a version of the story that they regarded as greatly superior—and which I myself see as clearly a version of "La Manekine." In this story, the brothers tell us, a father wants to take his daughter as his wife, and, upon her refusal, cuts off her hands (and breasts), makes her put on a white shirt, and drives her out into the world. The Grimm brothers never published their new version with these details as its beginning: instead, they retained the initial details of the version that appeared in their first edition. These are the familiar ones that a miller, fallen on hard times, strikes a bargain with the devil, promising him whatever is standing behind his mill in exchange for untold wealth, only to discover that it was his daughter who was standing behind the mill at the moment the bargain was struck. Such initial details lead to a departure from home stranger than the departure of La Manekine (where, from a superficial view, a father acts upon outrageous emotions). The severely injured girl tells her father she must leave to seek her fortune: she cannot stay at home ("'Hier kann ich nicht bleiben'"), even though, as her father tells her, she can now live at home with material comforts; she sets out, with her severed hands packed on her back. In the rest of the story, as it appears in the later editions, the girl arrives outside a royal garden, is helped to enter it by an angel, and is seen there by the gardener, who informs the king; the king later marries her, and gives her silver hands. The devil does the intercepting of the letters, in this version, and the exile journeys take place on foot; finally, the king's seven-year search, during which he does not eat or drink, ends, with divine assistance, at the small house in a wood where an angel has sheltered his wife and son. The version of the story in the first edition is similar, but shorter, without the angels and with the additional detail that the girl looks after the court chickens.⁸ In all versions, her hands grow again as before.

Recent studies of the work of the Grimm brothers suggest that the removal of material relating to incest and intrafamily violence is consistent with their work in general,⁹ and it appears to be fortunate that they have left us a record of the details removed, in this case. But, once other considerations, besides the desire to retain the plot intact, are present and can prevail, crucial details will be altered by many a narrator. We are given to understand that the version of "The Girl with No Hands" in the Grimm brothers' first edition was altered elsewhere. How far has the story actually been altered, in any case? A father has made a pact with the devil, and the result is that his daughter is to be given over to the devil, for what must be sexual purposes. I suggest that the story has not been altered as much as appears, and would work well as a magical plot dealing with more than one area of sexual guilt. It is a striking plot: nowhere does the purification purpose of the La Manekine group emerge more clearly. The events show great extremes in a short space—from severe ritual punishment to divine restoration.

The ritual punishments of some of these purification plots help us to consider exactly how the events in a magical narrative differ from those of other kinds of narrative. We are used to viewing savagery in narrative as the crime of a wicked character, but, in the case of a magical narrative, it has to be viewed as being there for the ritual use of the participant. It is there to be performed and experienced, and, when it has successfully played its part, it is in some way *un*done, in the bringing about of victory. The characters are all figures in these performances. Moreover, we have to understand that all the suffering in a magical plot is that of the participant and that the characters undergoing ritual punishment always represent the participant in some way, even where they seem to be quite distinct from the chief character. We do not have situations in the narrative where one character is cruel to another in the usual fictional sense, however much such cruelty may mirror experiences of the participant outside the text. At the happy ending of the narrative, it is quite irrelevant to look at the cost in suffering: the purification rituals are designed to relieve suffering.

The *Vita Offae Primi* Version

The oldest known version of the Accused Queen story is to be found in Matthew Paris's Latin *Life of Offa I,* usually dated in the mid-thirteenth century.[10] This version I find to be more distinctly a hero plot, in contrast to the heroine plot of *Emaré,* but it does work as both a hero and heroine plot, just as *La Manekine* can accommodate a hero. While using much the same material as these other versions, the *Life of Offa I* version has a magical plot more reminiscent of the Apollonius of Tyre plot, a hero plot where female characters play the most important parts in the purification rituals, Apollonius himself undergoing separation and penance.

My chart of the *Life of Offa I* plot (chart 11) shows how Offa's marriage is preceded by purification and defenses. The woman is proved to be one who will never engage in an incestuous relationship (so any idea of incest haunting the marriage cannot be true), and, while the woman becomes part of Offa's household after their meeting, their relationship can only be chaste, their first night being spent with the Solitary and the woman being constantly with members of the household thereafter. The Latin words might be understood to mean that the woman is entrusted to the servants' care, but in "diligenti custodia" there is also a sense that she is guarded.[11] She spends some years in Offa's household before their marriage, and, at the end of this time, all who know her love and praise her. Offa, meanwhile, is presented as having no particular thought of her, or of marriage, until he is under pressure from others (a defense also used in Apollonius of Tyre).

These arrangements make the marriage possible, but their power comes to an end once the marriage has taken place and children are born (as in the case of the other versions). At this point, the plot provides further violent purification rituals. The use of the king of Northumbria as interceptor of the letters would be a quite inexplicable feature, were it not that the interception is a mere device, a setting for the accusation that takes the plot on to the necessary family separation, ritual punishment, sojourn in the wilderness and then with a holy man, and finally sackcloth and ashes. After these rituals have been performed, there can be a final reunion, presided over by the holy man.

If this narrative is magical, as I suggest, we appear to have the spectacle of a hero healing his anxieties by subjecting his wife and children to savage suffering, while he does no more than don sackcloth and ashes for a while (or, alternatively, the spectacle of a heroine subjecting children to the greatest suffering in the story). But moral approaches of this kind never serve in the case of magical plots, as I have already indicated. In the King Offa narrative, all the characters involved in the rituals represent the situation to be purified; the purification requires the playing out of several parts simultaneously. It may be that the plot employed is an exclusively heroine plot in origin, but the Apollonius of Tyre plot is a hero plot that gives the major burden of purification to the female characters, while the chief character performs penances. The magical plot reflects what has worked among audiences, no more and no less.

I think it is correct to see all the events I give in the chart as playing roles in the rituals. Doing so presents us with a piling on of rituals both before and after the marriage. The woman who prefers death to incest is nevertheless shown repeatedly to be in a chaste relationship with Offa and at a distance from him in his household, before he marries her. After the marriage, it is necessary to begin all over again, with a further sequence of powerful rituals. Such an intensive build-up of rituals is typical of magical plots.

The Catskin Tales

In my consideration of narratives related to that of *Emaré*, I have so far concentrated on examples using more or less the same material, this being the ritual punishment material of exposure or mutilation prior to marriage and parenthood, and then of repeated exposure or exile, family separation, and perhaps penance. The interception of letters has been the crude device used to initiate the later rituals. But there is a group of narratives close in purpose to *Emaré* that use quite different material, and I shall examine an example here that represents the group well.

The group is known by the name Catskin, although the heroines use a variety of skins, and frequently a donkey skin. The Grimm brothers and Charles Perrault have left us versions—"Allerleirauh" and "Peau d'Asne"—but I prefer to use folktales collected by later, more disciplined folklorists wherever this is possible, and have chosen Delarue's "La Peau d'Anon," recorded in Nivernais, in about 1885 (Delarue and Tenèze 2: 256–60).

This French folktale should really be quoted in full, since the narration illustrates the ritual character of the story well, but it is more practicable here to give an account of the details in chart 12. The tale also represents the Catskin group well because it includes an exceptional amount of the detail characteristic of the group. Essentially, this group has a heroine plot with a more decidedly dual function than the previous plots discussed. Its plot, whichever details it includes, provides rituals for both the bringing about of desires and the removal of guilt related to those desires.

While the plot of *Emaré* is more directly concerned with purification, the role of the robe links it with the Catskin group, where garments given to the daughter by the father, for the purpose of winning her, are used ritually for the winning of a prince. Accompanying rituals provide the all-important expiation and purification, not by using the devices of the Accused Queen plots, but through the use of devices providing for extreme self-abasement. Some versions give more details of this self-abasement than does the folktale I cite here. In the Grimm version, the narrator refers to Allerleirauh in her skin coat as "it"; she is taken to her place of drudgery tied up behind a cart, and she is given tiny quarters under the stairs, where no light of day ever comes. In the Grimm brothers' first edition, she has to go upstairs each evening to pull off the boots of the king she will eventually marry, and every time he then throws the boots at her head. The detail scarcely presents the king as Prince Charming, but such reflections are not to the point here: the heroine is in exile among the cinders, in order to deal with her guilt; she is acting the role of an outcast, making use of humiliating experiences for the purpose of expiation and cleansing.[12] Even Perrault's version, which trivializes the tale to some extent, gives full attention to the rituals of expiation and purification. His Peau d'Asne cannot find employment because no one wishes to employ so foul-smelling and filthy a creature. She could solve the problem by discarding the donkey skin and washing in a stream, but, instead, she trudges grimly on until at last she finds work on a farm, where she washes the clouts and cleans out the pigsties. She is the common butt for the tricks and low jokes of the menservants.[13] This is a good example of how the decisions a character makes can be a clue to the presence of a magical plot. Delarue's version devotes less artistry to conveying the chief character's circumstances in exile, but instead it shows with great clarity—in ritual alternation three times over—the bringing together of the two contrasting forces: the talismans representing the power to win a king and the rituals of self-abasement. The culmination is the marriage in the presence of the father.

On the chart, I use italics where the rituals of self-abasement are dominant. As the two contrasting sequences of rituals take place concurrently through much of the narrative, this seems the most practical measure. In a text taken from oral tradition like this, it is all the more important to consider the significance of every detail—indeed, of every word—together with the order in which they appear in the text, and I have taken care to present as much of these as I can on the chart.

Chaucer's *Man of Law's Tale*

I shall now consider a version of the Accused Queen story that does not have a magical plot. This is Nicholas Trivet's version, his "Life of Constance" in his Anglo-Norman chronicle of the early fourteenth century, which Gower and Chaucer both use for their tales of Constance.[14] Chaucer's *Man of Law's Tale* is the best-known and most attractive tale in this group. The plot is as follows.

> A Syrian sultan wishes to marry Constance, daughter of the Emperor of Rome, having heard of her great goodness and beauty, and he will have himself and his people converted to Christianity so that he can do so. The Christians see the marriage as to their advantage against Islam, and Constance has to comply. Then the sultan's mother kills her son and the Christians at the wedding, and takes over power. Constance is put in a rudderless sailing vessel and she drifts for three years, protected by God and fed by Christ.

She is rescued on the coast of Northumberland by the constable of the castle. He and his wife Hermengyld care for her, and she converts the couple to Christianity. Satan retaliates by filling a young knight with love for Constance, who, when she refuses him, takes revenge by killing Hermengyld and making it look as if Constance has committed the murder. King Alla of Northumberland finds out the truth and marries Constance—against the will of his mother Donegild. Alla then goes to the wars in Scotland, and Constance bears a son Maurice. Donegild plays the role of interceptor, substituting letters, and, as a result, Constance is set adrift with her son. God cares for her once again during her five years at sea. On one occasion, she is protected by the Virgin Mary when a steward tries to rape her on a heathen shore.

Meanwhile, the Emperor of Rome takes revenge on the Syrians. On his way home, the senator leading this expedition meets Constance in her boat, and she is brought back to Rome to be cared for in his household. King Alla, for his part, has punished his mother with death, and he then, repenting, sails for Rome to receive his penance. The senator and young Maurice go to a feast Alla gives in Rome. The king notices the child, and the senator tells him how he was found; he extols his mother's virtue. Since the child resembles Constance, Alla goes to see his mother, and the couple are reunited when Constance knows the king was not responsible for her sorrows. Constance is then also reunited with her father, the Emperor.

Here, the initial vision of incest is absent, and other material appears in its place, both before and after the first voyage. This material is not of a kind that would lead to purification rituals or any other type of magical sequence. All the events in the narrative relate closely to each other as the misfortunes of a woman that come about through her goodness, and which are endured with exemplary fortitude.

The most likely explanation for this version is that its ultimate source was a magical Accused Queen narrative, adopted for development. The purification story, consisting as it does of one form of suffering after another, is admirable material for a (nonmagical) tale of fortitude. It provides the exposures at sea and exiles, and the motif of the accusation, which, like the wicked queen, is repeated in the material added by the developer. It also provides material for the reunion. Meanwhile, the magical plot, being of no interest, has vanished silently in the process.

2

The King Lear Stories and Cap o' Rushes

This chapter continues the discussion of the last chapter, with a consideration of the purification stories in the Cap o' Rushes group, stories closely related to those of the Catskin group, and the development of this material that gave rise to a tradition of nonmagical stories, the King Lear tradition. The Cap o' Rushes tales are exclusively heroine stories—since they include a sequence of rituals for the winning of a prince—and they are distinguished by their initial sequence, which is described by some folktale analysts as "King Lear judgement—Loving like salt—Outcast heroine" (Cox 80–86). The events that follow this beginning are rituals of the same kind as those of the Catskin tale "La Peau d'Anon." The stories of the King Lear tradition use the same initial events, replacing the enigmatic loving like salt with explicit material concerned with personal relationships, and then provide a sequence of events in which the king/father is the chief character and he undergoes a learning experience. The most striking alteration is that the story has been turned around so that the father, not the daughter, is the chief character, but the result is not a hero magical plot. The King Lear story is, by contrast, a moral tale. It seems likely that the moral tale is a development of the magical story in the same way that Trivet's "Life of Constance" is apparently a development of a magical story: in the case of the King Lear tale, the first step must have been an interest in the king that eclipsed the heroine and her magical plot.

A consideration of this intriguing situation draws into the investigation other interesting matters. Our knowledge of the King Lear story starts with Geoffrey of Monmouth, who may himself have adapted the magical tale for his use as the (moral) tale of King Lear. I shall argue that his treatment of the initial love-test scene suggests he found a theme of incest, either lurking or prominent, in his original, a theme that does not feature in his own Lear story. Many literary versions of the Lear story follow Geoffrey's (in a tradition that belongs peculiarly to Britain), and my discussion includes a chart comparing the treatment of the initial love test in a number of these. The lurking idea of incest appears in two texts—one of them Geoffrey's—and is absent in the others, and I shall explore these features and the reasons for them. Each version is an interesting study in light of the probable ancestry of the story in use.

One outcome of the investigation into the various treatments of the King Lear moral tale is the light thrown on the enigmatic love test of the Cap o' Rushes story, with its loving like salt answer. It is with the complete Suffolk tale of "Cap o' Rushes" that my discussion will begin.[1]

Cap o' Rushes

Well, there was once a very rich gentleman, and he'd three daughters, and he thought to see how fond they was of him. So he says to the first, "How much do you love me, my dear?"

"Why," says she, "as I love my life."

"That's good," says he.

So he says to the second, "How much do *you* love me, my dear?"

"Why," says she, "better nor all the world."

"That's good," says he.

So he says to the third, "How much do *you* love me, my dear?"

"Why, I love you as fresh meat loves salt," says she.

Well, he were that angry. "You don't love me at all," says he, "and in my house you stay no more." So he drove her out there and then, and shut the door in her face.

Well, she went away on and on till she came to a fen, and there she gathered a lot of rushes and made them into a cloak, kind o', with a hood, to cover her from head to foot, and to hide her fine clothes. And then she went on and on till she came to a great house.

"Do you want a maid?" says she.

"No, we don't," says they.

"I haint nowhere to go," says she, "and I'd ask no wages, and do any sort o' work," says she.

"Well," says they, "if you like to wash the pots and scrape the saucepans you may stay," says they.

So she stayed there and washed the pots and scraped the saucepans and did all the dirty work. And because she gave no name they called her "Cap o' Rushes."

Well, one day there was to be a great dance a little way off, and the servants was let to go and look at the grand people. Cap o' Rushes said she was too tired to go, so she stayed at home.

But when they was gone she offed with her cap o' rushes, and cleaned herself, and went to the dance. And no one there was so finely dressed as her.

Well, who should be there but her master's son, and what should he do but fall in love with her the minute he set eyes on her. He wouldn't dance with anyone else.

But before the dance were done Cap o' Rushes she slipped off, and away she went home. And when the other maids was back she was framin' to be asleep with her cap o' rushes on.

Well, next morning they says to her, "You did miss a sight, Cap o' Rushes!"

"What was that?" says she.

"Why, the beautifullest lady you ever see, dressed right gay and ga'. The young master, he never took his eyes off of her."

"Well, I should ha' liked to have seen her," says Cap o' Rushes.

"Well, there's to be another dance this evening, and perhaps she'll be there."

But, come the evening, Cap o' Rushes said she was too tired to go with them. Howsumdever, when they was gone, she offed with her cap o' rushes and cleaned herself, and away she went to the dance.

The master's son had been reckoning on seeing her, and he danced with no one else, and never took his eyes off of her. But, before the dance was over, she slipped off, and home she went, and when the maids came back she framed to be asleep with her cap o' rushes on.

Next day they says to her again, "Well, Cap o' Rushes, you should ha' been there to see the lady. There she was again, gay and ga', and the young master he never took his eyes off of her."

"Well, there," says she, "I should ha' liked to ha' seen her."

"Well," says they, "there's a dance again this evening, and you must go with us, for she's sure to be there."

Well, come the evening, Cap o' Rushes said she was too tired to go, and do what they would she stayed at home. But when they was gone she offed with her cap o' rushes and cleaned herself, and away she went to the dance.

The master's son was rarely glad when he saw her. He danced with none but her and never took his eyes off her. When she wouldn't tell him her name, nor where she came from, he gave her a ring and told her if he didn't see her again he should die.

Well, afore the dance was over off she slipped, and home she went, and when the maids came home she was framing to be asleep with her cap o' rushes on.

Well, next day they says to her, "There, Cap o' Rushes, you didn't come last night, and now you won't see the lady, for there's no more dances."

"Well, I should ha' rarely liked to ha' seen her," says she.

The master's son he tried every way to find out where the lady was gone, but go where he might, and ask whom he might, he never heard nothing about her. And he got worse and worse for the love of her till he had to keep his bed.

"Make some gruel for the young master," they says to the cook. "He's dying for love of the lady." The cook she set about making it when Cap o' Rushes came in.

"What are you a doin' on?" says she.

"I'm going to make some gruel for the young master," says the cook, "for he's dying for love of the lady."

"Let me make it," says Cap o' Rushes.

Well, the cook wouldn't at first, but at last she said yes, and

Cap o' Rushes made the gruel. And when she had made it she slipped the ring into it on the sly before the cook took it upstairs.

The young man he drank it and he saw the ring at the bottom.

"Send for the cook," says he.

So up she comes.

"Who made this here gruel?" says he.

"I did," says the cook, for she were frightened.

And he looked at her.

"No, you didn't," says he. "Say who did it, and you shan't be harmed."

"Well, then, 'twas Cap o' Rushes," says she.

"Send Cap o' Rushes here," says he.

So Cap o' Rushes came.

"Did you make my gruel?" says he.

"Yes, I did," says she.

"Where did you get this ring?" says he.

"From him as gave it me," says she.

"Who are you then?" says the young man.

"I'll show you," says she. And she offed with her cap o' rushes, and there she was in her beautiful clothes.

Well, the master's son he got well very soon, and they was to be married in a little time. It was to be a very grand wedding, and everyone was asked far and near. And Cap o' Rushes' father was asked. But she never told nobody who she was.

But before the wedding she went to the cook and says she,

"I want you to dress every dish without a mite o' salt."

"That'll be rarely nasty," says the cook.

"That don't signify," says she.

"Very well," says the cook.

Well, the wedding-day came, and they was married. And after they was married all the company sat down to their vittles. When they began to eat the meat, that was so tasteless they couldn't eat it. But Cap o' Rushes' father he tried first one dish and then another, and then he burst out crying.

"What is the matter?" said the master's son to him.

"Oh!" says he, "I had a daughter. And I asked her how much she loved me. And she said, 'As much as fresh meat loves salt.' And I turned her from my door, for I thought she didn't love me. And now I see she loved me best of all. And she may be dead for aught I know."

"No, father, here she is!" says Cap o' Rushes. And she goes up to him and puts her arms round him.

And so they was happy ever after.

In this complete text taken from oral tradition, the ritual nature of the tale emerges clearly; the verbal repetition and the absence of any attempt at rationalization suggest it, in particular. The text also offers clues as to the function of the loving like salt element, even though—as tends to be the case with magical material—meaning remains ambiguous and elusive. Its function appears to be the multiple one of being a declaration of love that appears to be a rejection of the father and the reason for the daughter's exile. If this is the case, the heroine will need all three functions, the statement of love, the statement of rejection, and the period as outcast. In the text, we can see that, from her position as outcast, she organizes her marriage, and that, afterwards, she uses the loving like salt element again to organize a relationship of love with the father; the father is given the clue to the meaning that she loves him. There is much evidence in the text that the story is a sequence of rituals removing the idea of incest from the heroine's marriage; nevertheless, further evidence is needed.

A French version of the Cap o' Rushes tale, "La Pouilleuse," provides some further evidence.[2] It begins as follows.

> Il était une fois un roi qui avait deux filles qu'il chérissait de tout son coeur. Quand elles furent grandes, il lui prit fantaisie de savoir si elles l'aimaient, en se disant qu'il donnerait son royaume à celle qui, par ses paroles, lui témoignerait le mieux son affection.

Il fit d'abord venir l'aînée des princesses et lui dit:

—Comment m'aimes-tu?

—Comme la prunelle de mes deux yeux.

—Bien, dit le roi en l'embrassant tendrement; tu es une fille dévouée et aimante.

A la cadette qui vint ensuite, il demanda comment elle l'aimait:

—A mes yeux, mon père, répondit-elle, vous êtes aussi aimable que le goût du sel dans les aliments.

Le roi, contrarié de ses paroles, ordonna à sa fille de quitter la cour et de ne jamais reparaître devant lui.

This version of the King Lear judgment, with its fuller detail, brings out clearly the father's concern with the love of the daughters. The bestowal of the kingdom is a detail, and a significant one, but it is not the reason for the love test: "il lui prit fantaisie de savoir si elles l'aimaient." In any case, no further mention of the bestowal of the kingdom is made in the story. There is also no mention of the king's approaching death or desire to retire. The question the father asks, and the daughters' replies, yield more information than in the case of the Suffolk version. The father asks the elder daughter how she loves him ("Comment m'aimes-tu?") and she replies, "As the apple of my eye." The younger, asked how she loves him, echoes details in her sister's reply while also giving a contrasting answer: "In my eyes, my father, you are as lovable as the taste of salt in food." The first reply uses a reference to food in a stock expression that means that the speaker has a special love for the king, above all else. The second reply uses a reference to food in an expression of a quite opposite kind: the original simile, referring to a down-to-earth pleasure (salt in food), speaks more convincingly of love, but also ambiguously, since salt is not a universal image of things we love, and its employment as such here can seem lacking in respect. Its employment successfully masquerades as the reason for the daughter's departure into exile. So, embedded in the equivocal language of the text there seems to be an idea of becoming a queen through love for the king, not through inheritance. The daughter's riddling answer expresses this desire, while appearing to deny it, and the father's anger has the double function of confirming the denial and explaining the exile.

Setting out into exile, the daughter makes herself unrecognizable and ugly to protect herself from the advances of "des méchants garçons." But she makes herself so filthy that people refuse to take her on as a goose-girl or shepherdess, and she does not modify her disguise. When she finally finds work, and is warming herself by the fire, she throws coarse salt on it, since salt makes the same sound as lice do when thrown on the fire; thus she earns the name La Pouilleuse (The lousy one). The rituals employed by La Pouilleuse in exile take a form similar to those of the Catskin group (a detail shared with many of these tales is her self-display in a field, rather than at a dance), and the story ends like the Suffolk tale, with the use of salt again to establish the father-daughter relationship.

In the recasting of the story as the King Lear tale, with the king as the hero, the loving like salt answer, with its multiple uses in the heroine plot, is replaced by another type of answer that suggests the quite different nature of the King Lear tale. In the Cap o' Rushes tale, the role of the test of love, with the daughter's response, eludes any final decisions as to meaning, and teases the mind; it is apparent, however, that it leads to a sequence of rituals important to the story. By contrast, in the texts using the King Lear tale, the daughter's answer has a rational and clear concern with matters such as personal relationships and power. This answer is, once again, one that leads to important subsequent events, events that are accessible to the rational mind: the king becomes an outcast himself and learns the wisdom of his daughter's answer.

The King Lear story does not also contrast with the Cap o' Rushes tale in being a tragedy. The tragic treatment of the story in Shakespeare's famous version was Shakespeare's own decision. It must be added that the defeat and death of Cordelia were present in some of his sources, and that these had become part of the tradition of the King Lear story through the accident that Geoffrey of Monmouth made these events part of a different story subsequent to his King Lear narrative. Geoffrey's King Lear narrative culminates in the restoration of Lear to his kingdom by his daughter and her husband, the king of France; when he dies, three years later, Cordeilla takes over the kingdom.

It is not the purpose of this chapter to discuss the various King Lear versions in full, for this has been done elsewhere,[3] and, here, my concern is to discover what can be learned from the comparison of the treatment of the love test in eight versions of the King Lear story. In the accompanying chart comparing the versions (chart 13), Geoffrey of Monmouth's passage from his *Historia Regum Britanniae* is placed beside the following corresponding passages: from Laȝamon's *Brut;* from a literal translation of one of the Welsh chronicles; from a manuscript of the *Gesta Romanorum;* from Holinshed; from the play of "King Leir" that preceded Shakespeare's play; from Shakespeare's *King Lear;* and from Aaron Thompson's translation of Geoffrey of Monmouth, entitled *Historia Anglicana*.[4]

I shall begin by saying that, although Geoffrey Bullough uses Aaron Thompson's translation to represent Geoffrey of Monmouth's original, in giving us the narrative and dramatic sources for Shakespeare's *Lear*, I find this a procedure more convenient than safe. There is, I think, an informative contrast between the texts of Geoffrey and Thompson, which I shall discuss here, considering Geoffrey's text in the 1929 edition of Griscom and Thompson's with the knowledge that Thompson will have been translating Commelin's 1587 edition of Geoffrey's text. In my chart of the eight treatments of the love test, I place Geoffrey and Thompson side by side, and below I compare two sentences of Cordeilla's reply.

Geoffrey's text in Griscom's edition	Geoffrey's text in Commelin's edition
Est uspiam pater mi filia quæ patrem suum plus quam patrem presumat. diligere? Non reor equidem ullam esse quæ hoc fateri audeat. nisi iocosis uerbis ueritatem celare nitatur.	Est uspiam, mi pater, filia quæ patrem suum plusquam diligere præsumat? non reor equidem vllam esse quæ hoc fateri audeat: nisi iocosis verbis veritatem celare nitatur. (13)
My suggested translation: My father, is there anywhere a daughter who presumes to love her father more than as a father? Indeed, I do not think there is any who dares to admit it, except where she endeavors to conceal the truth with joking words.	Aaron Thompson's translation: "My Father," said she, "Is there any Daughter that can love her Father more than Duty requires? In my Opinion, whoever pretends to it, must disguise her real Sentiments under the Veil of Flattery."

There is, in fact, no significant difference here between the two editions of Geoffrey, while the two translations have entirely different content. Thompson's rendering is one interpretation of Cordeilla's words, but he does not allow for the play on meaning in Geoffrey's text. Nor does my translation, which emphasizes the meaning lost in Thompson. In "plus quam patrem," there is a suggestion that Cordeilla is replying to a request from her father that she love him in some other way than as a parent. The second sentence, translating "fateri audeat" as "dares to admit" rather than as "ventures to make known," takes this suggestion further; Cordeilla appears to be referring, with subtle humor, to an inadmissible love. Her father's question would not seem to invite this response, but the love test needs more explanation than it receives. We are told that the king decides the time has come to divide his kingdom among his daughters and supply them with suitable husbands for the government of their share, but we are not told why there should be the giving of a more important part of the kingdom as the result of visiting each daughter in turn to find out which loves him more than the others ("Set ut sciret quæillarum parte regni potiore dignior esset. adiuit singulas ut interrogaret quæipsum magis diligeret," Griscom 262).

Cordeilla's third sentence in Geoffrey's text (identical in Griscom and Commelin) is "Nempe ego dilexi te semper ut patrem. & adhuc a proposito meo non diuertor," which Thompson translates as "I have always loved you as a Father, nor do I yet depart from my purposed Duty," while I think Cordeilla also says, "I am not to be parted from my intent on this point." If we consider Leir's reply to Cordeilla, we find that he says, "Quia in tantum senectutem patris tui spreuisti. ut uel eo amore quo me sorores tue dedignata es diligere" ("Because you have so scorned the old age of your father as to think me unworthy of the love that your sisters express for me"), a translation in agreement with Thompson's. This material is not the product of Cordeilla's subtlety, and yet the double level of meaning persists: Leir is expressing a sense of rejection as an old person, where he feels he should receive respect, and, meanwhile, we might recall that being scorned as too old for filial love cannot be as common as being scorned as too old for sexual love.

These hints of an incestuous love do not reappear in most of the versions I quote in my eight-text chart: they are eliminated, not only in Aaron Thompson's translation but also in Laȝamon's *Brut,* the Welsh chronicle, the *Gesta Romanorum* version, and Holinshed. They do not reappear, either, in the love-test scenes of the two Lear plays. What does appear in these versions is an avowal of filial love that, in some cases, seems to have an interesting link with the avowal in Geoffrey's version: (in my translation) "I have always loved you as a father, and I am not to be parted from my intent on this point." Whether or not this link is there, the material plays a quite different role in the text concerned from the role it appears to play in Geoffrey's version. The most striking text is Shakespeare's:

Cordelia: Sure I shall never marry like my sisters,
To love my father all.
Lear: But goes thy heart with this?
Cordelia: Ay, my good lord.

Lear: So young, and so untender?
Cordelia: So young, my lord, and true.

(Hunter, 1.1.103–7)

These words reveal the nature and extent of the transformation of the meaning hinted at by Geoffrey's Cordeilla. Geoffrey's Cordeilla seems to be speaking ironically of a love she herself might feel (a direct link with the Cap o' Rushes tales), while Shakespeare's Cordelia is seriously addressing her father's excessive demands for love, and the effects this has in terms of the elder daughters' use of them and the father's credulity. In all the versions of the King Lear story—including Geoffrey's version—the idea of loving the father more than as a father has been transformed so that it means, on the father's part, an excessive demand for love and, on the elder daughters' part, calculating pretense. Only in Geoffrey's version is there also a decided connection with the theme of incest in the folktale.

However, a few lines preceding the love test in the old play of *Leir*—which I quote in my chart—appear to contain incestuous material relating to the king and of a quite different quality from that in Geoffrey's treatment. Leir's choice of language, as he plans a love test that will put Cordella in the position of having to accept the husband he has chosen, suggests an undercurrent of meaning that conflicts with this stratagem:

> Then at the vantage will I take *Cordella*,
> Even as she doth protest she loves me best,
> Ile say, Then, daughter, graunt me one request,
> To shew thou lovest me as thy sisters doe,
> Accept a husband, whom my selfe will woo.
> This sayd, she cannot well deny my sute,
> Although (poore soule) her sences will be mute:
> Then will I tryumph in my policy,
> And match her with a King of Brittany. (Act 1, ll. 83–91)

Leir's expressions "Then at the vantage will I take *Cordella*" and "She cannot well deny my sute" are the more interesting in relation to some of the lines in his speech as he awaits his daughters' arrival for the love test. I give these lines in italics:

> *Oh, what a combat feeles my panting heart,*
> *'Twixt childrens love, and care of Common weale!*
> *How deare my daughters are unto my soule,*
> *None knowes, but he, that knowes my thoughts & secret deeds,*
> *Ah, little do they know the deare regard,*

> Wherein I hold their future state to come:
> *When they securely sleepe on beds of downe,*
> *These aged eyes do watch for their behalfe:*
> *While they like wantons sport in youthfull toyes,*
> *This throbbing heart is pearst with dire annoyes.*
> As doth the Sun exceed the smallest Starre,
> So much the fathers love exceeds the childs.
> Yet my complaynts are causlesse: for the world
> Affords not children more conformable:
> And yet, me thinks, my mind presageth still
> I know not what; and yet I feare some ill. (ll. 202–17)

In such a context, even the king of Brittany, who is politically entirely distinct, becomes an echo of the king of Britain, Leir himself. This kind of writing, apparently unconnected with the rest of the text, is probably an unconscious response to the material before the author.

It has been argued that the folktale plot, with its theme of incest and its heroine point of view, is never really absent in Shakespeare's play.[5] My own research has found Shakespeare an author who will re-create a magical plot when such material is before him, but, on this occasion, the material is not magical. Instead, it is transformed material with insufficient transformation of the love test, which is left too much like the ritual in the Cap o' Rushes tale and without a satisfactory motive. This situation may explain the material in the old play: the king has become the hero, but the latent material—and related heroine tale—could still have an influence. Does this situation explain France's choice of words in Shakespeare, when expressing his surprise at Lear's casting-off of Cordelia: "This is most strange, That she . . . should . . . Commit a thing so monstrous to dismantle So many folds of favour. Sure her offence Must be of such unnatural degree That monsters it"? (1.1.213–19). I would say it does not: the words used do not have to refer to incest—they can refer to quite other "unnatural" and "monstrous" offenses—and, although there might appear to be a link with the Cap o' Rushes tale, where the heroine considers herself cast off for such an offence, the comment is too isolated. Surfacing latent material of this kind is more likely to be a direct expression of feeling—perhaps disturbing in the text—and given to Lear or Cordelia. I have not found such material, but a few instances have been cited, one of these being Lear's reply to Cordelia at their final meeting, when she suggests they see Gonerill and Regan:

> No, no, no, no! Come, let's away to prison.
> We two alone will sing like birds i'the cage;

> When thou dost ask me blessing I'll kneel down
> And ask of thee forgiveness; so we'll live,
> And pray, and sing, and tell old tales, and laugh
> At gilded butterflies, and hear poor rogues
> Talk of court news; and we'll talk with them too—
> Who loses and who wins, who's in, who's out—
> And take upon's the mystery of things
> As if we were God's spies; and we'll wear out,
> In a walled prison, packs and sects of great ones
> That ebb and flow by the moon. (5.3.8–19)

It is hard to feel any conviction that Lear pictures himself and Cordelia as "lovebirds" (Dundes 235) in an incestuous sense, and this speech seems to be profoundly about matters quite different.

Geoffrey's treatment of his material contrasts in a curious way with the treatment of it in the other versions, while it reveals a decided link with the stories of the Cap o' Rushes group. So much is unknown, not only about how Geoffrey came to use the story but also about the sources of the other versions, that it is difficult to hazard a guess as to the reasons for this contrast. The most likely explanation does, however, seem to be that Geoffrey was handling a version of the Cap o' Rushes tale, transforming it for his own purposes. The resulting subtleties in his treatment, meanwhile, will not be likely candidates for transmission in tradition. It is hardly surprising that they do not reappear, while—by contrast—the mnemonic "quantum habes. tantum uales. tantumque te diligo," which forms the last sentence of Cordeilla's speech, sometimes reappears word for word (most strikingly in Holinshed and the version from the *Gesta Romanorum*). This last sentence lies at the heart of the new moral tale: it lies behind the fortunes of Geoffrey's Leir at the hands of his older daughters, leading him to an acknowledgment of its truth. Meanwhile, the hints of a theme of incest in Geoffrey's treatment assist the study of the enigmatic love test in the Cap o' Rushes tale.

The King Lear story has been confined to a British and literary tradition, while the Cap o' Rushes tale has been transmitted entirely in oral tradition, mainly—it seems—on the Continent. It is for these reasons that it is agreed that the oral story must be the original. It was once believed that Geoffrey's narrative was the source of the oral tradition, because of its age and distribution, and because it was believed that the analogue in the *Gesta Romanorum* was widespread on the Continent. Only when Hermann Oesterley showed that the analogue was peculiar to the English ("Anglo-Latin") recension was this belief dropped.[6] Geoffrey Bullough comments, "Geoffrey adapted the tale but altered it, omitting the 'salt' and making more of the natural relationship between children and parent" (272). Other traditions will have provided material for the events following the King Lear judgment: several were current concerning aged parents and their good and bad children (Perrett 21–23; Bullough 7:271). It is possible that the combination of these sources had already been made when Geoffrey was looking for a story for Leir, so that he only had to apply it to this figure from Celtic mythology, but the contrast between his treatment and that of the other Lear versions makes me more inclined to feel that Geoffrey himself created the King Lear story.

3

Cinderella and Other Sovereignty Tales

In the old play of *King Leir*—which is not, like Shakespeare's play, a tragedy—the two elder daughters assume something of the character of Cinderella's ugly sisters. Gonorill and Ragan, ugly in character and not in face, envy their younger sister and plot to make her the hated rather than best-loved daughter.[1] Their stratagem is to flatter their father so much during his love contest, declaring they will marry anyone he wishes—even a beggar—that their sister, who is reluctant to marry, must appear unloving. After Cordella's answer, they both speak before Leir replies, so as to influence his response:

>Gonorill.　Here is an answere answerlesse indeed:
>Were you my daughter, I should scarcely brooke it.
>Ragan.　　Dost thou not blush, proud Peacock as thou art,
>To make our father such a slight reply? (ll. 281–84)

Folktale analysts have included the Cap o' Rushes story in the Cinderella group,[2] but the ugly sisters do not belong to it and are introduced into this King Leir play, as their role in the love test shows. The elder sisters do not play a significant role in the Cap o' Rushes story, while they become the ugly daughters in the King Lear story, a role quite distinct from that of Cinderella's ugly sisters. In this chapter, I shall examine the Cinderella tale and make a sharp distinction between it and the Cap o' Rushes and Catskin tales, which are closely related to each other. Then I shall examine other stories that are not regarded as Cinderella stories by the folklorists, but which share important characteristics with them and also with the Cap o' Rushes and Catskin tales.

It is with the full text of a Scottish version of the Cinderella tale that my discussion will begin.[3]

Rashin Coatie

There was once a king and a Queen, as mony anes been, few have we seen, and as few may we see. The Queen, she deeit, and left a bonny little lassie; and she had naething to gie to the wee lassie but a little Red calfy, and she telt the lassie whatever she wanted, the calfy would gie her. The king married again, an ill natured wife, wi' three ugly dochters o' her ain. They did na like the little lassie because she was bonny; they took awa' a' her braw claes that her ain mither had geen her, and put a rashin coatie on her, and gar't her sit in the kitchennenk [*Folk-Lore*: kitchen neuk, 289], and a' body ca'd her Rashin Coatie. She did na get ony thing to eat but what the rest left, but she did na care, for she went to her red calfy, and it gave her every thing she asked for. She got good meat from the calfy, but her ill natured step mother gart the calfy be killed, because it was good to Rashin Coatie. She was very sorry for the calfy, and sat down and grat. The dead calfy said to her

"Tak me up, bane by bane

And pit me aneth yon grey stane.

And whatever you want, come and seek it frae me, and I will give you it."

Yuletide came, and a' the rest put on their braw claes, and was gaen awa to the kirk. Rashin Coatie said, "oh, I wad like to gang to the kirk too," but the others said, "what would you do at the kirk, you nasty thing? You must bide at home and make the dinner." When they were gone to the kirk, Rashin Coatie did na ken how to make the dinner, but she went out to the grey stone, and she told the calfy that she could not make the dinner, and she wanted to win to the kirk. The calfy gave her braw claes, and bad her gang into the house, and say

Every peat gar ither burn,

Every spit gar ither turn,

Every pot gar ither play,

Till I come frae the kirk this good Yule day.

Rashin Coatie put on the braw claes that the calfy gave her, and went awa to the kirk, and she was the grandest and the brawest lady there. There was a young prince in the kirk and he fell in love with her. She cam awa before the blessing, and she was hame before the rest, and had off her braw claes, and had on her rashin coatie, and the calfie had covered the table, and the dinner was ready, and every thing in good order when the rest cam hame. The three sisters said to Rashin Coatie, "oh, lassie, if you had only seen the braw bonnie lady that was in kirk to day, that the young prince fell in love with!" She said, "oh I wish you would let me gang with you to the kirk tomorrow"; for they used to gang three days after ither to the kirk. They said, "what should the like o' you do at the kirk,—nasty thing,—the kitchen neuk is good enough for you." The next day they went away and left her, but she went back to her calfy, and he bade her repeat the same words as before, and he gave her brawer claes, and she went back to the kirk, and a' the world was looking at her, and wondering where sic a grand lady came from; and as for the young prince he fell more in love with her than ever, and bade some body watch where she went back to. But she was back afore any body saw her, and had off her braw claes and on her rashin coatie, and the calfy had the table covered, and every thing ready for the dinner.

The next day the calfy dressed her in brawer claes than ever, and she went back to the kirk. The young prince was there, and he put a guard at the door to keep her, but she jumped ower their heads and lost one of her beautiful satin slippers. She got home before the rest, and had on the rashin coatie, and the calfy had all things ready. The young prince put out a proclamation that he would marry whoever the satin slipper would fit. All the ladies of the land went to try on the slipper, and with the rest the three sisters, but none would it fit, for they had ugly broad feet. The hen wife took in her daughter, and cut her heels, and her toes, and the slipper was forced on her, and the prince must marry her, for he had to keep his promise. As he rode along, with her behind him, to be married, there was a bird began to sing and ever it sang,

Minched fit, and pinched fit

Beside the king she rides,

But braw fit, and bonny fit

In the kitchen neuk she hides.

The prince said, "what is that the bird sings?" but the hen wife said, "nasty lying thing! never mind what it says," but the bird sang ever the same words. The prince said, "oh, there must be some one that the slipper has not been tried on"; but they said, "there is none but a poor dirty thing that sits in the kitchen neuck, and wears 'a rashin coatie.'" But the prince was determined to try it on Rashin Coatie, but she ran awa' to the grey stone, where the red calf dressed her yet brawer than ever, and she went to the prince, and the slipper jumped out of his pocket, and on to her foot, and the prince married her, and they lived happy all their days.

The story of Rashin Coatie has a superficial resemblance to that of her namesake, Cap o' Rushes: each heroine wins her prince in a menial situation. But this menial situation is playing a quite different role in the text. The king is married and Rashin Coatie is a menial in his household; he does not desire her to love him more than as a father, and she is instead a daughter cruelly treated by a stepmother and ugly sisters. While Cap o' Rushes's initial situation is one of a vision of incest, to be followed by descent into a menial position for purification purposes, Rashin Coatie's initial situation is a menial position without this purification purpose. Instead of the vision of incest and penance for the removal of guilt, I find a vision of the heroine as having been deprived of her rightful status, which she then restores (bringing about a new vision) with the help of the calfy. No provision has been made for the removal of guilt, which must mean that no such provision is necessary. The Cinderella plot structure has received various treatments in texts. Charles Perrault's version has presented the initial situation as a testing one in which the heroine proves her fitness to be queen (while her sisters fail the test).[4] She has to prepare her sisters for the ball and performs her tasks well, without self-pity or servility and without pleading.[5] In the case of "Rashin Coatie," we have a determined heroine, not greatly in need of magic as she takes her rightful place at the kirk and proves herself rightful queen, but more clearly a magical heroine, attaining sovereignty in the face of (her sense of) the obstacles. Such a plot structure can carry a range of meaning, according to audience demand—hence its great usefulness.

In "Rashin Coatie," power can be invested in the life-giving qualities of a loving mother, who appears in the form of an animal. The calf provides all Rashin Coatie's needs and desires: food, good clothing, and support in making her own way and achieving what she wants; moreover, while she is away, it does her household tasks for her. The opposite qualities are gathered together and embodied in a stepmother and her daughters. The sex and age of the helpful beast do not seem to matter: its important property is that the queen has bequeathed it to her daughter, saying that whatever she wants will be given her through this gift. The stepmother has no power over this gift, and her failed attempt to destroy it leads to its becoming protected and hidden (buried, like the mother). Power can also be invested in the threefold visits to the kirk, and in the ugly sisters' words confirming Rashin Coatie's triumph there, but the scope for enjoyment provided by this sequence seems to be its chief function in the text.

Perrault's version has provided us with the fairy godmother who, with a touch of her wand, turns a pumpkin and six mice into a coach and horses and creates a ball dress of gold and silver with glass slippers. In essentials, the story is close to that of "Rashin Coatie," and yet there is probably a distinction between these two texts where their use of magic is concerned. The Cinderella story does not need powerful magic and, unlike "Rashin Coatie," some texts may not provide for much investment of power; what provision there is may be more playful than designed to meet serious need. It is not easy to distinguish a magical plot from one not magical in this borderland area. Ultimately, the magical activity is on the part of members of the audience, who may or may not choose to employ opportunities provided by a text, and all the critic can do is examine the opportunities provided. In the case of the Cinderella tales, this is easier to do in relation to such a strange fairy godmother as the calf: it can be seen to be a collection of maternal properties making readily available to the heroine the benefactions of an ideal mother. In the case of a plot where it is more difficult to do, the safest judgment must be that where the single point of view "works," the characters and events making sense as agents in a progression towards a victory for a hero or heroine, there will be some scope for a magical engagement.

But we can also take into account that both godmothers and helpful animals traditionally have attributes that recommend them for magical use. Hilda Ellis Davidson has investigated the history of the fairy godmother and brought her essential qualities to our attention ("Enter Fairy Godmother" 171–78). Godmothers were originally sponsors and witnesses at a baptism, and, in stories, their gifts at christenings are not material ones: they bestow the child's destiny, for good or ill. Fairy godmothers and wise women also have origins in goddesses. In Germanic and Celtic tradition, goddesses had the power to assume bird and animal forms, and Hilda Davidson thinks that animal and female helpers have been closely linked from antiquity. Furthermore, fairy godmothers may have origins in supernatural female guardians and protectors of children and young girls. Magic will make use, where it can, of agents already invested with power, and—however playfully she may be treated—a character with such attributes traditionally attached to her may still be invested with a great deal of power if the plot concerned has the structure of a magical plot.

There are versions of the Cinderella tale with such a structure, which lack the godmother in either human or animal form. An example of these, showing minimal provision for magical use, is "La Cendrouse," a story from Poitou, cited by Delarue (2:245–48). This story has no stepsisters: there is simply a family with three daughters, two of whom are proud ("fières, fières!," 245) and one who is despised; this last does not enjoy herself like the others and she always stays apart, by the fireside. When the two elder go out for a walk, they ask her to join them and she turns down their invitation:

> "Allons, Cendrouse, tu ne veux pas venir avec nous autres te promener?"
>
> "Ah non! Je ne veux pas y aller de fait (bien sûr)!"
>
> "Ah, Cendrouse! Tu ne seras toujours qu'une Cendrouse, va! Toujours gratter les cendres! Toujours rester dans le coin du feu!" (245)

When their father goes to a fair and asks his daughters what they would like him to bring back for them, the elder sisters ask for beautiful dresses and Cendrouse asks for a hazelnut. On Sunday, the sisters put on their beautiful dresses and go to mass. After they have left, Cendrouse opens her nut and finds a carriage, horses, and clothes more beautiful than those of her sisters. She goes to mass and "personne ne pouvait s'imaginer qui était cette belle demoiselle." When the sisters return to tell her about the unknown girl, more beautiful than anyone has ever seen before, Cendrouse replies, "'Oh! Qu'elle soit tant belle qu'elle voudra, elle n'est pas plus belle que moi!'" (246). Her sisters exclaim over what she is saying. The next Sunday, they tell Cendrouse she must come with them to mass to see the beautiful girl and Cendrouse refuses. After they have left, she opens her nut again and goes to mass, where everyone wonders who she can be. On leaving, she loses one of her slippers, and the king's son picks it up, saying he will marry the girl it fits. But the slipper fits no one. The sisters return to tell Cendrouse the beautiful girl was there, and Cendrouse replies, "'Qu'elle soit tant belle qu'elle voudra! Elle n'est pas plus belle que moi'" (247). The following Sunday, she presents herself to try on the slipper, not this time in her carriage, but as Cendrouse. The slipper fits: "'Ah, mon Dieu! Le fils du roi se mariera avec la Cendrouse! Le fils du roi se mariera avec la Cendrouse!'" The last words of the tale are: "Ainsi la Cendrouse était beaucoup plus belle que ses soeurs, après!" (248).

"La Cendrouse" is very much the story of a triumph, with provision for miraculous display. But, whatever form the Cinderella tale takes, it is a radically different kind of story from the purification stories often connected with it. The magic in a magical plot is most powerful in the provisions made for dealing with guilt and fear: such provisions are found in most plots, and they have to be the criteria for the division of magical plots into groups. Stories that make no such provisions have a marginal position where my subject is concerned. The Cinderella tale I regard as a simple sovereignty story, "sovereignty" having its usual wide interpretation.

I shall now examine two narratives that transport the heroine or hero to a kingdom, while also using a great deal of magic, because of the presence of a related guilt, the sense of being a usurper. Their sovereignty theme links them with the Cinderella group, while their use of exorcism, penance, and ritual punishment gives them some similarity to the purification stories.

Roswall and Lillian and "The Goose-Girl"

The Scottish romance *Roswall and Lillian*, composed probably in the late fifteenth century, has been called a "male Cinderella" story, while I shall show it to be much more similar to the story I shall exemplify with the Grimm brothers' "The Goose-Girl."[6] Their plots are placed side by side in chart 14 (see appendix). The most obvious resemblance between the two plots is the use of the usurping servant, and we also find, once more, the winning of a kingdom from a menial position. The usurping servant plays the role that is to be exorcized, while the chief character plays the role of usurped and nonusurper. In "The Goose-Girl," the chief character is engaged in rituals for purification and for acquiring a sense of having a right to be a queen.

My entry into the Goose-Girl plot is through the role of the talking horse. The horse says nothing about the usurpation when the princess and her maid first arrive in their reversed positions: only when it is a severed head displayed under the gateway does it declare the girl's queenly status and speak of the grief her mother would feel over the goose-girl status. It speaks of the mother's grief in the same words used by the three drops of the mother's blood, which are her gift to her daughter and the source of her daughter's power as a princess on her way to marry a king's son. Associated with the horse's words are the rituals relating to the girl's hair, which convey the same message to the goose-boy—that she is secretly a queen with a golden crown; in this way the heroine brings herself to the attention of the king. Her purification will be complete, making her ready to be a queen.

The role of the horse can only be illuminated by careful attention to the detail in its context; we should not seek answers to the difficulties it presents by looking outside the text—for example, by comparing it with the role of the calf in "Rashin Coatie." It appears that the Goose-Girl narrative makes use of sacrifice or ritual punishment (or both) for the purification of the journey to the kingdom, expressing this through the horse employed for the journey.

The Goose-Girl rituals take a threefold form, and similar threefold rituals are found in *Roswall and Lillian,* where Roswall, who is playing the role of a cup-bearer lacking in the skills of a knight, reveals that he is a supreme jouster, and in this way brings himself to the attention of the king. He does this by changing places with the prisoners he has freed. While the chief source of power in "The Goose-Girl" is the declaration of the sacrificed horse, in *Roswall and Lillian* it is the freeing of the prisoners. These prisoners are traitors to the king, Roswall's father, and their release is to be punished by hanging; however, Roswall is sent to the king of Bealm instead. The essential properties of the prisoners seem to be that they are traitors to the king who have been released by Roswall with impunity. Their release propels Roswall on his journey towards his kingdom. The progress towards the kingdom is a step-by-step removal of a sense of being a traitor to the king (of being a usurper). It must be noted that Roswall's devoted mother and the princess share the same name, Lillian.

There are clear differences between these two narratives in both content and use of magic. The more profound in feeling a magical narrative is, the more it will make use of magic and the more interesting this use will be. "The Goose-Girl" is a much more profound story than *Roswall and Lillian:* it is intensively concerned with the struggle to acquire a sense of having a right to be a queen. The magic is powerful, using the gift of drops of the queen's blood (a primitive form of identification) and the sacrifice of the horse (which represents the journey to the kingdom). *Roswall and Lillian* and "The Goose-Girl" seem more alike than they truly are because they use some similar devices for exorcizing the idea of usurpation. *Roswall and Lillian* does not make comparable use of magic even in the area of penance (although it would be useful to discover the meaning of Roswall's adopted name Dissawar, especially as two characters comment on it as having a regrettable significance).

Exorcism, in narrative, is the ritual removal of the (irrational) idea that the participant's wishes and actions are evil. The study of this form of magic, like the study of ritual punishment and primitive identification, reveals the purposefulness behind the processes for making magic—purposefulness in the causes of eliminating unwanted ideas and bringing about desired feelings. This intensity of purpose varies from plot to plot. In fact, the more one learns about magical plots, the more wary one becomes about dividing them into groups or even comparing them; each is highly individual, however much it may truly resemble other plots. The provisions made by magical plots for dealing with guilt and fear are the most difficult features of all to study, being made almost impenetrable by the combined effects of the hidden point of view, the ambiguous, unexpected thought processes, and the eclectic, often highly original means of making magic. It is important that nothing hinders the study of each individual text. Moreover, each text offers the opportunity to learn more: making a fresh approach to the particular characteristics of a new plot, one can turn a new corner in one's knowledge of the magical narrative.

The Ugly Duckling

Finally, a story that might seem to have some profound connections with "Rashin Coatie" and "The Goose-Girl" is H. C. Andersen's *The Ugly Duckling*, a nonmagical story. Its chief character is transferred from a Cinderella situation to sovereignty, encountering many an "ugly sister," and this is essentially a process of discovering his identity, transferring from being a swan who does not know it to one who does. This story has deep meaning at the level of the Duckling's feelings about himself, and it also explores the outer truth of how the world behaves towards someone who is different. A perfect balance between inner and outer experience creates this unmatched tale.[7]

In *The Ugly Duckling*, an "ugly," wrong identity is experienced and explored and then altered to a beautiful, right identity. Magic, by contrast, does not explore feelings in relation to reality: instead, it seeks to change or acquire them through a sequence of strategies that forms the narrative. The ugliness and wrongness would be assigned to other characters and used there in ritual arrangements of character and event—rather as, in *Meriadoc,* the treachery is transferred to the emperor. Within magic's irrational arena, irrational anxieties create wicked characters and so too do magical strategies for enhancement. Such strategies can most clearly be seen in intensely magical narratives, but they can also be seen in the Cinderella tales.

So a key aspect to be considered is the role of the ugly sisters. In *The Ugly Duckling,* we are given two comparable characters in the hen and the cat, instantly recognizable to both our inner and outer experience. The hen and the cat, favorites of their mistress because of the things they can do, are two rulers of the world living in a hovel that is only standing up because it does not know which way to fall.

"Can you lay eggs?" [the hen] asked.

"No!" [replied the duckling].

"Then you had better hold your tongue!"

And the cat said, "Can you arch your back, and purr, and give out sparks?"

"No!"

"Then you mustn't have any opinions when sensible people are talking!"

So the duckling sat alone in a corner in a very bad mood. Then he thought of the fresh air and sunshine, and he was seized by such a strange longing to swim on the water that he could not help saying so to the hen.

"What's the matter with you?" said the hen. "You have nothing to do, and that's why you have these whims. Lay eggs or purr, and they will go away." (my translation)

The hen and the cat play negative roles, and these are explored, not used to enhance the protagonist. By contrast, the ugly sisters in "Rashin Coatie" might indeed appear to be "framed" by magic.

4

Cúroí's Castle and Its Tests

Many critics have shown the variety of connections between the Irish *Bricriu's Feast*, the English Carl of Carlisle texts, and a number of other texts, including *Le Chevalier à l'Épée* and *Sir Gawain and the Green Knight*.[1] This chapter is designed to show the nature of my own contribution to this discussion. My concern is not with the well-known narrative material that these texts have in common, but with the very different systems of thought I find using this material. Where the thought in a text is of a kind quite as unlike other kinds as I find magic to be, the text itself must be entirely distinct, even where the narrative material it employs is the same. I shall demonstrate this total distinction I find by considering the two Carl of Carlisle texts in relation to *Bricriu's Feast*.

The Carl of Carlisle texts and *Bricriu's Feast* have been thought to be similar narratives, in which three heroes are tested by a supernatural being and one is found supreme. But the adventures in the Carl of Carlisle texts do not work well as tests, and these problems have led me into an investigation where I find that both Carl of Carlisle texts have a magical plot—in which there is no concern with testing—while *Bricriu's Feast* does not, and is indeed about testing—although in a special, narrative sense. The adventures in *Bricriu's Feast* show the winner among the three contestants to have no equal for courage, skill, and honor (in the words of Cúroí at the end of the story). There has actually been no real contest, for Cúchulainn is so superior to the other two contestants that the narrative is really an exuberant—and humorous—celebration of the powers of a superhero, for which the tests provide the setting. The adventures all take place as a result of a quarrel at Bricriu's feast over who should receive the champion's portion: it is decided to seek a judgment as to which of the three contestants is supreme, and the narrative has devices for preventing an early decision so that there is no early end to the account of Cúchulainn's exploits. Nevertheless, the adventures make good sense as tests. In the case of the Carl of Carlisle texts, there is clearly something wrong with the material if it must be understood as a sequence of tests, and nor, in fact, are the adventures ever called tests in these texts. The adventures initiated by the curious orders of the Carl (whose behavior resembles that of the Imperious Host of tradition) present Sir Gawain with no real challenge. The quality he must show is obedience, and his tasks are to throw a spear at the Carl's face and to kiss the Carl's wife in bed, but there is no sense of an ordeal—or, indeed, of a submission—equal to Cúchulainn's obligation to turn up for a return blow. On the contrary, we are told that, in both these adventures, Gawain obeys with a fervor that provokes the Carl's rebuke (in the first adventure of one text) and his order to stop (during the second adventure). The adventures would make no more sense if we were to understand them as tests of courtesy, since the "ire" and lust Gawain shows are not approved by the Carl; his demeanor with the spear and the Carl's wife does not compare with his earlier gentleness towards the Carl's horse.

Once we have broken away from the extratextual explanation that these adventures are tests, we can examine the illogicalities surrounding the theme of doing the host's bidding in these texts. On the morning after the adventures, the Carl shows Gawain a great heap of bones, the remains of disobedient guests. Logically, these guests must have been men who refused to engage in actions that, in other contexts, would be treacherous—and also, conversely, men who engaged in a treacherous act by disobeying the Carl's order to stop, when making love to his wife. Only the idea of doing the bidding of the Carl—the Imperious Host who must be unquestioningly obeyed—stands in the way of our considering what these men must actually have done, and, when we consider what they must have done, we find they fall into two contradictory groups. Illogicalities of this kind are worth examination, especially as there is a sense in which the adventures appear to be presented from the wrong point of view. An idea of treachery lurks unacknowledged, while there is some verbal evidence for its presence, in the thoughts of Gawain and Kay (read by the Carl) as they admire the Carl's wife.

It will be my argument that the adventures are correctly seen as magically defended adventures. The magical structure of the defended narrative accounts for all the details in each text, each detail emerging as having a function in its particular position in the narrative, without there being any evasion of problems. Defended narratives are more difficult to study than magical narratives of other kinds, because they lack the move structure that provides so much guidance. Their magical structures are also more difficult to present clearly on a chart, and, in the case of the Carl of Carlisle texts, such a chart would be more complicated than useful. Instead, I must present the details of the two rather different versions the texts give us.

In the outline I give of the narratives of the two versions (chart 15), I have borne in mind that those wishing to refer to the exact points of resemblance and difference between the texts can do so in Auvo Kurvinen's parallel edition, "*Sir Gawain and the Carl of Carlisle* in Two Versions." For this reason, I have aimed for clarity in my chart, rather than for the provision of all the smaller differences. The chart makes the romance *Syre Gawene and the Carle of Carelyle*, found in MS Porkington and written in the late fifteenth century, its chief text; details from the version entitled *Carle off Carlile*, in Bishop Percy's Folio Manuscript, dated about 1650, are given only where they represent important differences from the first text.[2]

Auvo Kurvinen's exhaustive study of these texts points out the curious features of each "test" (89–104). Kurvinen comments that, while all the tests in *Bricriu's Feast* are tests of prowess, in which the competitors are aware of imminent personal danger, the heroes in the Carl of Carlisle texts are in danger only on their arrival, when the Carl's "whelps" are about to kill them. Moreover, the adventures in the Carl of Carlisle texts are never called tests: after their return to Arthur, the heroes tell the king what "wonders" (l. 581) (or "adventures," l. 452, in the second text) they have seen. The underlying ideas are also opposite, Kurvinen continues: in the visit to Cúroí's castle, in *Bricriu's Feast*, it is in the hero's interest to fight his antagonists and overcome them, while the main principle at the Carl's castle is absolute submission to the will of the host. However, the "framework of the story" is the same in *Bricriu's Feast* and the Carl of Carlisle narratives: three heroes are lodged in a castle and tested by the host, who has a beautiful wife. One of the heroes is successful in all the tests, declared superior to the others, and rewarded with a gift of gold. The testers, Cúroí and the Carl, Kurvinen also finds similar (87–88).

Auvo Kurvinen sees the presence of six tests, falling into two groups: the "whelps" and horse tests, which are shared by the three companions, and the tests of the spear-throwing, the wife, the daughter, and the beheading, in which Gawain obeys the Carl's explicit orders. She comments that the horse test "is obviously one of courtesy, while the tests put to Gawain alone appear to be tests of obedience." For her, the eccentricity of the Imperious Host's orders test Gawain's courtesy: "only a perfectly courteous knight can refrain from objection"; such a test, found elsewhere, is drawn to its extreme in the Carl of Carlisle texts, but, partly for this reason, the story has no hint of a moral lesson.[3]

My comment here is that we need to be prepared for the presence of totally different purposes behind the use of similar material: material used for a testing theme in one text may be used for quite other purposes in another. But this, of course, is well-known, and Auvo Kurvinen's assumption that the Carl of Carlisle texts are concerned with tests is probably due to the absence of any means of explaining their baffling narratives otherwise.

An investigation of the thought process using the material involves confronting the apparent absurdities in the texts and taking them seriously as they stand, with a conviction that this will lead us in a direction more fruitful than will the finding of ready-made explanations. The most complex illogicalities and contradictions can be those that provide the soundest information, because they provide more evidence for both the presence and character of any unrecognized thought system in the text. This is why I bring forward the problem of the heap of bones at the beginning of this chapter: it is the kind of problem that suggests that the entire narrative may make sense if we looked at it from another point of view.

If I use the model of the defended narrative, the correct point of view appears to be provided. The use of the Imperious Host and the obeying of his eccentric orders become defenses for actions the hero wishes to take. Moreover, further defenses can be seen, surrounding the adventures. The episode with the horses becomes an opening defense: the chief character, Gawain, appears to be making a statement of respect for the Carl's property, this being placed in contrast with the disrespect acted out by the bishop and Kay.[4] Earlier in each text, when Gawain, Kay, and the bishop plan to lodge with the Carl, space is given to Kay's aggressive talk, talk in which he declares that he will beat his host until he stinks and despoil his house. Gawain, by contrast, speaks of the respect he will show for the Carl's property and the courtesy he will use so that they might be welcome guests. Closing defenses also become visible: after the subversive adventures, in which the hero is protected by his being under the host's orders, there appear to be rear-guard arrangements, declaring terms of friendship and affirming the restoration of the status quo. The meeting between the Carl and the king would play a part here.

A number of problems remain outstanding, and one of these concerns the role of the daughter. The central feelings in a magical plot tend to be highly ambiguous, and the texts before us lack both the detail and move structure that would provide information about these feelings. However, it is more than likely that the daughter's chief function can be explored in relation to the closing defense structures. She can be seen to seal both the friendship with the Carl and the restored status quo.

Another problem is the role of the fierce beasts. There may be a connection between the Carl's control over his fierce beasts and his control over the feelings of his guests. In the Porkington text, the orders he gives to the beasts, commanding their instant obedience, are echoed in those he gives to Kay. Kay takes heed when the beasts creep under the table, and both he and the beasts are ordered to be still. "'Ly style'" (l. 241) the Carl orders the beasts and "'Sytt styll'" (l. 376) he orders Kay, reading Kay's thoughts about his wife and himself at table. That the Imperious Host has entire control over fierce beasts would be an important attribute behind his eccentric orders, used here to protect the hero as he ventures into forbidden experience.[5]

What would be the role of the heap of bones in the defended narrative I propose? Here, as always, the position of a detail in the text is essential, and Gawain's sight of the heap of bones comes on the morning following the night of adventures, in a place where the narrative would be concerned with providing closing defenses. As part of the closing defenses, the heap of bones would state that Gawain had to obey the Carl or die. The illogicalities it creates at rational levels of thought are of no account in a magical plot, for the disobedient guests will have no existence as characters. We have a ritual heap of bones—no more, its role confined entirely to the place where it appears, any magical plot being strictly a linear sequence of rituals.

The beheading of the Carl, meanwhile—which only appears in the Percy text—does not seem to play the same kind of magical role I have found such material playing in the text of *Sir Gawain and the Green Knight*. It appears to have nothing to do with ritual punishment or even with the defense structures I find in the Carl of Carlisle texts. Instead, it appears simply to be part of the clumsy but effective "explanation" apparatus. In the Porkington text, the Carl has made a pointless vow, while, in the Percy text, he has been transformed, and the beheading provides an exciting, well-established type of transformation scene. The transformation itself plays a part in the defense structures, providing a cause for the Carl's gratitude to Gawain. The Porkington vow, by contrast, lacks these useful roles, and it leaves the Carl with a suspect character at the end, where this is not appropriate. It is more than likely that the beheading scene was lost from the Porkington scribe's sources, as has been suggested, and the vow substituted as an explanation (Kurvinen 71–72).

My conclusion here is that the Carl of Carlisle texts provide structures for the defense of adventures into forbidden experience. But, in the case of these particular texts, it is easier to show the presence of defenses than it is to show the use of magic. The structures do not have the distinctive step-by-step organization apparent even in defended narratives, and I need more detail for study than these texts provide. But this is an opportunity to consider how the structures I see differ from disguise. Disguise safeguards the text from social and moral censure—a purpose outside the concern of magic—and it makes the material look like something else to external view. This latter situation occurs in any case in magical narrative, because the outsider does not take up the point of view of the participant, and the concerns and imagery of magic are hidden from the conscious mind. Magical defenses safeguard the participant "inside" the narrative, rather than the survival of the text in society, and there is evident concern with this kind of protection in the Carl of Carlisle texts. It is clearest of all in the use of the all-powerful host, who has total control over Gawain and all that takes place, and who is indestructible. The hero can give expression to feeling with a sense of safety. As always in magic, the essential process is an investment of power in the devices provided, for the immediate use of the participant concerned.

I shall now give brief attention to *Bricriu's Feast,* to show how I find similar material used for the nonmagical purpose of testing heroes. The text of *Bricriu's Feast* is well-known in its longer form, but I shall be concerned with its shorter form, the primary form in which it appears in the text of the scribe Mael Muire (known as M), one of the two scribes involved in the narrative as we now find it in the twelfth-century Book of the Dun Cow.[6] M's text and the long form differ mainly in the number of adventures testing the heroes: in M's text, there are three such adventures—the attack of the Crúachan cats, the night watch at Cúroí's stronghold, and the beheading bargain with Cúroí at Emain Macha. Leaves are missing from the end of the text, but the lost material can be supplied from the fragment in the Edinburgh Gaelic MS. XL.[7] The story is as follows.

> Bricriu Nemthenga prepares a great feast for Conchubur and all of Ulaid. He is well-known for inciting people against each other, and his guests prepare for this, but he nevertheless succeeds in doing so by telling three warriors in turn—Lóegure, Conall Cernach, and Cúchulainn—that once the champion's portion is his at Bricriu's feast, it will be his forever. He also tells each warrior's wife in turn that if she enters the house first that night she will always be first among the women of Ulaid. During the dissensions that follow at the feast, Lóegure and Conall each break off a pole their own height from Bricriu's house, so that their wives can enter, but Cúchulainn

lifts the side of the house so high that his wife Emer and her fifty women, and the fifty women of each of the other two wives, can enter. When he lets the house down again, the fort shakes so much that Bricriu's bower falls, and Bricriu and his wife are thrown onto the garbage heap in the courtyard, among the dogs.

It is agreed that a judgment should be sought from King Ailill and Queen Medb in Crúachu, concerning both the champion's portion and—dependent on this—the precedence among the women.

There follows a great procession of the Ulaid to Crúachu, for the judgment. Ailill is an unwilling judge and asks for three days and three nights to think it over. The Ulaid go home, cursing Bricriu, and the three contestants remain. That night, while the contestants are being given their food, three cats—druidic beasts—are loosed from the cave of Crúachu. Lóegure and Conall leave their food to the beasts and flee to the rafters of the house, where they remain all night. Cúchulainn does not move. He strikes a cat but cannot injure it, and, when the cat settles itself, Cúchulainn neither eats nor sleeps until morning. At dawn, the cats leave, and the warriors are found in the places where they have spent the night. "'Does this contest not suffice for judgement?'" Ailill says. "'Not at all,'" Lóegure and Conall reply, "'for it is not beasts that we fight but men'" (239).[8] When Ailill tells his wife Medb it is difficult to judge them, Medb says it is easy, and she devises the awarding of three cups, a bronze one for Lóegure, a white gold one for Conall, and a red gold one for Cúchulainn. She tells each warrior he deserves the champion's portion as she awards him his cup. Each is instructed to conceal his cup and then display it on his return home. When they display their cups before Conchubur and the chieftains, the champion's portion is awarded to Cúchulainn, but Lóegure accuses Cúchulainn of having purchased his cup from Ailill and Medb so that he might not be disgraced.

So the three warriors go to Cúroí's stronghold for judgment and are welcomed by Bláthnait, Cúroí's wife. Cúroí, knowing they are coming, has absented himself, instructing his wife in the hospitality they are to receive. One of them is to keep watch over the stronghold each night until Cúroí returns. Lóegure watches the first night, and, towards morning, he sees a giant approaching out of the western sea. The giant throws stripped oak trunks at him, which miss, and finally stretches out his hand to seize him; he grinds Lóegure between his palms and then drops him over the stronghold wall into the ditch at the entrance to the royal house. Those in the stronghold think Lóegure has leapt over the wall as a challenge to the other contestants. The same events occur the next night, when Conall Cernach keeps watch. On the third night, when it is Cúchulainn's turn, it is the night that the Three Greys of Sescend Úairbéoil and the Three Cowherds of Brega and the Three Sons of Dornmár Céoil gather to destroy the stronghold. It is also the night that the monster in the lake nearby will devour everything in the stronghold. Cúchulainn kills all nine of the first attackers, making a heap of their heads and goods, and then he destroys the monster. Finally, the giant from the western sea comes, and Cúchulainn avoids his grasp with his salmon's leap and hovers over the giant in a circle like a mill wheel. The giant grants Cúchulainn the supremacy, the champion's portion, and precedence for his wife, and departs. Cúchulainn then tries to make the leap he believes the other two to have made over the stronghold wall, and eventually succeeds. Cúroí, returning with all Cúchulainn's trophies, declares Cúchulainn the champion and rewards him with gold and silver.

When they return to Emain Macha, it is assumed that they will not be contesting the champion's portion any more, because they will have received judgment. But Lóegure and Conall say that Cúroí has not awarded anything to Cúchulainn. Cúchulainn says he will not contest the champion's portion, since the good of having it would be no greater than the trouble involved.

Then a huge, ugly churl comes to Emain Macha and announces his challenge of the beheading bargain: since the Ulaid surpass all other warriors, let them keep faith with him in this matter. The churl will cut off the head of anyone who dares to take up the challenge, and then he can have a return blow the next day. Lóegure, Conall, and Cúchulainn are not there, and Muinremur takes up the challenge, turning the bargain around so that the churl is beheaded first. Muinremur pledges to keep his part of the bargain the following night. The beheaded churl rises, gathers up his head, and leaves, streaming blood. The following night, he returns but Muinremur avoids him. The churl then asks which of those contesting the champion's portion of Ulaid will fulfill the bargain with him, and he asks for Lóegure. Lóegure is pledged, but, like Muinremur, he fails to appear the following night. Conall Cernach also fails to keep the bargain. The churl tells the men of Ulaid, on the fourth night, that they covet the champion's portion, yet are unable to contest it. He asks for "'that pitiful stripling'" they call Cúchulainn. Cúchulainn wants no bargain with him. "'No doubt you fear death, wretched fly,'" says the churl (254). At once, Cúchulainn leaps forward and beheads him.

The next night, Cúchulainn presents himself and stretches his neck on the huge block, which is too large for it. "'Stretch out your neck, you wretch,'" the churl says. "'You torment me. . . . Kill me quickly,'" says Cúchulainn (254). He finally stretches himself to the extent that a warrior's foot would fit between each rib, and the churl raises his axe so that it reaches the rafters of the house. He brings it down with the blade turned up and tells Cúchulainn to rise, supreme in courage, skill, and honor. The champion's portion is his and his wife has precedence before all the other women. The churl then vanishes. He was Cúroí, who had come to fulfill his promise to Cúchulainn.

Bricriu's Feast emerges with great clarity as a beautifully constructed sequence of testing adventures, and, while many of the events are fantastic and Cúchulainn uses supernatural powers, there is no magical system of thought at work in the text. The thought using the story elements is of a kind immediately accessible to the rational mind: the critic can, in fact, see exceptionally easily the main trend of the adventures and have no cause to suspect the presence of a hidden structure with quite different purposes.

It is also apparent that the role played by Cúroí's wife in no way resembles the role played by the Carl's wife and also that Cúroí's role does not truly resemble that of the Imperious Host. There is no Perilous Bed in this text or hint of love between Bláthnait and Cúchulainn, and there are no unexpected orders: the orders are all strictly to do with the contest, and Cúroí's role is parallel to that of Ailill.

The Imperious Host and *lit périlleux* appear in the Old French *Le Chevalier à l'Épée*,[9] which is also not a magical text. The characters are a sinister knight and his beautiful daughter, whom Gawain wins as a result of surviving the *lit périlleux*: a magic sword has killed those attempting intercourse. This material evidently has connections with material in Chrétien's *Lancelot* and "Gauvain" (the second part of *Le Conte du Graal*), and a concern of the narrative is the hero's embarrassing experiences in relation to a woman (Johnston and Owen 4–7). Put to this humorous, rational use, the host and his *lit périlleux* have a quite different character from the similar material in the Carl of Carlisle texts. The narrative is straightforward, the host's orders have entirely to do with throwing his guest and daughter together, so that the guest should be tempted, until, finally, the couple have to spend the night together in company with the magic sword, which watches every movement. Gawain is warned of his danger at strategic points, and in ways that build up suspense, and, when a full explanation comes at last from the host, it follows on logically from the preceding sense of the narrative. By means of the cruel test, a cruel knight has found the best knight for his daughter—and, seen from the daughter's point of view, which exists in this narrative, she has gained her chosen knight by warning him as she had not warned his predecessors. Gawain has not really passed the test quite as his host believes, and his enforced chastity gives us a comical *lit périlleux*. But the daughter has liked him, finding him courteous, and the test—while fantastic—makes thorough good sense as a test. There is no sealing of friendship between host and guest at the end. Gawain refuses the host's offer of gold and castle, accepting only the daughter, and this is appropriate. In the defended narrative of the Carl of Carlisle texts, there needs to be a sealing of friendship and also a declaration of the host's change of character, with some explanation of his previous behavior.

When one considers the contrasting uses of material such as the Imperious Host, the *lit périlleux,* and the beheading game, the question arises: was this material first invented by magic and adopted later by other forms of thought for different purposes, or was magic the borrower? However, to refer to this material also raises the question as to how much actual connection there is between these various hosts and various adventures frequently linked under the name of Cúroí's Castle.

5

The Tristan Verse Romances and *The Pursuit of Diarmaid and Gráinne*

There have been various obstacles in the way of my making a study of the Tristan material. One has been the fragmentary state of the texts I would need to work on. My methods require complete texts, although I have occasionally—as in the case of Chrétien's *Perceval*—been able to study an incomplete text. Other obstacles have been the many difficulties presented by the surviving material, but a sufficient number of these receded when, after I had finished my revised study of the plot of *Sir Gawain and the Green Knight,* I had the use of a new model—that of the defended narrative. Using this model, I am now able to present an argument for there being a magical plot in the German Tristan narrative known as the work of Eilhart von Oberge; I have also found evidence for the presence of the same magical plot in the incomplete French Tristan narrative attributed to Beroul.

This defended narrative I have identified in the texts of Eilhart von Oberge and Beroul is absent in the apparently parallel narratives of Gottfried von Strassburg and the Scandinavian *Tristrams saga ok Ísöndar,* even though the four texts use very much the same material. This gives me an opportunity to show by comparison how a narrative with a magical structure and a narrative without one can be distinguished from each other. Meanwhile, my study of the Irish work *The Pursuit of Diarmaid and Gráinne* shows how a magical plot—in this case, the Tristan defended narrative—can reappear in a text where the surface detail has been greatly altered. Despite appearances, the alterations made for the versions of Gottfried and the saga are greater than those made by the Irish writer, who adapts the tale of Tristan and Mark so that it becomes one about Diarmaid and Finn.

Since the magical structure I find in the Tristan narrative is one defending adventures, concentrating most of its ritual activity in particular parts of the narrative, rather than using the step-by-step sequence throughout the narrative, my examination of the details will concentrate on certain parts of the text. The structure does not include the exile (after the parting of the lovers), but my discussion of my findings in relation to some of the debates concerning the texts pays particular attention to the narratives recounting the exile.

I shall begin the discussion by offering a chart of the defense structures I have found in the Tristan narrative known as the work of Eilhart von Oberge (see chart 16). This narrative was composed some time in the last decades of the twelfth century, and it enjoyed long popularity. It has come down to us in the small fragments of three manuscripts belonging to about 1200 A.D. and also in three late manuscripts—only two complete (a Czech translation and a chapbook version)—all belonging to the fifteenth century, though based on much earlier sources.[1] It is impossible to reconstruct the exact language of the original, but there is close agreement with regard to plot, and we have a reconstruction of the thirteenth-century version that was the common source of the versions, in Franz Lichtenstein's *Eilhart von Oberge* of 1877. For my study, I use Lichtenstein's reconstruction and the chapbook version; the line and page numbers I give refer, as always, to the editions and translation cited in my notes and bibliography.

I have not found the many questions raised about the texts a good guide in the case of the Tristan verse romances, but the presence of a defended narrative would address a few of these questions. The perplexing separating sword episode only makes sense if it is understood to be a ritual in anticipation of the lovers' discovery by the king—and as an emblem of both the true situation and its opposite, the situation that the king must believe if he is to be able to take back his queen and forgive the hero. Another question addressed by the defended narrative is the one relating to the limited duration of the love potion. Fedrick notes that there "is something intrinsically odd about limiting the duration of the love potion's efficacy" (21) and D. de Rougemont asks why the philtre is so limited when it is destined for a married couple (33).[2] But in a defended narrative, the limited duration of the potion's power is essential: it must be just as it is, overwhelming for the limited period and then (strategically) releasing the lovers; in both instances it plays its part in the defenses. Meanwhile, there are my own questions, some of them discussed in my section on Eilhart's text in the chapter "Questions, Definitions, and Practice," and these relate to the incongruities, contradictions, and absurdities in the events in Ireland and elsewhere. Among them are the circumstances in which Tristrant gives Isalde to Mark and the juxtaposition of this gift and Tristrant's oath to the Irish king that he will treat Isalde honorably as Mark's bride. Equally indicative of the presence of a magical purpose is the method in the madness connected with the roles assigned to the hermit and the kings.

The questions highlight the scenes in Ireland, the potion, and the events leading up to the return of the queen, and these I have identified as defenses. The step-by-step arrangement of the king's forgiveness during the scenes in Ireland have a ritual appearance suggestive of a piling on of safeguards, and the potion could also play a role in the opening defenses of the narrative. If there are indeed opening defenses present, then there will be closing defenses, and the arrangements made to return the queen to the king constitute precisely the defenses needed. The events relating to the hermit Ugrim form the main part of these, while the separating sword episode would also play an important part, because the king's belief in the lovers' innocence depends upon it. The role of the potion as a magical defense would not be comparable with its role in Gottfried as an excuse to the world; a magical defense safeguards the participant so that a frightening inner experience (perhaps one breaking taboos) can be enjoyed, and there is no concern at that level with the opinion of the world.

I shall now examine several texts in detail, and begin by presenting chart 17 of Beroul's plot. The version of the Tristan story attributed to Beroul is preserved in a single manuscript, and it is a large fragment, some 4500 lines long.[3] The text begins during the tryst under the tree, where Tristan and Yseut stage a conversation, having realized they are being spied upon: it therefore begins early in the section of my chart entitled Defended Adventures. If the plot is a defended narrative, the opening defenses will be lost, but we should have the closing defenses in entirety; there is also additional material that I have included in the chart under the heading Additional Defenses. The Beroul version belongs to about 1200 A.D., and is therefore later than the French sources used by Gottfried von Strassburg (known as the version of Thomas), and yet it represents a more "primitive" version, as also does Eilhart, and it can therefore be regarded as "older." In my chart, I have reconstructed what I can of the lost narrative, from references to the lost events made in the existing text.

While the Beroul text has lost the all-important events in Ireland, I shall argue that the existing text provides good evidence for the presence of the defended narrative I find in Eilhart. When one is examining magical structures, some differences between texts can turn out not to be differences at all, while apparent similarities can turn out to be radical differences. Beroul is well-known for his fervent identification with his story: he constantly intervenes in the narrative to express his sympathy with the lovers, no matter what their moral position, and his enmity towards their accusers. This warmth and identification is, I believe, all a part of Beroul's faithfulness to the magical plot, while it is also a factor behind differences in his treatment, these not being real differences in terms of function. Beroul intensifies some of the magical arrangements, thus making them clearer, and this makes it all the more lamentable that the first part of his text is lost. For example, Beroul gives us more detail relating to the king's rituals after he finds the lovers asleep with the sword between them. Eilhart tells us only of the exchange of swords and the laying of the king's glove on Isalde:

> Dô nam he Tristrandes wâfin
> den tûrlîchen beiden
> und zoug daz sîne ûz der scheide.
> Tristrandes stackte he wedir în
> und legete dô daz swert sîn
> dâ jenez hâte vor gelegin
> . . . .
> der koning sînen hantschû
> ûf die vrauwen legete. (ll. 4630–35, 4638–39)

> [He took Tristrant's weapon from the noble pair and drew his own. He placed Tristrant's in his scabbard and laid his sword where the other had lain. . . . The king then laid his glove on the lady. (J. W. Thomas 100)]

Beroul gives us a convincing explanation for what the king is doing, that he is giving the lovers a sign so that they will know for certain that someone found them asleep and took pity on them, and that neither the king nor anyone else in the kingdom is in any way seeking their death (Fedrick 93). The king exchanges the swords, referring to Tristran's separating sword as the sword that killed Morholt ("Morhot" in Beroul's text quoted below), and places his own in the strategic position between the lovers; this detail is precisely as in Eilhart and it must have an important ritual function. Equally important must be the laying of his gloves (glove, in Eilhart) on the queen. Beroul's king also takes the queen's ring, which had been his own gift.

> "Je lor ferai tel demostrance
> Ançois que il s'esvelleront,
> Certainement savoir porront
> Qu'il furent endormi trové
> Et q'en a eü d'eus pité,
> Que je nes vuel noient ocire,
> Ne moi ne gent de mon enpire.
> Ge voi el doi a la reïne
> L'anel o pierre esmeraudine,
> Or li donnai, molt par est buens;
> Et g'en rai un qui refu suens:
> Osterai li le mien du doi.
> Uns g(r)anz de voirre ai je o moi,
> Qu'el aporta o soi d'Irlande;
> Le rai qui sor la face brande—
> Qui, li fait chaut—en vuel covrir;
> Et quant vendra au departir,
> Prendrai l'espee d'entre eus deus
> Dont au Morhot fu le chief blos."
> . . . .
> L'espee qui entre eus deus est
> Souef oste, la soue i met. (vv. 2020–38, 2049–50)

Beroul rationalizes some of his material, perhaps, in having the king leave the lovers a sign to reassure them and in having him shield the queen's face with the gloves, but the feelings he gives the king are entirely in tune with the plot: these are feelings desired in the king at this point. Gertrude Schoepperle Loomis wonders that Mark, in finding the lovers asleep as he does, departs without making an effort towards a reconciliation (1:79), but Beroul's treatment of the magical plot brings out the fact that he does indeed demonstrate a reconciliation. Eilhart gives us the fundamental rituals, through which the king is probably expressing his ownership of the woman, while Beroul gives us these rituals too, together with further details that convey the reconciliation in more human terms; moreover, through giving the king loving feelings, Beroul invests more power in the rituals. Beroul seems to develop the material both imaginatively (as a conscious artist) and at the deeper, magical level.

The same contrasting treatment of Eilhart and Beroul is apparent in the hermit material of the two versions: Eilhart's treatment is baldly ritualistic compared with the fuller and warmer treatment of Beroul. Eilhart uses the hermit's power as the king's confessor, while the letter sent to the king in Beroul is more complex, drawing strategically on defenses organized earlier in the plot. As Eilhart's Tristrant throws the hermit's letter through the window to the king, he gives him added messages from the hermit that, if his father confessor is dear to him as a confessor, the king should heed the letter; his confessor grants him God's salvation, and imposes this letter as a penance for all his sins, so he should accept it gladly (102). In Eilhart's words:

> "dîn bîchteger Ûgrîm
> sendit dir desin brîf
> und entbût dir, ab he dir sî lîf
> zu einem bîchtegêre,
> daz dû vornimest dese mêre,
> swaz dar ane geschrebin sî,
> und entbût dir dâ bî
> daz he dir wol heiles gunde:
> vor alle dîne sunde
> wil he dir zu bûze gebin,
> sô mochtestû daz gerne nemen." (ll. 4804–14)

The king performs his penance as soon as it is day, and the letter reads,

> "hêre, dû nemest wedir
> mîne vrauwin daz wîp dîn,
> des betet dich sêre Ûgrîm
> in gotlîcher minne.
> her heizzet sie bringen
> Tristranden dir engegene
> mit luzeler menige.
> mit lîbe saltû sie entvân
> unde salt Tristrandin lân
> abir an dînen huldin:
> daz mag her wol vorschuldin
> mit sîme lîbe swâ he sol:
> hêre mîn, daz weistû wol
> vil baz denne ich.
> dorch gotes liebe bite ich dich,
> Ûgrîm der meistir dîn,
> daz dû ez willest gût lân sîn
> dorch got und mîner bete willen." (ll. 4844–61)

["Sir, Ugrim beseeches you in holy love to take back my lady, your wife. He bids Tristrant come with few troops and bring her to you, and you should receive her fondly and should again show Tristrant your favor. He can indeed earn this with his strength wherever he ought, as you, my lord, know better than I. I, Ugrim, your teacher, beg you for the love of God to be gracious, for God's sake and because of his plea." (J. W. Thomas 102)]

Beroul's hermit, instead, thinks up several strategies that the letter to the king could use. The chief is that Tristran should challenge anyone who accuses him of loving the queen dishonorably; this must succeed as no one would dare to take up the challenge. So it proves, when the letter is read out: there is not a baron in Cornwall who does not say, "'King, take back your wife. The men whose accusations of the queen we have just been reminded of acted unwisely'" (Fedrick 106; "N'i a baron de Cornoualle / Ne die: 'Rois, ta feme pren. / Onques cil n'orent nul jor sen / Qui ce distrent de la roïne, / Dont la parole est ci oïe,'" vv. 2624–28). The accusations—which are essential to the plot—have throughout been characterized as those of three wicked, lying barons. Among its other arguments, the letter claims that Tristran rescued the queen when she had been given to the lepers as her punishment, since he could not fail her when she had been condemned to death for his sake. This refers to one of the strategies resorted to during the defended episodes. The strategy that the letter look for "'suitable falsehoods'" to remove the shame and cover up the wrong (100; "'Por honte oster et mal covrir / Doit on un poi par bel mentir,'" vv. 2353–54)—to quote words assigned to the hermit—is sanctified by means of making it entirely the work of the holy man in question. The letter also has an important, ritual opening, presenting the two contradictory defenses organized during the episode in Ireland, that the queen had been rightfully given to Tristran and that he has then rightfully given her to the king. "'Sire, remember well your marriage with the king of Ireland's daughter. I crossed the sea to Ireland and I won her by my prowess. I killed the huge, crested dragon, for which she was given to me. I brought her to your country, sire, where you took her to wife, as all your knights saw'" (104):

"Rois, tu sez bien le mariage
De la fille le roi d'Irlande.
Par mer en fui jusque en Horlande,
Par ma proece la conquis,
Le grant serpent cresté ocis,
Par qoi ele me fu donee.
Amenai la en ta contree;

Rois, tu la preïs a mollier,
Si que virent ti chevalier." (vv. 2556–64)

Beroul's letter draws on the power of various defenses and strategies already provided by the plot. The Eilhart and Beroul versions vary in the actual detail of their devices, but their magical arrangements are, in fact, the same in this part of the plot, where the two versions can be compared: in particular, both rely most on the Christian magic of the hermit.

I shall now examine the details of the scenes at the Irish court in Eilhart's version and compare it with the details of the chapbook version, based on Eilhart, and, afterwards, with the details of Gottfried von Strassburg's version. First, I shall show how Eilhart's rituals in Ireland are constructed in detail; their step-by-step progression is outlined in my chart of his plot.

Eilhart's Tristrant arrives in enemy territory (the kingdom of Morolt's people) and sends a message that he has brought twelve sailing vessels of food to relieve the famine in the land. But, before a reply is received, a dragon doing great harm to the country is introduced: if someone were to kill it, the king would, without doubt, give him his daughter. Tristrant decides to risk his life to win the lady and save his comrades; if he is to die (in his dangerous situation in enemy territory), he would rather die fighting a dragon. Of the motives given here, the operative one in the magical plot is winning the lady. Tristrant wins the lady and she heals him of his wounds; at this time, she recognizes him as her uncle Morolt's killer and threatens to reveal him to her father the king. But the plot has introduced a false aspirant for the lady's hand, the lord high steward who pretends to have killed the dragon, and Brangene stops Isalde, saying that Tristrant is noble and her husband will otherwise be the steward; if Tristrant had slain all of her family, she could bear it more easily than marriage to such a thief ("'sulchin dîb,'" l. 1957). Thus Isalde accepts that Tristrant is to be her husband: Tristrant is noble and not a false thief; the roles of the unworthy aspirant and thief are played out by another character in order to be ritually eliminated from the situation. Isalde treats Tristrant throughout with love and honor, through the use of the steward, but the use of this thief averts a different kind of threat: that the lady has discovered the hero to be the enemy of the king and herself. Morolt is an invader who threatens the king's sovereignty, and the hero becomes the king's champion, defending him against such an invasion. Through this very act, he becomes the king's enemy in Ireland, and, meanwhile, Morolt's activities express the hero's vision of his own activities that he does away with. All these conflicting roles for Morolt play an important, and different, part at various stages of the plot. The important matter in Ireland is that the hero sees himself as the king's enemy, and it is the function of the rituals in Ireland that they bring about a sense of the king's forgiveness, even as they also bring about a sense of the king's permission that he receive the lady; he establishes his right to her and ends the rituals by acknowledging the king's prior right. The difficult task of deciding on meaning in a magical plot is one depending entirely on context, the contexts dictated by the particular plot emerging in the text concerned.

The rituals in Ireland make the hero's identity known to the king in stages, arranging the king's forgiveness at each stage. First, Isalde tells the king she knows the real dragon slayer (as opposed to the false steward) and tells him he deserves his favor. The king asks where he is.

"wâ ist her nû?" "hîr vil nâ,
dâr ich in wol gevinde."
"sô heiz in vor mich bringen!"
"sal he dîne hulde hân?"
"jâ, swaz he mir hât getân,
daz sî om umme daz vorgebin."
"Kusse mich, vatir, vor den degin
und mache die sûne vullen stête!"
"swaz he mir tede unde hête
getân, daz vorkîse ich."
"Sô saltû vor in kussen mich!"
"waz wiltû mêre daz ich tû?"
"sô hâstû lûtirlîchin nû
vorkorn?" "jâ, ich hûte hân."
"sô mag he wol her vor gân." (ll. 1988–2002)

["Close by, where I can find him."
"Then have him brought to me."
"Will he receive your favour?"
"Yes, whatever he may have done to me will be forgiven because of this."
"Kiss me, father, for the warrior, and make a complete and lasting peace with him."
"I forgive anything he has done to me."
"Now kiss me in his place."
"What else do you want me to do?"
"Have you fully pardoned him now?"

"Yes, as of this day."
"Then he can indeed come forth." (71)]

The king and Tristrant gather their people, and the steward thinks he is to receive the princess at this gathering. In front of the gathering, Isalde takes Tristrant firmly by the hand and leads him to her father. The king asks who he is, but the princess says he should first kiss him. The king is quite willing and does as his daughter asks; he grants a firm pardon to Tristrant and all his family. Eilhart describes the scene below:

> Dô nam die vrauwe hêre
> Tristranden vaste bî der hant
> und ging dâ sie iren vatir vant.
> . . . .
> der koning abir begunde
> vrâgin, wer he mochte sîn.
> Dô sprach die junge koningîn,
> daz her in ze dem êrsten kuste.
> dem koninge des vil wol geluste:
> he ted, als in sîn tochtir bat.
> eine stête sûne her im gab
> vor in und al die sîne. (ll. 2112–14, 2122–29)

"'Now I'll let you know who he is,'" Isalde says, "'if you can be trusted to observe the pardon which you granted the hero and which he can well earn. He killed the finest man on whom the sun ever shone: my dear uncle'" (72). In Eilhart's words:

> "nu wil ich dir lâzin schînen"
> sprach die vrauwe "wer he ist:
> wen dû sô wârhaftig bist,
> daz die sûne sî stête
> die dû dem helde tête,
> und he die wol gedînen kan.
> he irslûg dir den tûrsten man
> den die sunne î beschein:
> daz was mîn lîbir ôhein." (ll. 2130–38)

"'God knows, Sir Tristrant,'" the king responds, "'if that had not been pardoned, you would be treated with scorn, but what you have done against me is fully forgiven.'" The princess says that this is only right, because Tristrant is a noble knight who has won great honor. He killed

Morolt unwillingly; there was no other way to save his uncle's land from the tribute. She continues, "'Now he has journeyed across the sea to show you a kindness: he fought the dragon single-handed and slew it. This was a great service to us all'" (73). In Eilhart's words:

> Dô sprach der koning zû hant
> "nû weiz got, her Tristrant,
> wêrez nû nicht vorsônet,
> ir wordet hî von mir gehônet:
> abir swaz ir mir hât getân,
> des sult ir gûten vrede hân."
> die vrauwe sprach, daz wêre recht
> "wen he ist ein gût knecht
> und hât êren genûg.
> daz he mînen ôm slûg,
> daz ted he âne sînen dang.
> he en mochte sînes nebin lant
> von dem zinse anders nicht irweren.
> nû vûr he dorch daz obir mere,
> daz he dir lîbez bescheine:
> den trachin bestunt he eine
> und hât im den lîp benomen:
> des habe wir alle grôzin vromen." (ll. 2139–56)

At this point, the steward protests and Tristrant challenges him. The steward then declares in front of everyone that he has not slain the dragon and that Tristrant should have the lady. Tristrant reminds the king of the reward of the lady, and the king does not refuse him ("der hêre im nicht vorsagete," l. 2228). Tristrant then tells the king that he wishes to give the lady to Mark, his dear uncle ("'ich . . . wil sie dâr gebin Marken mîme lîbin nebin,'" ll. 2235, 2237–38): Mark is a famous king, while he himself is too young to take a wife. The king is glad that Mark should be the one to have the princess, since Tristrant has caused her much grief, and he places Isalde in Tristrant's charge, on his oath that he will consider her fully with honor and bring her to his uncle:

> he gab sie im bî den hendin
> und beval sie im ûf sîne trûwe,
> daz he die schône juncfrauwe
> mit êren wol bedêchte
> und sie sîme nebin brêchte. (ll. 2254–58)

Since it is Tristrant's wish to give Isalde to Mark, and she has, in any case, been his to give, it is strange that the king should require this pledging of his faith, but in the magical plot it makes entire sense that he should do so: the hero's pledging his faith is his important statement to the king of his intentions—that he is giving the lady to the king. The potion, which takes over at this point, takes care of the rest.

Essentially, we have a piling on of defenses here: where we might expect one or two to be enough, more and more are added. There is a progression of rituals through which the hero removes the danger of the king's anger and gains his full acceptance that he should take the lady. He takes her as the one with prior right to her and yet yields her up to him who also has prior right. The rituals in Ireland can only achieve this contradictory situation, so the potion is an essential magical device for the final enjoyment of the lady. Why should the hero give the lady to the king, creating the contradictory situation, when neither Mark nor the king of Ireland would insist on it? The king of Ireland does not refuse Tristrant the reward of the lady, and Tristrant has only arrived in Ireland accidentally on a search for a queen for Mark that Mark himself does not desire. The answer must be that this lady is the king's in any case: her belonging to the king is an essential attribute. Hence Tristrant's pledge to the king of Ireland that he will honor this fact; it is an important ritual at that point that he should acknowledge the king's right. That the lady should be represented otherwise (as a marriageable woman and as an undesired, unknown lady), and that the kings themselves say nothing about it, is of no importance in the magical plot; the kings have no point of view, in any case.

At this point I shall take a look at the chapbook version of the scenes in Ireland. This prose version in early New High German reflects the continuing popularity of the Eilhart story of Tristan: there were two editions of the chapbook at the end of the fifteenth century, ten in the sixteenth century, three in the seventeenth, none in the eighteenth, five in the nineteenth, and three in the twentieth (J. W. Thomas 37). The chapbook's author has adapted his material for a contemporary and less sophisticated audience, but these matters will not concern me so much as the version's faithfulness to Eilhart's plot.

That the chapbook version is very faithful to Eilhart could have explanations that have nothing to do with the re-creation of a magical plot. Nevertheless, I find the chapbook strikingly faithful to the rituals in Ireland and also to the hermit Ugrim strategy, and I shall illustrate this closeness here, by giving detail of its version of the ritual exchanges between the princess and the king. When the chapbook princess tells the king she knows the true dragon slayer, and the king asks that he be brought before him, the princess says she will do so when she is assured that he will have peace and safe-conduct where all he has ever done to the king is concerned:

> Hierauff antwurt die schŏn Isald: "Das will ich gern thon. Aber vor allen dingen will ich, das der held frid und geleit habe umb alles, was er dir ye gethon hat." (36)[4]

The king replies that he shall have peace and safe-conduct, and shall be forever forgiven anything he has done to him:

> Do sprach der künigk: "Frid und geleit sol er haben, und was er mir halt geton hab, das sej ym ewigklich vergeben." (36)

The princess then asks the king to kiss her in his stead, to confirm this forgiveness. The king does so and says, "With this kiss all the wrong this man has done against me is forgiven":

> Do die fraw das erhŏrete, do sprach sy zů dem vatter: "So mach den frid stet, und küß mich an des helden stat." Das tet der künig, und sprach: "Mit disem kuß ist nach gelassen und verkoren alles, das diser wider mich verschult hab." (36)

When the princess brings Tristrant to her father, before the assembled company, holding him by the hand, the king asks who he is. The princess says he must kiss him first and the king kisses him, confirming thus the forgiveness and safe-conduct he gave him in his absence:

> Do der künig das sahe, fragt er fraw Isalden, wer der held wer. Sy sprach: "Du solt yn vor küssen." Zůhant ward seiner tochter gebot volbracht: er küst den helden und bestetet damit den frid und geleit, so er vor geben het in abwesen herr Tristrants. (38–39)

The princess then says she knows that he will keep firm and constant what he has vowed, so she will say who the hero is:

> Als das geschahe, sprach fraw Isald: "Ich weiß, das du gelobste und redest, das du das stet und untzerbrochen haltst, so will ich auch sagen wer der held ist." (39)

She then announces that he is the man who killed her uncle, and the king, though saddened, confirms that he has forgiven all the wrongs done to him by Tristrant. I have quoted enough here to show that Eilhart and the chapbook use quite different language and yet are strikingly close. There is also a remarkable force in the chapbook's version of these extraordinary scenes, in which a daughter persuades her king father to go through solemn declarations of forgiveness without allowing him to know what he is doing.

There is also a remarkable force in the chapbook's faithfulness to Tristrant's extraordinary words to the king, when he delivers the hermit's letter: the hermit's power as the king's confessor is once again used, and the letter asking the king to take back his queen is laid upon him as a penance for his sins:

> Herr Tristrant sprach: "Dein meyster und beichtvater Ugrim embeüt dir sein gebet, und heist dich vermanen, ob er dir lieb sey zů einem meyster, das du dann wőllest leisten, darumb er dir geschriben hat. Er ratet dir das auch mit treüwen: so soltu das auch gern tůn, wann er will es für dein sünde zů bůß geben." (104)

This is the kind of faithfulness I look for when asking whether a version has re-created a magical plot. The continuing presence of the magical plot is the best explanation for the continuing presence of the absurdity.

What do I find in Gottfried von Strassburg's treatment of the scenes in Ireland? Gottfried's version, of the beginning of the thirteenth century, uses much the same material as Eilhart, yet the rituals of Eilhart and the chapbook are not there. It is, in fact, obvious that Eilhart's magical plot is not present in Gottfried's text, because the rituals needed to close the plot—those relating to the hermit—are absent. There is no hermit and no letter, and while the separating sword is included, Gottfried gives us, for its culmination, the intervention of love the reconciler ("Minnè diu süenærinne," l. 17540). This intervention leads to the king's desire for the return of Isolt and Tristan, and the lovers return for reasons of honor and their station in society. Alternative magical arrangements might conceivably be used, but they are nowhere to be found. Nothing secures the safe return of the queen beyond love the reconciler, a courtly concept, even though the text takes us beyond Tristan's departure from court and up to the point where he contemplates marriage with Isolt of the White Hands. If an essential part of a magical plot is not there, then none of it can be there; the plot has to be in some way complete. Either Gottfried or his chief sources transformed the narrative, so that its magical plot disappeared, and we have, instead, a work that is throughout a great work of the imagination, the story of a passion beyond the law. I shall return to a consideration of Gottfried's chief sources; meanwhile, there is evidence that he also used Eilhart, and we know that Eilhart was well-known enough to be a much more important source for other Tristan literary works, and also tapestries, than it was for Gottfried.[5] Gottfried had a quite different vision of the narrative, but his having to adhere to much of the detail of his sources—as a storyteller must when handling a well-known traditional tale—still created problems for him, even without the exigencies of the magic. A. T. Hatto points out Gottfried's problems with Loyalty and Honor: they lose to Love after the potion has been drunk, which does not strike us as unthinkable, yet, "when Gottfried has to land the lovers in Cornwall at a time when they were free to go to Tristan's country, Loyalty and Honor (for what they are worth) are momentarily in the ascendant—probably the poorest piece of work in the story" (25).

But, while Gottfried's version shows conflict with his raw material, the absence of the magical plot leaves him free to discard much small detail that would otherwise conflict seriously with his development and themes (this material may already have been discarded in his sources). Gottfried's alterations, where the Irish scenes are concerned, have mainly to do with the development of the women, who are three in number—the princess Isolt, her mother the queen, and Brangane, who is the queen's niece in this version. Gottfried's Tristan has already met Isolt, when he sets out for Ireland; he met her during his healing in Ireland, and his praise of her to Mark leads the king to choose her. So here we have a more precise mission on Mark's behalf, yet also a dangerous mission. The chief consideration upon arrival is gaining protection until the mission can be accomplished, and the killing of the dragon plays its part here. The queen grants Tristan protection, as the dragon slayer, and he commends himself and his ship to her honor. Meanwhile, the queen says she needs help over the false steward's claim, and Tristan says he will be at her service. They nurse him back to health. When they discover his identity through the splinter, the queen's pledge to him saves his life. Brangane also reminds them that through Tristan the steward's fraud will be exposed. Tristan then tells the women his mission, and the four of them make plans for the reconciliation with the king. All that is needed to persuade the king is a single, sensible discussion between the queen and the king, in which the queen persuades a relaxed king to take the killer of Morold into his favor, in the light of the fact that his mission is to their advantage. The queen sends for the king:

"seht, hêrre," sprach si "nemet war:
ir sult uns einer bete gewern,

der wir drî ernestlîche gern:
tuot ir'z, ez kumt uns allen wol."
"ich volge, swes ich volgen sol;
swaz ir welt, daz sî getân."
"habet ir'z danne an mich verlân?"
sprach aber diu guote künigîn.
"jâ, swaz ir wellet, daz sol sîn."
"genâde, hêrre, des ist genuoc:
hêrre, der mînen bruoder sluoc,
Tristan den hân ich hinne;
den sult ir iuwer minne
und iuwer hulde lâzen hân.
sîn gewérp der ist alsô getân,
daz diu suone fuoge hât."
der künec sprach: "triuwen, disen rât
den lâze ich bältlîche an dich:
er gât dich mêre an danne mich.
Môrolt dîn bruoder der was dir
nâhèr gesippe danne mir.
hâstu'z umbe in varen lân,
wil dû, sô hân ouch ich ez getân."
sus seite sî dem künege dô
Tristandes mære rehte alsô,
als er ir selber sagete.
diz mære daz behagete
dem künege wol und sprach ir zuo:
"nu sich, daz er'z mit triuwen tuo." (ll. 10634–62)[6]

["Listen, my lord," said the Queen. "You must grant us a request which the three of us earnestly desire. If you comply, we shall all reap the benefit of it."

"I will deny you no reasonable request. Whatever you wish shall be done."

"Is the matter entirely in my hands?" asked the good Queen.

"Yes, whatever you wish shall be done."

"Thank you, Sire, I am satisfied. My lord, I have the man who killed my brother—Tristan—here in the Castle! I want you to receive him into your grace and favour! His errand is such that a reconciliation is justified."

"Upon my word, I leave it to you to decide, without any hesitation. As a nearer relation your brother Morold concerns you more than me. As you have renounced his quarrel, I shall do so, too, if you wish."

(The Queen) now told the King of Tristan's mission just as the latter had told her himself, and the King was well pleased by it. "Now see that he keeps his word," he answered her. (Hatto 181)]

After Tristan has proved that he is the dragon slayer, the king announces his identity to the assembled company and then asks Tristan to ratify the agreement, as he had promised, and Tristan duly does so. He and his men swear that Isolt will be mistress of all England, and she is solemnly handed over to Tristan. The potion that follows does not have a limited duration.

It is much easier to show how a magical plot is present than how it is absent, but it is instructive to compare Gottfried's treatment of the scenes in Ireland with the parallel passages in Eilhart and the chapbook. In Gottfried we find thorough development of motive, using the traditional ingredients, and the development of strategies that would work in the world at large, using these same ingredients. The characters, detached from the ritual roles I find in Eilhart and the chapbook, have been developed as individual personalities, without there being conflict with a magical plot lurking underneath.

The magical plot is also absent in the early-thirteenth-century Scandinavian version *Tristrams saga ok Ísöndar,* known as the version of Friar Róbert. All the hermit material is absent, as in Gottfried, and the separating sword episode is rationalized to the extent that we are told it has occurred accidentally: the king's huntsman looks in and sees Tristram and Ísönd asleep at opposite ends of the room; they have lain down to rest because the heat is so great, and they are sleeping so far apart because they have gone out to amuse themselves ("Sá hann inn ok leit Tristram sofanda ok ǫðrumegin í húsinu Ísond, ok hǫfðu niðr lagzt at hvíla sik, þvíat hiti var mikill, ok sváfu þau því svá fjarri hvárt ǫðru, at þau hǫfðu gengit at skemta sér," 80, ll. 28–31). A large sword is lying between them, presumably in the middle of the room. These rationalizations are typical of the kind I find, lacking connection with each other and making less sense than the material they seek to rationalize, but here they are not dealing with living magical material. The potion, meanwhile, is given brief attention and it does not have a limited duration. The treatment of the crucial scene in Ireland, where the king's forgiveness is obtained, is much as in Gottfried, and I shall give the details here.

Both Princess Ísönd and her mother wish to slay Tristram on discovering his identity as Morold's slayer, but they forbear when Tristram begs for mercy. Then they send for the king.

> ok er han var kominn, þar fellu þær til fóta hánum: "Herra!" sǫgðu þær, "játit oss eina bœn, er vér viljum biðja yðr!" "Gjarna," kvað konungr, "er mér sómir at veita!" "Hér er nú kominn," kvað dróttning, "Tristram, er drap bróður mínn. En nú síðan drap hann drekann, ok bið ek, at þér fyrirgefit dauða Mórholds, með þeim formála, at hann frelsi ríki várt ok dóttur okkar ur klandi ok rangindum ræðismanns, svá sem hann hefir heitit oss!" 'Þá segir konungr: "Með því at ek játaða yðar bón ok þú hefir meira látit enn ek, með því at þit vilit báðar fyrirgefa hánum dauða Mórholds—enginn hefir í þessu meira látit enn þit, ok vil ek af þessu gøra sem ykkr líkar bezt!" 'Þá fell Tristram til fóta konungi ok þakkaði hánum. . . . 'Þá mælti hann til konungs: "Hlýðit, herra konungr! Hinn mildi ok ríki Markis konungr yfir Englandi sendir yðr sína orðsending, at þér gefit hánum Ísondu, dóttur yðar, ok ef þér vilit satt vita, ok með þeim hætti sáttir gøra . . . er hun þá dróttning yfir Englandi." (54, ll. 31–36; 55, ll. 1–9, 12)[7]

> [When he arrived, the two women fell down at his feet.
>
> "Sire," they said, "grant us a request that we wish to ask of you."
>
> "Gladly," said the king, "if it beseems me to accede to it."
>
> "This man," said the queen, "who has come here is Tristram, who slew my brother. But now he has also slain the dragon. I beseech you to forgive the death of Mórold with the stipulation that he free our kingdom and our daughter from the molestation and wrongs of the steward as he has promised us."
>
> Then the king said, "Since I have already promised to grant your request—and you have lost more than I—and since you both wish to forgive him for the death of Mórold—no one has lost more through this than you—I wish to act in this matter as pleases you best."
>
> Then Tristram fell to the feet of the king and thanked him. (68–69)][8]

Tristram gives the king his message from King Markis asking for his daughter's hand; he proclaims that, if the king agrees, Ísönd will be queen of England. While there are differences in treatment from Gottfried, the material not being so developed and the queen's reasons why Tristram should be forgiven being different, the treatment is still that of a writer who has no magical plot to work with.

The loss of the magical plot in the saga suggests to me that the source used by both the saga and Gottfried contained no magical plot, and this is made the more likely by the evidence provided by the Cambridge fragment, known as a fragment of the largely lost version of Thomas of Britain, the reputed source of Gottfried and the saga.[9] This fragment relates the parting of the lovers after the king finds them asleep together in the orchard, when Tristran's exile begins, and this is the alternative parting of the lovers found in Gottfried and the saga, a parting quite distinct from that of the magical plot I find in Eilhart and Beroul, where there is a separation of the lovers upon the return of the queen to the king. A comparison of the Cambridge fragment with the corresponding passages in the saga and Gottfried provides some useful information for both the present discussion and what is to follow. A study of the chart I supply with this discussion (chart 18), comparing the fragment with the saga, shows immediately that the two versions are almost identical. Gottfried's version is also strikingly close, though Gottfried develops the thoughts of the king and the lovers so that his narrative is nearly four times as long.[10] That the Cambridge version represents the source followed by both authors is more than likely. It is also clear that it contains a skillful, fast-moving narrative, deeply informed by courtly knowledge. I think its content also suggests that—while the magical plot is not there—the theme of the desire for the love of a queen figure is retained, and, without the boundaries set by the magical plot, there is a development of this primitive theme, so that the narrative relates the story of that fundamental dream of love and the exile from it that humankind permanently feels.

All these matters lead me to the question of the relationship between the narrative up to the parting of the lovers and the narrative concerned with Tristan's exile. Most of the exile material is found in Eilhart, the saga, and the Thomas fragments. Here again, the Cambridge fragment must play a part in the discussion, because, as Constance B. Bouchard points out, this fragment's concise style contrasts strongly with the style of the other Thomas fragments, all of which relate to Tristan's exile (70).

First of all, it seems to me that Gertrude Schoepperle Loomis is not only right in concluding that Eilhart's version was the best representative of the lost *estoire* but also right in concluding that the story was originally much shorter than the *estoire:* she argues that the story ended with the return from the forest and that its popularity led to the creation of the additional narrative for the supposed *estoire,* which deferred the conclusion.[11] She must be right in rejecting the theory of the unity of the *poème primitif.* Bouchard, meanwhile, argues persuasively that there never was a full-length Thomas of Britain version (66–72). She argues for there having once been a later twelfth-century French poem of the story of Tristan, which claims—as a literary convention—to be repeating the true story according to Thomas and which breaks off at the point where Tristan goes to Brittany, before he marries Isolt of the White Hands. The extant second half, known as the Thomas fragments, may be considered as the work of a second author (the Cambridge fragment should not be included in this material). Among the problems Bouchard addresses in her argument is the fact that Gottfried's version breaks off precisely where the Thomas fragments begin (a striking coincidence) and—more particularly—the fact that the continuators of Gottfried do not use Thomas as a source, as Gottfried claims to do; they use Eilhart. Why do they not use Thomas? It makes sense to suppose that Gottfried's source breaks off where Gottfried's version breaks off (whether or not he himself intended to continue his narrative), and, Bouchard comments, "It is at any rate difficult to see where the story can go after Tristan has left Isolde and gone to Brittany" (71). Bouchard also draws our attention to anomalies that point to there being two independent sources for the Scandinavian version: one for the narrative up to the exile and another for the exile. There is, of course, the well-known contradiction in the saga as to who offered the potion to the lovers, but there is a more important anomaly than this. If the saga author used only one source, whether actually the version of Thomas of Britain or not, this one source is, in its first half, "inexplicably much terser than the same author's work in the second half" (70). Bouchard continues that it seems clear Gottfried and the saga writer both used, for the narrative up to the point where Gottfried breaks off, a source that was so simple that Gottfried felt free to add to it, while the saga writer felt no need to condense it. All the first half of the saga material appears, in some way, in Gottfried, so we know the saga writer cannot have cut it significantly, and yet we know he cut his source for the second half of his saga severely—Bédier believes by more than half its length (2.64–75). The Thomas fragments are—far from being terse and simple—both long-winded and convoluted. Bouchard concludes that future Tristan studies "may be greatly benefited if the fragments themselves are viewed as a substantial part of a poem written well along in the development of this tradition from an earlier common source, rather than as a mutilated portion surviving from that source" (72).

The conclusion to be drawn from these arguments would be that we have only one representative of the lost *estoire*, and that is Eilhart.[12] The Cambridge fragment, meanwhile, is all that remains of another shorter work which did not include an extended narrative of the exile, and it represents Gottfried's source and also the source for the events up to the parting of the lovers in the saga. For its exile material the saga then used yet another poem, a long-winded one concerned only with the exile. There was no Thomas version as we have imagined it. If we can accept the arguments, we see there being three twelfth-century French poems used as sources. I would argue that the *estoire* was composed of the magical plot, followed by a narrative of the exile, and that the shorter work represented by the Cambridge fragment was a transformation of the magical plot, removing the magic. The author of the saga, writing in 1226 A.D. (according to his prologue), found the third, long-winded poem (Thomas) and produced a much shorter version of it for his account of the exile. Gottfried, writing perhaps in 1210 A.D., may have known this poem too and decided not to pursue the matter of Isolt of the White Hands, leaving her as an undecided dilemma for the exiled Tristan. Gottfried's continuators preferred the *estoire* version as retold in their own German Eilhart to a long-winded French poem that had nothing to do with Gottfried's sources. What about Beroul? What we have left of Beroul is the magical plot on its own, with some brief additional material of disputed authorship, which, I believe, plays a role in the magical plot. Did Beroul's lost ending in fact complete the *estoire* version, in a fashion parallel to Eilhart?

It does not seem that there is any way of knowing. There are good arguments for considering Beroul the author of all the material in the text as we have it. Gweneth Whitteridge argues that Beroul took Yseut's trial (in the additional material) from his sources (it appears in the narrative preceding the parting of the lovers, in Gottfried and the saga) and then—to follow—gave his audience Tristran's revenge against his enemies, a vengeance promised by the narrator in lines 2755–64, just before the narration of Yseut's return to the king. Beroul is sometimes forgetful and contradictory as a storyteller, and his style changes when he ceases to follow a written source closely. Gweneth Whitteridge argues further that the contradictions may well be deliberate: Beroul may overlook the fact that one of the three barons is already dead because he wishes to show completely how Tristran avenges himself on his enemies. She sees Beroul as having used the *estoire* as his source up to the time of the return of the lovers from the forest, and then to have become involved in his theme of vengeance, inventing some material for it (337–56). Would Beroul, with his ardent justification of Tristran the lover, have been sufficiently interested in Tristran the exile to have pursued the subject after vengeance had been wreaked? Unlike Eilhart's King Mark, Beroul's Mark speaks of the possibility of the exile not being for longer than a year or two (vv. 2671–74), and Beroul's wishes for the end of his romance may well have been reflected in those words of Mark, that he might decide to have Tristran return to himself and Yseut. Alison Adams and T. D. Hemming, considering how Beroul would have ended his narrative, do not think Beroul would have followed the tradition represented by Eilhart. They think the narrative may have ended with the vengeance of the king. Beroul's surprising turns of events and paradoxes support the likelihood of the lovers being killed unawares by Mark's anger; Adams and Hemming point to the alternative conclusion in the prose version, in which Tristan, stabbed by Mark, smothers Iseut in a last embrace (449–68). Gertrude Schoepperle Loomis comes to the conclusion that the original French romance ended with the return of the lovers from the forest and the death of Tristan at the hands of Mark—a conclusion she draws from her examination of Irish material (395–446). One of the Irish works she studies is *The Pursuit of Diarmaid and Gráinne,* a work that gives me an opportunity to examine this theme of vengeance within a "Tristan" defended narrative.

While James Carney in his *Studies in Irish Literature and History* presents a number of Irish works as connected with the Tristan tradition, only *The Pursuit of Diarmaid and Gráinne (Tóruigheacht Dhiarmada agus Ghráinne,* and henceforth referred to as the *Tóruigheacht)* is relevant to my argument.[13] The *Tóruigheacht* is one of the best-known tales of the Finn cycle, and an Early Modern recasting of a much older tale, which was probably the tenth-century *Aithed Grainne ingine Corbmaic le Diarmaid ua nDuibne* (The elopement of Gráinne, daughter of Cormac, with Diarmaid grandson of Duibne), a lost work, though its title has been preserved. James Carney argues that the Irish works are not sources for the Continental *Tristan:* in their structure and composition they all show—with the exception of *Deirdre*—that they are secondary adaptations. Both they and the Continental works show signs of having diverged from a lost Celtic source, which must be substantially anterior to 900 A.D. (Carney 195). In the *Tóruigheacht* we find the Tristan story adapted to a Fenian background, and this must also have been the case with the tenth-century *Aithed:* Finn, as the jealous husband, is playing a role inconsistent with the role he plays elsewhere, and the story has to end with Diarmaid's death fighting the Wild Boar of Ben Gulban—a tradition too well-known to be changed (220). The details in the last column of chart 19 of the *Tóruigheacht's* plot show that the adapter was inventive in the attempt to give the Tristan story, using Diarmaid.

Chart 19 shows that the daring splash of water (an incident belonging to the exile in the Tristan material) reappears in the *Tóruigheacht* (although many versions of the work omit the incident). The chart also shows that the adapted use of this and other familiar incidents in the *Tóruigheacht* makes more coherent sense of them than we find in the Continental *Tristan* material. The splash of water incident comes after Diarmaid's signs for Fionn, telling him he has not taken Gráinne sexually (signs parallel with the Continental separating sword), and just before the couple become lovers; Diarmaid explains to Gráinne that he has been keeping himself from her "through fear of Fionn" (Shéaghdha 47). If we look at the succeeding events, we find that, immediately after they become lovers, Diarmaid makes a contract with a giant, getting permission for partial, not total, rights to use his terrain, and, later, he kills the giant, takes everything, and informs Fionn that he has done so. In spite of the presence of additional material (which is quite skillfully fitted in, using the theme of Fionn's seeking compensation for the death of his father, demanding either Diarmaid's head or the quicken berries of Dubhros), the defended adventures I show on my chart make a coherent sequence. They show a progression not unlike the sequence I find in the bedchamber/hunting scenes of the defended adventures in the plot of *Sir Gawain and the Green Knight*. The hero takes the lady gradually, under continual threat from the pursuing Fionn (to be compared with the hunting Green Knight), offering tokens to prove his loyalty as he does so. But once the comparison is made, the important differences become the more apparent. The tokens of loyalty are changed to tokens of conquest, when Diarmaid sends the quicken berries to Fionn. The Green Knight plot is full of fear, and the lady timidly borrowed, while, in the *Tóruigheacht,* the plot is one in which the hero boldly takes the lady and keeps her—much more completely than he does in the Tristan plots of Eilhart and Beroul.

The end of the plot is correspondingly different. Diarmaid traditionally has to die by the Wild Boar of Ben Gulban, an event not involving Fionn, and which could, in this narrative, have been placed among the last details in the way these matters often are in stories: how Diarmaid eventually dies might have been briefly added to an account of his prosperity after the story. But here the storyteller goes to great lengths to make

Fionn the cause of Diarmaid's death, inventing a healing property for him that he does not use to save Diarmaid. The reason might not seem far to seek: the lady is not returned, and so Diarmaid has to die by Fionn, not by the boar. In a defended narrative, the energies of the magic are concentrated on making the adventure safe, and—hitherto—the restoration of the status quo has been one of the essential defenses I have found. Fionn's eventual revenge is a means of restoring this status quo. However, Diarmaid's death appears to play a different role, giving us a different kind of defended narrative.

It seems that a defended narrative can also be used for bringing about desires that are retained, and thus for bringing about a victory for the hero or heroine. In most respects, the plot of the *Tóruigheacht* is a model defended narrative: there is a great concentration of defenses at the beginning of the plot, which defend the entire adventure, up to the end. Other powerful agencies are introduced later, and there is little need for closing defenses. Most important of all is the use of Gráinne's *gessa*, her magical injunctions or bonds, threatening strife and destruction for Diarmaid if he does not do what she wishes. Nessa Ní Shéaghdha tells us that the oral versions have had difficulty with the *gessa*, since they became obscure in the modern Irish period, and some have left them out, while one has substituted a magic wand (xxvii). The *gessa* are Diarmaid's excuse to the last, when he begs Fionn for his life: in reply to Fionn's words that he ill-deserves his healing because he took Gráinne, he says, "'That is not true . . . for I was not guilty of that, but Gráinne put injunctions on me and I would not violate my injunctions for the gold of the world'" (93). Diarmaid speaks of the *gessa* here as if they relate to his honor. Whatever the *gessa* mean, anywhere in the text, the hero is "'not guilty'" of taking Gráinne, to the last: he has assigned the responsibility to the lady. The *gessa* play a similar role to that of the love potion (Gráinne also uses a potion—the sleeping potion—but this does not play a role in the defenses). Apart from the *gessa*, the most important defenses opening the plot are the ritual statements—those of Diarmaid and those of his friends, all given in detail in my chart: Diarmaid declares the elopement wrong, while his friends declare it right; the hero presents himself as entirely loyal to Fionn and overruled by the lady's powers and by his friends.

The *Tóruigheacht,* James Carney argues, transfers the story from a Christian scene to a pagan Irish past (220). Whatever the case, the foster-father Aonghus is a primitive Irish divinity, and he is used in the plot to play powerful roles similar to those played by the hermit Ugrim and more extensive than those played by the hermit. Diarmaid has his assistance and support from the beginning of the defended adventures till after his own death, and Aonghus plays an even more outrageous role than the hermit in sorting out the affair, arranging for Diarmaid to keep Gráinne, with huge transfers of land from her father and her rightful husband. Sixteen years of prosperity follow under the protection of Aonghus, and Aonghus is chief mourner at Diarmaid's death, so that his death becomes a proclamation of his honor.

The storyteller has Fionn responsible for Diarmaid's death, rather than the boar, and Fionn's resentment as the wronged husband is the cause, not his honorable vengeance. Fionn is morally guilty of Diarmaid's death, as Oisín states (Shéaghdha 97). The various texts disagree somewhat over what happens to Gráinne, but only one has her return to Fionn, while they all stress her grief for Diarmaid. The Fiana also grieve. It seems that the treatment of Diarmaid's death has but one purpose: to proclaim the hero.

Death is never a tragedy in a magical plot, because it is a device chosen for ritual use. Could an early tradition have ended with the death of Tristan at the hands of Mark, after the return of the lovers from the forest? I think this is possible. The death would have been used as part of the mechanisms for the restoration of the status quo, the hero paying the price in some way, with honor. However, this view should not be arrived at by comparison with the *Tóruigheacht*: in the *Tóruigheacht*, there is no full return to the status quo, for the lady is not returned, and the death of Diarmaid imparts honor to the hero, while not to the king. In the Tristan defended narrative, the death would, I think, impart honor to both parties. Whether or not this vengeance was present in an older tradition, I doubt its presence in Beroul. Beroul's version would have had to change direction from its repeated concern with the vindication of the lovers and vengeance on the accusers for there to have been a magical vengeance for the king. Perhaps the spirit of justification in Beroul and the *Tóruigheacht* is a truer reflection of the early Tristan tradition than the use of the king's vengeance.

6

The Hamlet Stories

This chapter is a reassessment of an early study I made of the Hamlet texts (*Magical Thought in Creative Writing* 114–39). It has been made necessary by the later developments in my methods and understanding of my subject. While there has been no radical change in my view of the plot Shakespeare has given us, my approach to Saxo Grammaticus's text is greatly altered. I am now interested in the relationship between his Hamlet narrative and that of *Bevis of Hampton* and also in the many resemblances to *The Story of Meriadoc*, and this chapter explores these first. Then, from the point this exploration takes me to, I reconsider Saxo's plot as a magical plot (see chart 20 in the appendix and chart 22 on p. 149), and also as a tale of vengeance culminating in the vengeance against the Claudius character Fengi. Finally, I shall reconsider it briefly in relation to Shakespeare's play.

It has been argued that Saxo's Hamlet material is correctly seen as a revenge story, followed by loosely added material relating the story of Queen Herminthrud and the death of Amleth in battle against the king of Denmark. Saxo's narrative is embedded in the greater matter of his *History of the Danes*, and it is important to consider how Saxo regarded the story.[1] It seems clear that Geoffrey of Monmouth's vision of the King Lear story did not include Cordelia's defeat and death: these belong to a later narrative in his history, and writers using Geoffrey's material brought them into the story. Saxo's Hamlet material appears at the end of his book three and the beginning of his book four, the division coming after Amleth returns from Britain and kills Fengi. This division suggests the separateness of the apparent revenge story, and the two Norse Hamlet stories *Ambales Saga* and *Brjáms-Saga* also suggest it, as they are both revenge stories ending at that point.[2]

A different view of Saxo's narrative emerges from Maldwyn Mills's study of it, showing that the material in its entirety has a symmetrical exile-and-return structure similar to that of *Bevis of Hampton*.[3] Using A, B, and C to represent each of the three geographical locations in the narrative (A designating home country, B the country of the princess, wife, and C a third location), Professor Mills reveals how much Saxo's Hamlet material has in common with the plot of *Bevis*. Chart 21 in the appendix presents this view of the two plots, omitting some of the ABC detail in *Bevis* and including the detail in each narrative that brings out the important resemblances. The plot of *Meriadoc* is also included, because, although it does not lend itself to exile-and-return methods, it presents a further illuminating comparison. The first part (or move, as Vladimir Propp understood "move") in all three plots has an appearance of being complete as a revenge story, and all three revenge stories are fundamentally the same story, except that there is no princess in *Meriadoc*. Then the departure from home at the beginning of the second part (move) seems in each case to be the beginning of a new story, having little connection with the preceding events and appearing to be a different kind of story. Motives seem forced and adventures incongruous. Each newly made ruler departs at once for a story world in which characters swing around to being the opposite of what they previously were, and the royal women are extravagantly irrational figures. These three second parts show fewer similarities and one sharp difference: Amleth's death as a usurper appears as the final A, while no fresh turn of events can be recorded in this position for the other two plots.

The use of my models, in addition to the exile-and-return approach, extends exploration of the similarities and differences among the three plots. In my introductory studies, I explore *Bevis* as a typical sovereignty plot and *Meriadoc* as another sovereignty plot with exceptionally heavy initial defenses. In *Bevis,* the moves towards winning a queen are made in the first part of the narrative (in a move sequence not represented on chart 21), and Bevis's marriage to the queen at the end of it provides a different reason for the existence of the second part than I find in the case of *Meriadoc*. Much of the second part of *Bevis* is a rear guard of purifications, giving us a different lady in C from the parallel sovereignty figures of the other two plots, and, meanwhile, Bevis has still to become king. In *Meriadoc,* the first part, and much of the second, is concerned with the defenses that make the winning of the queen possible. In the magical plot of both *Bevis* and *Meriadoc,* the revenge story is just one of the devices making possible the winning of sovereignty: the hero is on the side of the kings, opposed to usurpers.

In the case of Saxo's text, the initial A^1 "conceals" a foster sister and material concerning the mother, and these, incidentally, relate to material omitted in the *Bevis* section of the chart, in which two knights observe a kiss and make an accusation that Bevis has lain with Josian, and where Bevis says to his mother:

> "Dame, why haste thou my fader be-trayde
> And wyll be wedyd to his foman?
> Alas, that euer thou waste woman!
> I-wys, moder, thou semyste full well
> To be an hore, an old Brothell!
> All fals horys, ffor thy sake
> The devill in hell I hem be-take!"[4]

My models, together with the chart, help to show how Saxo's plot in its entirety might be found to work as a magical plot. A step-by-step progress can be seen in the women: foster sister, slave-princess wife, and then queen sovereignty wife. The chart also shows, with remarkable symmetry, an overall theme of usurpation and revenge, with a final restoration of the status quo: the usurper dies and the queen marries the king. Amleth's death as a usurper is anticipated by a theme of death haunting every step forward. He arrives in Britain, where he is to marry the princess, under Fengi's sentence of death, and he divines that the feast at the court comes from corpses; he then returns to kill Fengi just as the court is performing his own last rites; and he is under the king of Britain's sentence of death when he seeks out Queen Herminthrud, killer of suitors. Finally, he defeats and slays the king of Britain by setting up his own slain men in battle array. It can also be observed that in all four engagements with the women characters—foster sister, mother, princess, queen—a king has been given the slip. This strange plot, in which the hero uncharacteristically—it would seem—fails finally to win, emerges as having a more regular structure than those found in *Bevis* and *Meriadoc*. It could also not be a sovereignty plot, but instead a purification plot, with the unusual arrangement of having the chief character—rather than a surrogate—undergo a ritual death, a device related to the rituals of reparation, penance, and sacrifice found in other plots.

At this point, I must give more attention to the apparent revenge story in the first part, examining both how Saxo regarded his material and how much evidence there is for a magical structure in this part of the narrative. Here, I shall argue that Saxo adopted a magical story and developed the first part of it at a quite separate level of thought, a not infrequent response among authors where aspects of an adopted tale attract them.

Saxo cuts his material in half, placing the vengeance against Fengi at the end of book three, and he may have done this in order to emphasize the vengeance. He had a great admiration for Amleth, expressing this particularly at the close of his third book, where he praises Amleth's courage and wisdom in the use of his disguise of stupidity for the purpose of survival and revenge. Hilda Ellis Davidson argues that Saxo's narrative was influenced by classical works; as a writer, he was inclined to bring classical material into his text when anything reminded him of it. It would therefore be quite possible that, in dividing his narrative, Saxo was influenced by Livy's account of Lucius Junius Brutus, where the material is divided into books one and two, the division coming at the point where Brutus's courageous disguise of stupidity culminates in the removal of Tarquinius and Brutus's appointment as consul.[5] Dr. Davidson also regards Saxo's book four material as additional to the tale of Amleth's vengeance and as made up of popular folktale motifs and ideas taken from the classics. She argues that the story of book three is outlined twice in book four: once in the speech to the people to tell them why Fengi has been killed and again in the description of the shield with its series of pictures illustrating Amleth's adventures. There are close parallels in the speech made by Brutus against Tarquin after the suicide of Lucrece as told by Valerius Maximus (whose writings we know Saxo read) and in Virgil's description of the shield of Aeneas. Dr. Davidson's conclusions are also influenced by Amleth's apparent change of character in book four, from a resolute avenger to a puppet who wins through by luck rather than ability. His final defeat and death she sees as an anticlimax, used by Saxo only to voice his poor opinion of the faith of women.[6]

Supporting Hilda Davidson's arguments is the appearance of the book three narrative as belonging to the common type of the revenge story, in which the hero feigns insanity or stupidity to save his life and avenge his father. The stories of Brutus, Ambales, and Brjám are all of this type. Another important factor is the resemblance of Amleth to the trickster hero, a resemblance that is scarcely apparent in the book four material.[7] In particular, Amleth uses trickery to kill Fengi, in his position as one man alone against Fengi and his court. Saxo's interest in these aspects of his narrative is evident.

There are, however, three episodes standing in uneasy relationship with this revenge story and indicating that it is an overlay. Hilda Davidson refers to the puzzling nature of the meeting between Amleth and his foster sister, and I shall begin with the illogicalities I find in this test.[8] We are told that people suspect Amleth is "concealing deep designs under a cloak of feeble-mindedness," and that "the best way to reveal his trickery [is] to bring him to some shady nook where a supremely attractive woman could lure his heart into sexual entanglement":

> Naturae siquidem tam praeceps in venerem esse ingenium: ut arte dissimulari non possit: vehementiorum quoque hunc motum fore, quam ut astu interpellari queat: ideoque si is inertiam fingeret, futurum: ut occasione suscepta voluptatis ilico viribus obtemperaret. (Gollancz, *Sources of Hamlet* 104)
>
> [Men's characters are so naturally inclined towards love that no subtlety may keep its existence secret. His cunning could not obstruct so violent an emotion and so, even if he simulated indifference, once the opportunity presented itself he would succumb to the powers of pleasure there and then.][9]

This is to be a test as to whether Amleth is simulating lethargy ("inertiam fingeret"), so the way to find him out, with the use of an attractive woman, is to find out that he remains indifferent in her presence — since the assumption in this silly test is that no man could really remain indifferent. If he does nothing, he is a simulator in everything. But this is not what we are told: we are told that no cunning could hide his passion and a feigned inertia would give way to sexual activity. If there is no possibility of his employing his cunning, what can this test prove? The testers could discover through it that Amleth was not entirely lethargic, but it would be in a context where they expected him to be active by nature. It would prove nothing about the rest of his behavior, the behavior they were concerned about: his suspected concealment of his intelligence and plans for vengeance.

It seems clear that there is another concern, entirely different from the concern of these characters, and it is also clear that the test is no test at all — that something else is concealed by it. Amleth certainly conceals that he has made love to the woman concerned, and we are also told that he is warned not to yield to dangerous sensuality ("periculosam... lasciviam," 108) by his foster brother, a warning that conflicts with the logic of the test, where his yielding to lust will prove nothing and his indifference must prove him a simulator. Amleth interprets his foster brother's warning sign as meaning that there is an ambush, and he finds another place for his intercourse with the foster sister, in "a remote and trackless fen."

After having intercourse with his foster sister, Amleth "earnestly [begs] her not to disclose the incident to anyone" ("Quam etiam peracto concubitu: ne rem cuiquam proderet: impensius obtestatus est," 108). He is indeed earnest (impensus) here. The foster sister readily promises her silence because they were brought up together, sharing the same guardians in childhood, and are close to each other. These details suggest a hidden incestuous relationship, material that cannot explain very much on its own but which may do so in relation to other material in Saxo's text. Meanwhile, it is interesting to look at how François de Belleforest treats the matter of the test, in his version of Saxo's narrative, published as one of his *Histoires Tragiques* in 1582.[10]

> Ainsi furent deputez quelques courtisans, pour mener le Prince en quelque lieu escarté, dans le boys, et lesquels luy presentassent ceste femme, l'incitans à se souiller en ses baysers et embrassemens, artifices assez frequent de nostre temps, non pour essayer si les grands sont hors de leur sens, mais pour les priver de force, vertu et sagesse, par le moyen de ses sansues et infernales Lamies, produites par leurs serviteurs, ministres de corruption.

It is translated in the anonymous *Hystorie of Hamblet,* published in 1608:

> To this end certaine courtiers were appointed to leade Hamblet into a solitary place within the woods, whether they brought the woman, inciting him to take their pleasures together, and to imbrace one another, but the subtill practises used in these our daies, not to try if men of great account bee extract out of their wits, but rather to deprive them of strength, vertue and wisedome, by meanes of such devilish practitioners, and intefernall spirits, their domestical servants, and ministers of corruption. (Gollancz, *Sources of Hamlet* 201)

Moralistic reflections are typical of Belleforest's treatment, but here he also reveals both his incomprehension of the material as a test and his sense of a danger in it. The foster-sister episode is absent in both *Ambales Saga* and the folktale *Brjáms-Saga,* two nonmagical texts.

Amleth's meeting with his mother is also presented as a test in the revenge story, once again to find out whether Amleth is a simulator or truly an imbecile, and it is equally unconvincing as a test. Fengi's friend, who plans the test, expresses the view that if Amleth had any sense at all (using the verb "sapio," with its connotations of discernment and prudence) he would trust his mother and not hesitate to speak openly in her hearing. While not so ill-fitting as the purpose given for the first test, the purpose given for this test has an air of being imposed upon an episode that is really about something else. Even a man possessing more self-assurance than shrewdness ("solertia"), as Saxo describes Fengi's friend, would probably not assume that a sensible son would trust his mother in circumstances where she has married his father's murderer (the facts are known in this text)—and he would be particularly unlikely to assume it if, as here, it is suspected that this son is plotting vengeance. Problems of motivation of just this kind are typical features in texts using a magical plot.

The third episode standing in uneasy relationship with the revenge story is the adventure with the king of Britain before the killing of Fengi. In the revenge story, this episode represents Amleth's turning of the tables on Fengi, displaying his great wisdom, but, once again, it seems really to be about something else not openly acknowledged. We are presented with a king delighted with a visitor who has divined the royal couple to be the offspring of slaves. The episode is a celebration of Amleth's powers of mind, so the motivations of a king who does not find his visitor too dangerous to remain alive are not of the first importance, but I still wonder why Amleth's powers of divination are displayed through material quite so unwelcome to any king—since the king is to be delighted.

It is likely that Saxo used a magical story that had become attached to the traditional character Amlothi, and that, over and above retelling this story faithfully, he also developed the first part of it as a revenge story and trickster tale. It is possible that a collection of riddles was associated with Amlothi and that Saxo, or earlier versions, made use of these as Amlothi's tactics (Davidson, *Saxo Grammaticus* 1:67). To retell a story faithfully was as characteristic of Saxo as was being attracted by resemblances to other stories.

In my full outline of Saxo's narrative, the greater part of the material is given in italics, particularly in the case of the three episodes standing in uneasy relationship with the revenge story. The magical plot I see in the text is a puzzling one, but it has clear structures for safeguarding the steps forward and providing purification. There appear to be nine moves having the functions given in chart 22. In the first move of this chart, I assume that the story Saxo adopted for development contained some form of the pretence of folly.

Saxo's revenge story has a happy ending, and Amleth's final defeat and death do not make the story as a whole a sad one. Amleth's ritual death would protect the preceding events, so that they can be enjoyed: it is not to be understood as we understand death in other kinds of narrative. It would be a death performed in the mind, having the status of a thought rather than of an event in the usual fictional sense. Such a mental ritual can act upon anxiety over thoughts felt to be wicked, working perhaps chiefly as a statement of punishment carried out. There is a sense in which

Chart 22. The Nine Moves of Saxo Grammaticus's Magical Plot

1	2	3
The usurpation. Amleth secretly plans revenge.	The meeting with the foster sister.	The meeting with the queen.
The role of avenger is a device that could be invested with the power to keep the participant safe during the taboo-breaking adventures to follow. The avenging of the king is fulfilled in the final move. The role of fool could also make identification with such adventures easier.	The initial step to sovereignty, protected by the defenses set up in the first move.	Reversal of the meeting with the foster sister. By upbraiding the queen for her incestuous union with a usurper, the hero removes the idea of such a union between her and himself. This removal is reinforced by his making her a partner in his revenge against the usurper.
4	5	6
In Britain. The marriage with the princess.	The vengeance against Fengi.	Amleth becomes king.
The next step to sovereignty, aided by the reduction of the status of the royal family.	This vengeance for the killing of the father and the usurpation of his position is placed in the middle of the plot and protects the participant in both directions. As an enacted vengeance, it is used in the strategies for moves 6 and 7 (the speech and the shield).	This move is defended by Amleth's speech presenting himself as avenger (not usurper).
7	8	9
Queen Herminthrud.	The defeat and death of the king of Britain.	The king kills the hero, and sovereignty (the queen) returns to the king.
The hero takes the queen, who declares herself sovereignty itself. The shield has a defensive role, but, at this stage of the plot, it is also triumphal.	The hero kills the king.	

the rituals of a magical plot can be continuous in the mind, enacted whenever needed. In living with the disturbing complexity of human thought and feeling, humankind has found various means of purification, some of these using storytelling and drama.

In Shakespeare's play I find a purification plot in which the hero carries out a magical vengeance against himself for his usurping thoughts. Saxo's plot appears to be close to Shakespeare's, the chief difference I see being that there is much more provision for the enjoyment of the thoughts of usurpation in Saxo's plot than in Shakespeare's, where there is a more concentrated concern with purification. Shakespeare's version syncopates the plot,[11] removing the marriages and many characters and intensifying some aspects of the magical material, particularly the thoughts of death leading up to the suicidal vengeance and the spying upon the scenes with the women. Over and above these developments, Shakespeare has added a great superstructure of themes (which includes Saxo's revenge story). While the play's superstructure is the creation of other levels of thought, it has some profound connections with the feelings in the magical plot (though not conscious connections with its thought): the result is a more unified work of art than can always be possible where a magical plot is used.[12]

The vengeance against the Feng character (the name Feng suggests "snatch" or "seize") plays the same roles in Saxo and Shakespeare. It is part of the defense structures, while it also plays its central role in the revenge story. Shakespeare's famous delay, however, is absent in Saxo, for it is Shakespeare's development of story material that does not provide the concerted advance towards revenge demanded by a true revenge story. It is given the theme of lack of resolution in Shakespeare's revenge story, and it draws on the magical plot for its preoccupations with usurpation and death. The magical necessity that the hero's vengeance be carried out against himself deeply informs this drama of hesitation and intense reflection on death.

Finally, my comparison of Saxo's plot with those of *Bevis* and *Meriadoc* brings out how ambiguous and multipurpose the structures of a magical plot can be; placing magical plots in categories is helpful only up to a point. Saxo's plot has the steps forward of a sovereignty plot and also the protective structures of a defended narrative, culminating as they do in the return of the queen to the king. But there is no final sovereignty and no final safe retreat for the hero, within the text itself. Audiences may, of course, use the narrative how they will. Its final reversal of the hero's subversion with the king's vengeance, magically undoing all that has been done, provides for their safety, and the payment of the ultimate price provides purification.

Appendix

Chart 3. The Sovereignty Plot in *Degarré*

1 Family Separations and Upbringing with Holy Man	2	3 "Goodmind" Move
A rich king of Brittany, never defeated in arms, has a greatly loved daughter who will only be won by the man who defeats her father.	*The holy man at the hermitage takes charge of the child, and christens him "Degarré" (the one almost lost"). The hermit's sister, wife to a merchant, cares for him during his first ten years, and then the hermit educates him.*	*On his way, Degarré comes upon an earl struggling with a dragon who has already killed his men. Degarré rescues him, killing the dragon.*
On a feast day commemorating her mother, the princess rides to the abbey where she is buried, and becomes lost in a wood. There, a fairy knight ravishes her. On parting, the knight tells her she will bear a boy, and he leaves her a sword for the child. When he is of age, he must seek his father with the sword: the sword's point was broken off in the head of a giant the knight once killed, and he will recognize his son by this sword, having the point in his possession.	*When he is twenty, the hermit gives him the letter and gloves, and Degarré swears he will not stop until he has found his kindred; he will know his mother by the gloves. He sets out, armed only with an oak sapling.* ll. 235–334	*The grateful earl offers Degarré all he has, "Rentes, tresor an eke lond" (l. 391) and Degarré asks first to see all the women—the earl's lady and the others, young and old. If the gloves fit any of them, then he will accept the earl's land; otherwise, he will take his leave. They do not fit and he leaves, knighted and armed by the earl.* [In the Percy text, the earl offers half his land and his daughter, ll. 329–31.] ll. 335–424
The boy is born secretly, the princess being afraid that people would think the king fathered it. She also fears the king would be unhappy if he knew of the child, all his joy being in her.		

Chart 3 · 153

	The child is abandoned at the door of a hermitage, with gold and silver and a pair of gloves sent to the princess by the fairy knight. A letter is also left in the cradle, saying that the child is noble and that he should be told to love only the woman whom the gloves fit, for they will fit his mother alone. ll. 1–234
A magical plot is magical throughout, since the thought behind it is magic, but the use of magic is more intensive in places, and the italics in my charts indicate these places. In the case of *Degarré*, almost the entire plot should be given in italics, so I have chosen to highlight the sovereignty move—the summit of the plot made possible by all that surrounds it—by giving it in roman type, in spite of its intensive magical use of the gloves.	

(continued)

4 Dangerous Sovereignty Move: Use of Powerful Safeguards	5 Strategic Use of Repeat Character and Surrogate Location	6 Removal of the Idea of Theft
On his next journey, Degarré comes upon a gathering of people and learns that the king offers his daughter and heritage to any man in arms who will remove him from his saddle. Many have tried to do this and all have failed. Degarré tells the king that "his lord" wishes to take up the challenge. At church, Degarré gives a florin to the Father, another to the Son, and a third to the Holy Ghost; the priest prays for him with all his heart. In the combat, the king seeks to break Degarré's neck, but Degarré is too strong: he survives three encounters and then thrusts the king out of his saddle. The King is generous in defeat, giving Degarré his daughter and making him his heir, while the princess is sorry she must	*Traveling in the forest where he was begotten, he comes upon a castle in the middle of a river. The drawbridge is down and the gate open, but, at first, there is no one in the castle. Then maidens who have been hunting appear, followed by a dwarf, and finally the beautiful lady of the castle with more maidens. Degarré behaves courteously and joins their meal, but no one speaks to him.* *Falling in love with the lady, he goes up to her chamber, where she is sitting on her bed with a maiden at her feet, playing the harp. Degarré is lulled to sleep by the harp, and the lady covers him up warmly, adding a pillow under his head, and gets into the bed herself.*	*On his journey, he meets a knight who accuses him of poaching. They fight until the knight sees that Degarré's sword has no point. He asks Degarré's origin and name, and he fits his point to the sword. Recognition follows, and they set off to see Degarré's mother.* *Degarré's marriage to his mother is dissolved, and the fairy knight marries her.* Then Degarré marries the lady of the river castle in the presence of his parents, the king, and the court. ll. 999–1084

marry someone she knows nothing of. They are married, and then, before they go to bed, Degarré remembers the gloves and the holy man's bidding that he take no woman unless the gloves fit her. He tells the king that he may not consider marriage with any woman unless she tries on the gloves and they are easily drawn onto her hands. The princess, her face as red as blood, asks to see the gloves, and they fit her easily. The couple joyfully acknowledge each other as mother and son, and the king is told about Degarré's birth. The princess says, "Ich am his moder and ek his wive" (l. 700).

Degarré now wishes to find his father, and his mother gives him the pointless sword for this purpose. He says that now that he has what he cares for, he will not rest until he sees his father.
ll. 425–724

The next morning, the lady tells him he should be ashamed that he did nothing but sleep, paying no attention to her women. He asks her about herself and this castle of women, and learns that the castle is undefended, her father being dead and she his only child. A suitor is seeking to seize her, and has slain all her men. Degarré offers to help, and she offers him herself and her land in exchange. He slays the suitor, and then continues his journey, saying he will return.
ll. 725–998

Chart 4. The Sovereignty Plot in *Bevis*

1	2	3
Bevis's mother desires a young, vigorous husband in place of Bevis's elderly father, the earl of Southampton, so she arranges that the emperor of Germany should kill her husband and take his place. Bevis opposes these deeds and his mother orders his tutor Saber to kill the boy. Saber pretends to have done so and disguises Bevis as a shepherd. Bevis attacks the emperor and his mother sells him to heathen merchants for a large sum. Kölbing, *Romance of Sir Beues of Hamtoun*, pp. 1–23	Bevis is given to the Saracen king Ermin of Armenia, to whom he tells his story and of his intention to avenge his father. The king offers him his daughter and his land upon his death. Bevis refuses since they are heathens, and he is made chamberlain instead, until he is knighted. His feats of arms are such that the king's daughter, Josian, falls in love with him. pp. 23–43	Bevis saves the king from an invader, King Brademond of Damascus, who is demanding Josian in marriage. The defeated Brademond offers Bevis cities, but Bevis refuses them because he is sworn to King Ermin. He makes Brademond become the king's liege man, keeping the peace with him. Bevis refuses Josian's request that he be her lover and retires to the town. But she wins him by promising to adopt the Christian faith, and he kisses her. pp. 43–57
4	5	6
Two knights freed by Bevis from Brademond witness this scene between the lovers and tell King Ermin that Bevis has lain with Josian. The king sends Bevis as an unarmed messenger to Brademond, bearing a letter. The letter asks Brademond to kill Bevis. On the way, Bevis meets	Josian is married to King Yvor of Mombraunt and preserves her virginity with a charm. Bevis escapes from prison, having killed his gaolers and having had his prayers answered. Having defeated his pursuers, he confesses his sins to the patriarch of	Bevis enters Mombraunt disguised as a poor palmer, and Josian recognizes him. She gives him his horse and his sword and begs him to take her. He says he would be wrong to love her: for loving her he has lain in prison for seven years, and the patriarch has charged him only to marry a virgin. Josian assures him that

Terri, Saber's son, who is searching for him, and he tells him Bevis has been hanged. He refuses to let the suspicious Terri see the letter. On his arrival in Damascus, Bevis kills a priest and throws idols into the dirt. King Brademond gladly throws him into a dungeon where, after killing two dragons with a stick, he spends seven years. pp. 57–75	Jerusalem, who enjoins upon him that he marry only a pure virgin. pp. 75–98	she is a virgin, so they escape together. Bevis defeats the giant Ascopart, who has been sent in pursuit of them, and takes the giant into his service. pp. 98–134
7 Bevis leaves for Hampton, while Josian remains in Cologne in Ascopart's care. The bishop, who is his father's brother, equips him with a hundred knights for this mission to avenge his father and claim his heritage from his stepfather, the emperor of Germany. pp. 135–44	8 *An earl, Miles, forces Josian into marriage with him, but she strangles him before the marriage can be consummated.* *She is sentenced to be burned, but is rescued by Bevis and Ascopart.* *They all go to meet Saber in the Isle of Wight.* pp. 144–53	9 Bevis defeats his stepfather and has him executed. His mother, overcome with grief, then falls to her death. He marries Josian and succeeds to his father's earldom. pp. 153–65

(continued)

(Continued)

10	11
When his horse kills the son of the king of England, Bevis goes into exile with Josian, Terri, and Ascopart. *Josian gives birth to twin sons and is then abducted by Ascopart, who has promised King Yvor to return her to him. Bevis and Terri find foster parents for the babies.* *Bevis wins the hand of a princess in a tournament, but she allows him seven years' grace to find his wife before consummating the marriage.* *Saber rescues Josian and together they search for Bevis for seven years.* pp. 165–83	The family is reunited and the princess marries Terri. Bevis is reconciled with King Ermin and defeats King Yvor on his behalf. One of the twin sons succeeds King Ermin and the other becomes heir to the king of England. Bevis kills King Yvor and takes over his kingdom. Bevis and Josian eventually die in each other's arms, in sanctity. pp. 183–218

Chart 5. The Sovereignty Plot in *Lanval*

1

There is a knight at the court of King Arthur to whom the generous king gives nothing. No one puts in a good word for this knight and he asks for nothing. His name is Lanval and he is a king's son, envied for his many knightly gifts.

One day, he rides out of town and lies down in a meadow. There, two beautiful damsels come to him with a message from their lady, inviting him to her tent. In the magnificent tent, he finds a maiden of great beauty lying on a bed in only her shift, and she tells him she has come from her country for his sake, since she loves him above all else. Lanval responds that he will abandon all others for her, and she grants him her love and her body. She also grants him everything he desires in terms of wealth. However, he must keep all these things secret: he will lose everything if this love becomes known.

At the end of the afternoon, the lady tells him he cannot stay longer, but she will always be there when he needs her.

On his return to court, he is generous with his new wealth, and happy, because he can see his beloved often and she does his will.

vv. 1–218

2

One day, in the company of the queen, and of other ladies and knights, Lanval stands apart, thinking of his beloved. The queen approaches him and offers him her love. Lanval refuses, professing his good faith to the king, whom he will not wrong. The queen is angry and accuses him of preferring young men to women. Distressed, Lanval tells her he has a lady of much greater beauty, wisdom, and goodness than she possesses. The queen is angry and humiliated and, when the king returns from hunting, she tells him that Lanval has shamed her. He has requested her love and, because she refused him, has insulted her with his boast of his lady. The king is angry and swears an oath that if Lanval cannot defend himself in court, he will have him burned or hanged.

Lanval, meanwhile, is unable to summon his beloved; she will not answer his appeals because he has revealed their love. He is taken to the king, who tells him he has wronged him greatly by shaming him and slandering the queen. Lanval denies that he has shamed the king and that he sought the queen's love, while he admits his boast of his lady. It is decided that there will be a trial, and Gawain and other knights stand bail for Lanval.

At the trial, the barons, considering their verdict, are perplexed. The king has accused Lanval of a felony and charged him with a crime, the cause being a love he boasted that angered

(continued)

(Continued)

| | the queen. They decide that, if Lanval proves the truth of his boast, he should be pardoned, since he did not boast to spite the queen. Then two beautiful maidens ride up to announce the arrival of their lady, followed by another two, and the verdict is delayed until the fairy mistress herself arrives, the most beautiful of all women. She tells the king that the queen is wrong, Lanval never having sought her love, and that if she herself can acquit Lanval of his boast, let him be released.

Lanval and his fairy mistress ride off together.
vv. 219–646 |

Chart 6. The Sovereignty Plot in *Meriadoc*

Safeguards to Protect the Hero during the Narrative	Adventures Safeguarded
Two brothers inherit the kingdom of Cambria, the elder, Caradoc, holding the fuller authority. Caradoc then suffers from premature senility, and his brother Griffin rules in his stead, finally murdering Caradoc and seizing the kingdom.	1. Pursuing a fleeing invader after recovering from him stolen goods, Meriadoc and his knights enter a dark forest of fear and come upon a splendid castle. There, the beautiful lady of the castle is throwing the dice in a game with her knights, and, when she sees Meriadoc, she says she has long desired to see him, having heard of his prowess. Meriadoc reclines at the high table with her alone for a splendid banquet. But no one speaks and the seneschal only makes faces in response to his questions. Meriadoc and his men flee in terror.
Caradoc's son Meriadoc and daughter Orwen, ten-year-old twins, are to be taken and hanged in the forest of Arglud. Planning to save the children, the executioners hang them clinging to each other face to face, with a rope that will break quickly.	
The children's foster father, Ivor, rescues them by means of trickery. He attracts a large number of wolves to the grove where the children are hanging from an oak tree, by cooking meat, and the twelve executioners hide in a hollow of the tree. Then he drives away the wolves by using his horn and makes a hot, smoking fire in front of the hollow. The executioners cry out for mercy, and Ivor agrees to push the fire away and let them out, in return for the children's freedom. Then, as each man comes out of the exit, Ivor cuts off his head.	2. Suffering a storm in the forest, they visit another castle, where Meriadoc's men are overcome by terror. Meriadoc steals bread and wine from the beautiful lady of the castle without speaking to her, as she sits at the table, and he also forages in the kitchen. He is attacked as a thief, and, after several fights, is allowed to go free, his opponents being overcome "by his pertinacity."
	Meriadoc meets a woman mourning her husband, a powerful knight killed by "two vile thieves," and he kills the thieves.
The children spend five years in the forest with their foster parents, hunting and gathering, and they are then abducted, Orwen by King Urien of Scotland (whom she marries) and	Meriadoc defeats the brother of King Gundebald in battle and takes over his kingdom. The emperor is informed of his success and replies that what he has

(continued)

(Continued)

Meriadoc by Kay, who takes him to King Arthur's court. Griffin is brought to justice by Urien and Arthur, at the request of Meriadoc and Orwen, and Meriadoc becomes king of Cambria with Arthur's approval. He hands over the rule to Urien, because he wishes to go out and prove himself as a knight. At Arthur's court, Meriadoc becomes the king's champion against three knights in succession, who all claim land due to them from the king. Having won his battle against the Black Knight, and been asked by the king to name his reward, Meriadoc asks that the king generously restore the Black Knight's property to him. The king refuses, but his household urges him to honor Meriadoc's request, and Arthur deeds the Black Forest to Meriadoc, who then restores it to the Black Knight in the presence of the king. The Red and White Knights similarly receive their land through Meriadoc. Each knight has sworn an oath of fealty and obedience to Meriadoc after being defeated by him, and they become his companions. Meriadoc becomes a mercenary knight with the emperor of the Alemanni in his war with King Gundebald, who has abducted his only daughter. Gundebald is king of the Land From Which No One Returns. pp. 2–104	acquired and will acquire will be his domain; if he rescues his abducted daughter, he may have her in matrimony, together with riches and glory in abundance. pp. 104–56

Sovereignty Move	Exorcism of the Ideas of Usurpation and Treachery
The fame of Meriadoc's daring has reached the ears of the emperor's daughter, and she sends messages suggesting that he come in a private party to rescue her and win Gundebald's kingdom. He sets off with only the Black, Red, and White Knights. The king and prefect of the city are both absent, and Meriadoc spends two days alone with the emperor's daughter. On the third day, she tells him that the king has not treated her like a prisoner, but as his daughter, and even as his lady, yielding to her will in all things: the sovereignty of all Gundebald's kingdom lies under her command. Yet she depends on Meriadoc for her rescue, and the people, too, wish to be rescued from Gundebald's tyranny. Only with her help, however, can Meriadoc defeat the king. She tells Meriadoc that Gundebald tests everyone wishing to be one of his knights, doing so in an area of bog known as the Land From Which No One Returns. The bog has an island and a road three feet wide leading across the bog to it. On this road the combat will take place. The king has overcome everyone so far, and they have been swallowed up in "the deep pit" of the bog. He has a superior horse that has played an important part in these contests. However, she herself will give Meriadoc an even	*However, war breaks out between the emperor and the king of Gaul. The king is plundering and razing the emperor's provinces, and the emperor is forced to negotiate for peace. The conditions for peace are that the emperor's daughter—about to be restored to him by Meriadoc, as he has been informed—must be given in marriage to the king.* *The emperor is careful that his daughter's betrothal to the king of Gaul is not revealed to Meriadoc. He knows the extent of Meriadoc's military skill and authority, now he has won two kingdoms for him, and wishes to subdue him to his own power.* *He proclaims Meriadoc lord and regent of the empire many times, and orders him to return with his daughter since he wishes the marriage to take place in his presence. On their return, he separates them, placing his daughter in a tower with a close watch on her. Meriadoc can visit her, and they are spied on so that the emperor can obtain a pretext for a just accusation against Meriadoc. The spies report secret words and passionate kisses, and the emperor announces that Meriadoc's marriage with his daughter will not take place: Meriadoc has forced and violated her, leaving her pregnant, and he deserves to be beheaded. Meriadoc seeks to defend himself, and is captured and imprisoned.*

(continued)

(Continued)

greater horse, presented to her by Gundebald, and she will also give him the splendid arms of the king, which are housed by her. Meriadoc is received by the king as one wishing to enroll as a knight, and, when he rides up on the narrow road for the contest, Gundebald recognizes the horse and his strength withers. He screams that Meriadoc's pact with the maiden has overthrown him. Meriadoc casts him into the pit. The courtiers acclaim Meriadoc worthy to be lord of the realm, and Meriadoc declares that he is under the orders of the emperor, having undertaken his task in order to rescue the emperor's daughter. The lords reply that he owes nothing to the emperor, but, if he is determined to transfer sovereignty to the emperor, it will go as he wishes because he holds dominion. They will place him in authority as if he were the king, in the meantime. pp. 156–88	*The king of Gaul, learning that his betrothed is pregnant, repudiates the marriage, and the treaty with the emperor therefore also ends. The king refuses to give up anything he has seized for himself, and the war is renewed; he ravages the emperor's provinces everywhere.* *The emperor now regrets the accusation of treachery, because he has lost a man valuable to him while the king of Gaul remains his enemy. He has Meriadoc released from his chains, and Meriadoc is consequently able to escape from prison and fight for the king of Gaul. He kills the emperor and distinguishes himself elsewhere in battle. The king of Gaul tells him he has requited the emperor as he deserved, for the emperor repaid his services with treachery. The king now takes over the empire, and he restores to Meriadoc his wife and all the territories he has conquered.* pp. 188–214

Chart 7. Purification in *The Basket of Flowers*

1	2
Marie and her saintly father Jacob, former gardener to the count of Eichburg, live in a cottage on the count's estate. Jacob has made a beautiful garden, and here he teaches Marie about God and how to pray. In her favorite flowers he points out the emblems of the virtues a young girl should possess. When she brings him a violet, he says, "Dear Marie, let the demure violet be for you an emblem of humility, reserve and quiet charity. It is clothed in the soft colours of modesty, and loves to bloom in secret.... May you also be a quiet violet ... doing good in silence." When Marie points at a lily, Jacob says, "Dear daughter, let the lily be for you an emblem of innocence.... Happy the girl whose heart is pure of all wickedness.... The lily can easily be spoilt ... and just so can innocence be damaged by one word or thought." Pointing to the rose, he says, "Let the rose be for you an emblem of chaste delicacy.... More beautiful than the colour of the rose is the blush of embarrassment. Safe is the girl who blushes at every indecent joke ... and is thus put on her guard against the danger of sin." When apple blossom is caught by frost, Jacob says that, just as frost spoils apple blossom, so sinful desire spoils the flower of youth. Chapter 1	One day, Marie gives wildflowers to the countess and her daughter Amalia, in the woods, and it is arranged that she will bring flowers to Amalia every morning. On Amalia's birthday, she gives her flowers in a basket made by her father, with Amalia's name and coat of arms on it. In return, she is given a dress of Amalia's, and the waiting-maid is angry because the cast-off dresses usually go to her. *Immediately after Marie leaves, the countess finds her diamond ring has disappeared and it is believed Marie must have taken it. Jacob believes his daughter's denial and counsels that all is the will of God. The bailiff arrests Marie and she is imprisoned. In court, the waiting-maid states that she saw the ring in Marie's hands, and Marie persists in declaring herself innocent. The judge has her beaten until blood is drawn, in order to extort a confession of guilt. He convicts her on the evidence of the maid because he has no other course. All are anxious about the sentence—the maid seeing Marie's bloody head in her dreams—but it is banishment for both Marie and Jacob, since Marie is young and of irreproachable reputation, while her father must have been an accomplice, if only in giving her a bad upbringing. As the old man and his daughter leave, the maid throws the basket at Marie's feet, saying her mistress wants nothing from such hands as hers.*

(continued)

(Continued)

	When Jacob becomes very weak on their journey, they are taken in by a kind farming couple at Pine Cottage. Here they stay three years, working hard, and Jacob makes a new garden. Then he dies, and Marie plants a rose tree on his grave and places the basket of flowers there. Chapters 2–12

3

The couple at Pine Cottage hand over the farm to their son and daughter-in-law, and the daughter-in-law, who cares only for money and has everyone in her power, ill-treats Marie. When a piece of fine linen disappears, she accuses Marie, having heard the story of the ring. Marie is turned out of Pine Cottage, and she goes to her father's grave, where the full moon is shining on the rose tree and the basket of flowers.

There Marie prays for an angel to show her the way and she hears a voice saying, "Marie! Marie!" It is Amalia. She tells Marie they have done her a great wrong, but her innocence has been discovered. Amalia is staying in the neighborhood, and knows about the grave because the forester's daughter took her to see it as something beautiful. There she recognized the basket of flowers with her name and coat of arms on it. The forester's daughter told her Marie's story, and then she went to see the priest, who confirmed it, praising Marie highly. Amalia then tells Marie that the ring was found in a magpie's nest—after they cut down a pear tree made unsafe by a storm that year. The count was shocked and had the waiting-maid arrested; she was made to suffer all that Marie had suffered. Amalia also tells Marie the effect of the news on the bailiff, an upright man, when he learned that innocence had been condemned.

Marie's story, related by the priest, brings tears to everyone's eyes. Then

Amalia and Marie enter with the basket of flowers, and the count asks Marie's forgiveness. He gives her the cottage and garden Jacob had rented on his estate. The countess kisses her and calls her daughter; then she puts the ring on Marie's finger. Marie is given a dress suited to her new situation. The daughter-in-law and waiting-maid die the deaths of sinners. Marie is joyfully welcomed back in Eichburg, and the bailiff asks her forgiveness. Later, she marries his son. A monument is made for Jacob's grave, with the basket of flowers carved upon it, and the priest tells the story of the basket of flowers to everyone visiting his parish.

Chapters 13–24

Chart 8. Purification in *Emaré*

1

Emaré (refined, excellent?), the motherless daughter of an emperor, grows up so beautiful that her father plans to marry her. He has a robe made for her out of rich cloth adorned with precious stones and famous lovers from romance. When Emaré puts on the robe, she seems no earthly woman. The emperor then reveals his desire to marry her.

Emaré replies that if they married they would be damned, and she refuses. Her furious father has her put out to sea in a boat, dressed in her robe. Later, he repents this deed. Emaré drifts for more than seven days, sorrowful and almost mad with hunger and thirst, until she is cast on a shore:

Now thys lady dwelled thore
A good sevennyghth and more,
   As hyt was Goddys wylle.
Wyth carefull herte and sykyng sore,
Such sorow was here yarked yore,
   And ever lay she styll.
She was dryven ynto a lond,
Thorow the grace of Goddes sond,
   That all thyng may fulfylle.
She was on the see so harde bestadde,
For hungur and thurste almost madde:
   Woo worth wederus yll! (ll. 325–36)

Emaré is cast ashore in Galicia and is rescued by the king's steward. He and his accompanying knights are astonished by the glittering sight in the boat. Emaré becomes a servant in the royal household, under the name Egaré ("the Outcast").
ll. 1–384

2

During a feast at court Emaré serves in her robe and seems no earthly thing. The king of Galicia sees her and falls in love. His mother protests that Emaré is an evil spirit, but he marries her. While he is away fighting Saracens, a son, Segramour, is born, with the double king's mark. A letter is written to the king, giving him the news, but the queen mother changes it for another saying that a devil has been born, not a son. The king faints, but sends instructions that Emaré should be well cared for. The queen mother intercepts this letter, too, substituting one saying that Emaré should be set adrift at sea, dressed in her precious robe and with her child.

Emaré drifts for more than seven days, sorrowful and almost mad with hunger and thirst, until she is cast on a shore:

Now thys lady dwelled thore
A full sevenenyght and more,
   As hyt was Goddys wylle;
Wyth karefull herte and sykyng sore,
Such sorow was her yarked yore,
   And she lay full stylle.
She was dryven toward Rome,
Thorow the grace of God yn trone,
   That all thyng may fulfylle.
On the see she was so harde bestadde,
For hungur and thurste allmost madde,
   Wo worth chawnses ylle! (ll. 673–84)

She is cast ashore in Rome and is rescued by a merchant. He is afraid at the sight of her in her glittering robe. She lives in his household for seven years, under the name Egaré.
ll. 384–744

3

The king returns to Galicia, punishes his mother with exile, and later leaves for Rome to do penance. He lodges where Emaré is living, and, under Emaré's instructions, the child Segramour brings about a reunion. First, she has the child serve at table so that he is admired: the king asks his name and, on learning it, thinks of his own son with regret. He asks to be given the boy. Next, Emaré tells Segramour the king is his father and she instructs him to bring the king to her:

"Soone when he shall to chambur wende
Take hys hond at the grece ende,
　For he ys thy fadur, ywysse.
And byd hym come speke wyth Emaré,
That changed her name to Egaré,
　In the londe of Galys!" (ll. 904–9)

The child carries out her instructions:

When the kyng shulde to chambur
　wende,
He toke hys hond at the grece ende.
. . . .
And sayde, "Syr yf your wyll be,
Take me your honde and go wyth me,
　For Y am of yowr kynne!
Ye shull come speke wyth Emaré,
That chaunged her nome to Egaré"
　　　　　(ll. 916–17, 919–23)

After the joyful reunion, Emaré's father arrives in Rome to do his penance for his deed. Emaré asks her husband to ride to meet the emperor, and she instructs Segramour to go also, receive the emperor's kiss, and then bring him to her: "'And bydde hym come speke wyth Emaré / That was putte ynto the see.'"

The child is kissed by the emperor and says to him, "Lord . . .

Ye shull come speke wyth Emaré
That changede her name to Egaré
　That was thy thowghthur dere."
　　　　　(ll. 1006–8)

A second joyful reunion follows.
ll. 745–1035

Chart 9. Purification in *La Manekine*

1

The king of Hungary promises his dying wife that he will only remarry if he finds a woman who looks like her. His barons urge him to remarry and he refuses, telling them his promise to the late queen. They search in vain for a woman who resembles the late queen; only Joie, the king's daughter, truly resembles her and the barons suggest to the king that he marry her. The king refuses, but he gradually gets used to the idea, and, since the clergy are sure of a dispensation from the pope, he agrees.

Joie is horrified and cuts off her left hand to disqualify herself. The hand drops into the river Yse. The king orders that she be burned alive, and his seneschal, moved to pity, burns a woodpile and sets the girl adrift in a boat. God hears her prayer and, on the ninth day, she arrives on the coast of Scotland, where the king shelters her.

At the Scottish court, she conceals her name and origin, and calls herself "La Manekine" (which must here be intended to mean "the woman with only one hand").

vv. 49–1346

2

The king falls in love with La Manekine and marries her, in spite of the opposition of his mother, who retires to live elsewhere on the day of the wedding. Some months after the marriage, the king goes to a tournament at the French court and, La Manekine being pregnant, he instructs the seneschal to send him news when the birth takes place. La Manekine gives birth to a son, and a letter with the news is sent to the king, but the old queen changes it for one saying that La Manekine has brought a monster into the world. The grieved king replies that the mother and child must be well cared for until he arrives home, and this message is changed for one saying *that La Manekine and her son must be burned alive. The seneschal burns images instead, and La Manekine is set adrift in the same boat as before, with her child. Once again, her prayer is heard and, on the ninth day, she arrives in the river Tiber and is rescued by fishermen, who sell her to a rich and noble senator. The senator is concerned that a woman clearly of gentle origin should be alone in Rome, her honor unguarded.*

The senator shelters her, accepting that she will tell him no more about herself than her name. The name she gives is La Manekine. The senator's daughters care for her, and she is loved and honored. The senator is a widower.

vv. 1347–5398

3

The king of Scotland returns home and learns what has happened. He walls up his mother and then sets out to search for his wife. After seven years, he arrives in Rome and stays where La Manekine is living. La Manekine has to tell the senator why the king must not see her. The king weeps on seeing La Manekine's seven-year-old son Jehan, because he is reminded of his own lost son. He confides in the senator. La Manekine is also weeping and does not notice when Jehan takes the ring given to her by the king when he married her. Jehan plays with the ring in the room where the king and the senator are having a meal, and it falls on the table in front of the king. The king looks at the ring for a long time and then asks the senator for the truth about the ring and the child. The senator tells him all he knows of La Manekine's story—but only after the king has sworn he will not harm anyone as a result of what he hears. The king then tells his side of the story. Finally, the senator brings La Manekine to the king, and they are reconciled. The couple remain chaste until the king receives the pope's absolution.

Meanwhile, the king of Hungary, tormented by remorse, comes to Rome to seek a pardon from the pope. Joie hears his public confession and goes up to him afterwards, before the pope and people, to say, "'Biaus dous peres, . . . Je sui vostre file Joïe'" (vv. 7145–46). They are reconciled.

Joie's hand reappears miraculously in a fountain, and the pope's prayer restores it on her arm.
vv. 5399–8590

Chart 10. Purification in "Penta the Handless"

1

The widowed king of Preta-secca has the idea that he should marry his sister. She locks herself in her chamber, and when, some days later, the king gives vent to these desires again, she comes out of her room to ask him what it is about her that he desires. He says it is her hand.

Penta returns to her room, has her hands cut off, and sends them to the king. The king is furious and has her put to sea, shut up in a chest.

Eventually, the chest is washed up on a shore, and sailors open it to find the beautiful Penta. The chief and most courageous of these people, Masiello, takes her home and asks his wife Nuccia to treat her with kindness. But, when he has gone, Nuccia puts her back into the chest and casts her once more into the sea.

2

Then the queen dies, asking the king to marry Penta. The king does so and Penta conceives. The king then sails for the kingdom of Antoscuoglio. Penta bears a son, and the messages to and from her husband are intercepted by Nuccia, at whose shore the messenger's ship calls on both journeys. Nuccia substitutes false messages, saying the queen has given birth to a dog and that the king orders the queen and her son to be burned at once. The king's counselors send them into exile instead.

Penta travels weeping to Lago-truvolo, with her child. In Lago-truvolo, she meets a magician and tells him her story. He cares for her as if she were his daughter.

3

The magician sends out an announcement that he will present a crown and scepter worth a kingdom to whoever relates at his court the greatest misfortune.

Meanwhile, the king of Terra-Verde comes home and avenges himself on Nuccia. At sea, on his way home from this revenge, he meets the king of Preta-secca, who tells him he is going to tell his story to the magician, as he is the most unfortunate man in the world. The king of Terra-Verde goes too, to tell his own story. They agree that, if either wins, they will share their winnings. The two kings tell their tales—which turn out to be about the same woman. The magician sends for Penta's son, Nufriello, bidding him kiss his father and then his uncle. Each in turn is

Chart 10 · 173

At last the chest is picked up by a large vessel, which has the king of Terra-Verde on board. The king gives Penta as maid of honor to the queen, and she serves the queen well, using her feet.

delighted with the child. Penta has been hidden by a curtain, and she now comes out, and all are joyfully reunited. The magician gives the prize to the king of Terra-Verde and also his own kingdom, and he restores Penta's hands. The couple live with the magician, while the king of Preta-secca rules in Terra-Verde.

Chart 11. The Purification Story in *Vita Offae Primi*

1	2	3
King Offa is hunting one day and is separated from his company when a storm comes on. As he wanders down unknown byways, he hears a lamenting voice and finds in the dense woodland a maiden of unparalleled beauty in royal clothing.	However, under pressure, King Offa begins to consider the matter and thinks of the maiden he found in the woods, who is both loved and praised by all who know her. He marries her, and she bears fine children.	Offa arrives home, after two months, victorious, and, after a period during which he is not told why his queen has not appeared to welcome him, he learns the truth.
Her story is that her father, a prince of York, desired her sexually and often tried to move her with threats, promises, and flattery, and to weaken her constancy with gifts, but she never gave in. She had preferred exposure or death to yielding. Her father ordered that she should be taken to a remote wasteland, to be cruelly killed and left for the beasts. But his men spare her life, moved by her beauty.	Then the king of Northumbria, harassed by the Scots, asks Offa for help, offering to marry his daughter and acknowledge him his sovereign. A pact having been made, Offa leaves for the North and quickly defeats the Scots. His messenger with this news calls at the court of the king of Northumbria, now Offa's son-in-law, and this king intercepts his letters, substituting others giving bad news of the expedition and having Offa say that it must be the judgment of God on account of their sins.	*He puts on sackcloth and ashes ("induit se sacco cilicino, aspersum cinere"). (Chaucer Society, 81)* Eventually, persuaded to hunt once more, he comes upon the hermitage. He tells the hermit his story, and the hermit reunites the couple.
King Offa takes her with him, and they spend the night at the home of a Solitary,		

who guides them back to Offa's kingdom the next day.

The maiden is placed in the careful custody of members of Offa's household ("familiaribus et domesticis generis sui sub diligenti custodia commisit"). (Chaucer Society, 75)

Some years later, Offa's nobles entreat him to marry, but he dismisses the subject with jokes.

The substituted letter goes on to say that Offa thinks his marriage is the cause: it was an ignorant and unfortunate thing to marry that abandoned witch, and she and her children must be taken to some unknown wasteland, a place of wild beasts, there to have their hands and feet chopped off and be left to perish.

Offa's amazed people dare not disobey, and the order is carried out; the mother only they spare in the wilderness, because of her beauty.

A passing hermit hears her lamentation, and the rending cries that the Lord draws out of the corpses. By means of prayer, he restores the children and then makes the sign of the cross over them. He takes them all to his own dwelling, where he cares for them.

Chart 12. The "Peau d'Anon" Plot

1	2
A dying princess tells her husband she wishes him to remarry only if it is with a woman who resembles her. The prince replies that he does not wish to remarry and that only her daughter resembles her. Some time after his wife's death, he tells his daughter that he wishes to marry again and only she accords with her mother's wishes. The daughter consults her fairy godmother, and her godmother says she must tell her father she would like to marry him, but first he must buy her a spinning wheel that spins by itself. The daughter goes to her father and tells him she would like to marry him, but first he must buy her a spinning wheel that spins by itself. The prince walks and walks till he finds one. The princess consults her godmother again, and she says she must tell her father she would like to marry him, but first he must buy her a dress like the stars. The daughter goes to her father and tells him she would like to marry him, but first he must buy her a dress like the stars. The prince walks and walks and walks till he finds one. Then, following the counsel of her godmother, she has him find her a dress like the sun, a dress like the moon, and a cabriolet harnessed to four rats going like the wind. Then her godmother tells her to go away in her cabriolet, with her dresses packed in trunks. *The godmother says that, on the road, she will meet shepherds, from whom she must buy a donkey. The donkey must then be skinned, and she must cover herself with the skin. Then she must get work on a farm as a shep-*	*When Sunday comes, the daughter and son of the house say they are going to a dance. The shepherdess asks to go too and is laughed at. But, after they have gone, the farmer's wife gives her a great blow with a dishcloth and says she can go for an hour and a half. She goes to her hidden cabriolet to change into her dress like the stars, and then she goes to the dance. As she leaves, the son of the house asks where she comes from, and she replies that she comes from the country of the Dishcloth. She returns to her vehicle to change and then returns to the farm. The next day, the daughter and son tell her she should have seen the beautiful girl at the ball.* "Elle n'était toujours pas plus belle que moi!," *she replies. Everyone laughs on hearing this. The following Sunday, the daughter and son go dancing again, and the shepherdess asks to go with them. At last, her mistress gives her a great blow with a broom and tells her she may go for two hours. She goes in her moon dress and is greatly admired. As she leaves, a young man wishes to escort her, but she refuses. He asks her her country, and she replies that she is from the country of the Broom. The next day, the daughter and son tell her of the beautiful girl at the ball, and she replies,* "Elle n'était toujours pas plus belle que moi!" *(2.258) Everyone laughs at her. The following Sunday, she is given three hours at the dance and a great blow with a poker.* She goes to the dance in her dress like the sun, and the king's son is there, having heard about her. When she arrives, he dances with no one else, and he wishes to escort her when she leaves. He asks her where she is from, and she re-

herdess, turkey-girl, or servant. The girl follows these instructions and finds work, both tending sheep and spinning; the spinning wheel does the spinning on its own. The cabriolet and the girl's possessions are hidden. (2.256–58)

plies that she is from the country of the Poker. He escorts her a little way, and, when she approaches her vehicle, she wishes him to leave her. However, he follows her without her knowing it, guided by her dress like the sun, shining in the night, and he sees her change into her donkey skin and return to the farm. (2.258–60)

The king's son falls ill with longing for her and says he wants to eat a cake made by the shepherdess at the farm. She arrives to make it wearing her dress like the sun under the donkey skin. While making the cake, she takes off the donkey skin for comfort, but, hearing the king's son coming, she puts it on again quickly. The invalid stands by her as she works and gently draws off the skin. "Chat, chat, chat!," she says without turning, "tu manges ma peau d'ânon." She pulls it on again quickly. The king's son begins to do it again. "Chat, chat, chat!," she says, "tu manges ma peau d'ânon" (2.259), and she pulls it on again. The king's son goes out and, when the cake is finished, she puts her ring in it. Then she returns to the farm, where everyone laughs at the idea of the king's son enjoying her cake.

The king's son eats the cake and finds the ring; he is cured at once and says he will marry the owner of the ring. Every girl, rich and poor, tries the ring on and fails. Donkeyskin comes last and it fits her perfectly. The king's son says he will marry her, and he pulls off the donkey skin. She is revealed in her dress like the sun and no one laughs at her. She writes to her father to tell him all that has happened, and he arrives. They are reconciled, and the marriage takes place.

Chart 13. The King Lear Judgment in Eight Texts Compared

Geoffrey of Monmouth	Aaron Thompson's Translation
At cordeilla iunior cum intellexisset eum predictarum adultationibus acquieuisse temptare illum cupiens aliter respondere perrexit. Est uspiam pater mi filia quæ patrem suum plus quam patrem presumat. diligere? Non reor equidem ullam esse quæ hoc fateri audeat. nisi iocosis uerbis ueritatem celare nitatur. Nempe ego dilexi te semper ut patrem. & adhuc a proposito meo non diuertor. Et si ex me magis extorquere insistis. audi cercudinem [Bern MS certitudinem] amoris quæ aduersum te habeo. & interrogationibus tuis finem impone. Et enim quantum habes. tantum uales. tantumque te diligo. Porro pater iratus [Bern MS ratus] eam ex abundantia cordis dixisse uehementer indignans. quod responsurus erat hoc modo manifestare non distulit. Quia in tantum senectutem patris tui spreuisti. ut uel eo amore quo me sorores tue dedignata es diligere. & ego dedignabor te nec unquam partem in regno meo. cum sororibus habebis. (Griscom 263–64) [Bern MS, ed. Wright, 19]	But *Cordeilla* the youngest, understanding how easily he was satisfied with the flattering Expressions of her Sisters, was desirous to make Tryal of his Affection after a different Manner. "My Father," said she, "Is there any Daughter that can love her Father more than Duty requires? In my Opinion, whoever pretends to it, must disguise her real Sentiments under the Veil of Flattery. I have always loved you as a Father, nor do I yet depart from my purposed Duty; and if you insist to have something more extorted from me, hear now the Greatness of my Affection, which I always bear you, and take this for a short Answer to all your Questions; Look how much you have, so much is your Value, and so much I love you." The Father supposing that she spoke this out of the Abundance of her Heart, was highly provoked, and immediately reply'd; "Since you have so far despised my Old-age, as not to think me worthy the Love that your Sisters express for me, you shall have from me the like Regard, and shall be excluded from any Share with your Sisters in my Kingdom." (Bullough 312)

La3amon's *Brut*, MS Caligula	Welsh MS LXI, Jesus College
Cordoille iherde þa lasinge. þe hire sustren seiden þon kinge. nom hire leaf-fulne huie. þat heo li3en nolden. hire fader heo wolde suge seoð. were him lef were him lað. . . . . Þa answarede Cordoille. lude and no-wiht stille. mid gomene and mid lehtre. to hire fader leue. Þeo art me leof al-so mi fæder. and ich þe al-so þi dohter. Ich habbe to þe sohfaste loue. for we buoð swiþe isibbe. and swa ich ibide are. ich wille þe suge mare. Al swa muchel þu bist woruh. swa þu velden ært. and al swa muchel swa þu hauest. men þe wllet luuien. for sone heo bið ila3e[d]. þe mon þe lutel ah. Þus seide þe mæiden Cordoille. and seoððen <set> swþe stille. Þa iwarðe þe king wærð. for he nes þeo noht iquemed. and wende on is þonke. þat hit weren for vnðeawe. þat he hire weore swa unwourð. þat heo hine nold iwurði swa hire twa sustren. þe ba somed læsinge speken. . . . . mid þere wræððe he wes isweued. þat he feol iswowen. Late þeo he up fusde. þat mæiden wes afeared. Þa hit alles up brac. hit wes vuel þat he spac. Hærne Cordoille. ich þe telle wlle mine wille. Of mine dohtren þu were me durest. nu þu eært me arle læðes[t]. Ne scalt þu næuer halden. dale of mine lande. (Brook and Leslie ll. 1514–16, 1520–32, 1535–40)	(Literal translation of Robert Ellis Jones) And then K*ord*aila, after seeing her two sisters deceiving him with false deceiving love, was minded to give him a moderate answer. And then he asked his Youngest daughter how greatly did she love her father. "My Lord father, it may be that some pretend to love their father more than they do; but, my Lord, I will love thee as a daughter should love her father. According to what grounds of affection there shall be, will I love thee, my Lord father." Then her father, thinking that she said this to him out of sheer willfulness of heart, was greatly angered and spoke thus: "In the way that thou lovest me in my old age, so will I love thee henceforth, for I will disinherit thee forever of thy share of ynys brydain and will give it to thy two sisters." (Griscom 263–64)

(continued)

(Continued)

Old Play of *King Leir*

LEIR. I am resolv'd, and even now my mind
Doth meditate a sudden stratagem,
To try which of my daughters loves me best:
Which till I know, I cannot be in rest.
This graunted, when they joyntly shall contend,
Eche to exceed the other in their love:
Then at the vantage will I take *Cordella*,
Even as she doth protest she loves me best,
Ile say, Then, daughter, graunt me one request,
To shew thou lovest me as thy sisters doe,
Accept a husband, whom my selfe will woo.
This sayd, she cannot well deny my sute,
Although (poore soule) her sences will be mute:
Then will I triyumph in my policy,
And match her with a King of Brittany.
(Act I, ll. 77–91)

LEIR. Oh, what a combat feeles my panting heart,
'Twixt childrens love, and care of Common weale!
How deare my daughters are unto my soule,
None knowes, but he, that knowes my thoghts & secret deeds.
Ah, little do they know the deare regard,
Wherein I hold their future state to come:
When they securely sleepe on beds of downe,
These aged eyes do watch for their behalfe:
While they like wantons sport in youthfull toyes,
This throbbing heart is pearst with dire annoyes. (ll. 202–11)

CORDELLA. I cannot paynt my duty forth in words,
I hope my deeds shall make report for me:
But looke what love the child doth owe the father,
The same to you I beare, my gracious Lord.
. . . .
LEIR. Why how now, Minion, are you growne so proud?
Doth our deare love make you thus peremptory?
What, is your love become so small to us,
As that you scorne to tell us what it is?
Do you love us, as every child doth love
Their father? True indeed, as some
Who by disobedience short their fathers dayes.
. . . .
CORDELLA. Deare father, do not so mistake my words,
Nor my playne meaning be misconstrued;
My toung was never usde to flattery.
. . . .
LEIR. Peace, bastard Impe, no issue of King *Leir*,
I will not heare thee speake one tittle more.
Call not me father, if thou love thy life.
. . . .
Looke for no helpe henceforth from me nor mine;
. . . .
My Kingdome will I equally devide
'Twixt thy two sisters to their royall dowre.
(Bullough 339–45, ll. 277–80, 285–91, 300–302, 312–14, 16, 18–19)

Shakespeare's *King Lear*	Holinshed
CORDELIA Nothing, my lord. LEAR Nothing? CORDELIA Nothing. LEAR Nothing will come of nothing. Speak again. CORDELIA Unhappy that I am, I cannot heave My heart into my mouth. I love your majesty According to my bond, no more nor less. . . . . You have begot me, bred me, loved me. I return those duties back as are right fit, Obey you, love you, and most honour you. Why have my sisters husbands, if they say They love you all? Haply when I shall wed, That lord whose hand must take my plight shall carry Half my love with him, half my care and duty. Sure I shall never marry like my sisters To love my father all. LEAR But goes thy heart with this? CORDELIA Ay, my good lord. LEAR So young, and so untender? CORDELIA So young, my lord, and true. LEAR Let it be so! Thy truth then be thy dower! (Hunter, 1.1.87–93, 96–108)	Then called he his yoongest daughter Cordeilla before him, and asked of hir what account she made of him, unto whome she made this answer as followeth: "Knowing the great love and fatherlie zeale that you have alwaies borne towards me (for the which I maie not answere you otherwise than I thinke and as my conscience leadeth me) I protest unto you, that I have loved you ever, and will continuallie (while I live) love you as my naturall father. And if you would more understand of the love that I beare you, assertaine your selfe, that so much as you have, so much you are woorth, and so much I love you, and no more." The father being nothing content with this answer . . . for the third daughter Cordeilla . . . reserved nothing. (Bullough 317) *Gesta Romanorum,* MS Addit. 9066 "Sir," she seide, "my systers han seide to you wordes of glosyng, but I say to you trouthe. I love you as mych as I owe to loue my Fadire, and for to make you more Certayne how mych loue is worthe, I shall say you, as mych as ye han, so mych are ye worthe, and so mych I loue you." leyre wenyd that she had skorned, and was wrothe, and seide, that she shuld neu*er* haue lande of hym. (Herrtage 49)

Chart 14. *Roswall and Lillian* and "The Goose-Girl" Compared

Roswall and Lillian	
1 Roswall is the son of the king of Naples and his queen, Lillian. One day, he sits outside the prison to overhear the prayers for freedom of three lords who had been traitors to the king. The king keeps the keys under his bedhead and Roswall steals them to free the prisoners, while his father is asleep. When the deed is known, the king vows he will hang the perpetrator. But, on learning from a report spread abroad that his son has done the deed, he is grieved, and his queen begs that the fault be forgiven. The only way to save his son from the vow is to keep him out of his sight; otherwise, his "own two hands his bane shall be." So Roswall is sent to the king of Bealm, with the king's steward as his servant. The queen entreats the steward to look after her son. *On the journey, Roswall is thirsty, and the steward alights to drink from the river, telling the prince to do so too. While he is on his belly at the river, the steward takes him by the feet and says he will throw him in the deep unless he swears an oath that he will resign his place to him and become his faithful servant. Roswall swears the oath and they continue on their journey. At Bealm, Roswall is left outside the town and the steward is welcomed by the king. Roswall is destitute and decides to take the name Dissawar. He calls at a little house and asks the old woman there for shelter; she cares for him and sends him to school with her son.*	**2** On the first day of the tournament, Roswall sets off early to hunt in the forest. There he meets a knight in white armor and on a white horse, who tells him they must change places and Roswall must go to the tournament to win praise and honor. The white knight will hunt in his stead and give him the venison when they meet afterwards. Roswall triumphs at the tournament and defeats the false steward. Then he runs into the forest, "As light as ever did a man" and The King cry'd with voice on hie, Go take yon Knight, bring him to me, And whoso brings him to my hand, Shall have an Earldome of land: But all for nought, it was in vain. . . . (ll. 505–9) Roswall changes into Dissawar's clothes in the forest and returns to court with venison for Lillian. She says he has beguiled her, and he replies that he has no skill at jousting. She tells him about the white knight and says he might see him if he stays with her the next day. He agrees to do so. But he goes early into the forest the next morning, and there he meets a red knight with whom he changes places. His triumphs at the tournament are even greater, and he humiliates the false steward again. Then he runs into the forest "As light as ever did a man" and The king cryed with voice on hie: Go take yon Knight, bring him to me, And whoso brings him to my hand

When she learns he is called Dissawar, she says,

> Dissawar, *wo is me,*
> *That is a poor name verilie.*
> *Yet* Dissawar *you shall not be,*
> *For good help you shall have of me....*
> (ll. 249–52)

Then the steward of the king of Bealm takes Roswall away to serve him at court. At court, he is loved as if he were a prince or a king, and the princess Lillian, to the steward's chagrin, takes him to be her cup-bearer. She is sure he is of noble blood and wants to marry him, while he continues to act the role of Dissawar. She says,

Dissawar, *I do you pray,*
Cast that name from you away;
Call you Hector *or* Oliver,
Ye are so fair without compare....
(ll. 367–70)

Then Roswall's parents receive a request from the king of Bealm that Roswall (the steward) be married to Lillian. Lillian despairs and tells Dissawar, saying that he must take part in the tournament that is to inaugurate the marriage festivities. Dissawar replies,

> *Lady, by my good fay,*
> *I nere was bred with such a play,*
> *For I had rather be at hunting....*
> (ll. 443–45)

Shall have an Earldome of land,
But all for nought: it was in vain. . . .
(ll. 579–83)

Roswall becomes Dissawar again and returns to court with a white hind for his lady. She tells him about the red knight and says she thinks it is he, but he says he has no skill at jousting. Against her wishes he returns to the forest the next day and changes places with a knight dressed in gold, with a red shield and green armor. He throws a ring at his lady when he arrives, and he surpasses Roland and Oliver. He breaks two of the false steward's ribs and then runs into the forest as swiftly as a falcon.

The King cryed with voice full shrill:
Go take yon Knight, bring him me till:
And whoso brings him to me here,
Shall have my land and daughter dear,
But all for nought, it was in vain. . . .
(ll. 647–51)

In the forest, the three knights reveal that they are the three prisoners Roswall freed. They tell him they will prevent the steward's marriage to Lillian. When Roswall returns to Lillian, she says that if he tells her father the truth, the king will give him his daughter "and all the land." But it is the freed prisoners who tell the king the truth and bring about this end.

(continued)

(Continued)

"The Goose-Girl"

1	2

The daughter of a widowed queen is betrothed to a king's son. When it is time for her to be married, she sets off with a waiting-maid, riding a horse called Falada, who can speak. The queen gives her daughter three drops of her blood on a napkin, telling her to preserve them well for they will help her in time of trouble on her journey. The princess places the napkin in her bosom.
 	
When she has ridden for an hour, the princess is thirsty and asks her maid to get her a drink from the stream. The maid tells her to dismount and lie down and drink out of the water, for she will not be her servant. The princess does so and is not allowed to use the golden cup. She sighs and the drops of blood reply, "If this your mother knew, her heart would break in two." She is humble, says nothing, and they ride on. The day is warm and she becomes thirsty again. She once again asks her maid to get her a drink in her golden cup, as she has long forgotten her ill words, and the maid replies even more haughtily that she must get it herself. As the king's daughter bends over the flowing stream, she weeps and sighs, and the drops of blood answer, "If this your mother knew, her heart would break in two." Then, as she is drinking, the napkin with the drops of blood falls out of her bosom and floats away without her noticing it, so great is her anxiety. The waiting-maid sees it and is glad, because she
	Passing under the gateway early next morning, the goose-girl says,
	    Ah Falada, there you hang,
	and the head answers,
	    Ah young queen, there you go,
	    if this your mother knew,
	    her heart would break in two!
	When they reach the meadow, the goose-girl sits down and unloosens her hair, which is pure gold. Conrad is delighted and tries to pull out a couple of strands. Then the goose-girl sings,
	    Blow, blow, little wind,
	    take Conrad's little hat,
	    and let him chase it,
	    until I have plaited my hair
	    and bound it up again.
	The wind blows and, when Conrad returns with his hat, she has arranged her hair and he cannot seize any of it. He is angry and will not speak to her. The next morning, as they pass under the gateway, the girl says,
	    Ah Falada, there you hang,
	and Falada answers,
	    Ah young queen, there you go,
	    if this your mother knew,
	    her heart would break in two!
	In the field she begins to comb out her hair, and Conrad runs up and tries to grab it, so she quickly says,
	    Blow, blow, little wind,
	    take Conrad's little hat,
	    and let him chase it,
	    until I have plaited my hair
	    and bound it up again.
	The wind blows and, when Conrad returns with his hat, her hair has been up again for a long time. In the evening,

now has power over the bride; without the drops of blood, she has become weak. She tells her to ride the other horse, not Falada, and put on her maid's clothes. She is made to swear that she will say nothing of what has taken place; had she not sworn, she would have been murdered. Falada takes note of all that has passed.

Upon their arrival, the maid is welcomed with great joy and taken upstairs, while the princess is left standing below. The old king sees the beautiful girl in the courtyard and asks the false bride about her. She replies that the girl should be given work to do, and the old king gives her the job of helping the goose-boy, Conrad.

The false bride then asks that Falada's head be cut off, because the horse has annoyed her on the way. She is really afraid the horse will tell. The princess hears of this and asks the knacker to nail the horse's head under the great gloomy gateway through which she passes morning and evening with the geese. The knacker does so.

Conrad goes to the old king to tell him he does not wish to herd geese with the girl any more. The king asks why, and he tells him how, in the morning, she speaks to a horse's head under the gateway, saying,

Ah Falada, there you hang,

to which the head replies,

Ah young queen, there you go,
if this your mother knew,
her heart would break in two!

Then Conrad relates what happens in the meadow. The old king follows them unobserved the next day and sees it all. In the evening, he asks the girl why she does all these things, and she tells him she has sworn not to tell her story. At last he bids her tell it to the stove: she creeps into it and pours her heart out, while he overhears. Then she is dressed in her royal clothes, and the young king is told the truth. At the wedding feast, the true and false brides sit on each side of the bridegroom, and the maid, who has not recognized her mistress, is tricked into pronouncing her own punishment.

Chart 15. The Porkington and Percy Versions of the Carl of Carlisle Tale

Porkington	Percy
King Arthur proclaims that the court will go to mass and then to the hunt. The adventure with the Carl begins when three of the party chase a deer and get caught in a mist.	
Gawain suggests they camp under a tree, and Kay wishes to find lodging for the night. Bishop Baldwin suggests they stay with the Carl of Carlisle nearby: the Carl beats his guests, and anyone getting away with his life has done so through God's dispensation. Kay agrees, saying that if the Carl makes trouble he will beat him until he stinks and despoil his house. Gawain says he will not lodge there against the Carl's will, if courtesy will make the lord glad to have them in his castle. He tells Kay to leave off his boastful talk; he is setting out to stir up trouble. (ll. 127–74)	ll. 83–130
At the gate, Gawain is courteous and Kay discourteous. The porter tells them the Carl has no courtesy, and that if he knew of their boastful words, they would either flee or die. When the porter tells the Carl that knights of King Arthur are asking for lodging, the Carl is pleased. (ll. 175–222)	ll. 131–70
The Carl is surrounded by horrible creatures ("whelpus"), a lion, a bear, a bull, and a boar, and they are under his control. He orders them to lie still, and they creep under the table; Kay takes heed of this. (ll. 223–46) The Carl himself is enormous and ugly. (ll. 247–70)	ll. 205–16 ll. 175–88

Porkington	Percy
Gawain kneels and the Carl tells him to get up, saying that he himself will not be courteous. The Carl drinks more than nine gallons of wine. (ll. 271–97)	ll. 189–204 The wine scene is placed after the horse scene in this version. This text has a scene before the adventure with the horses, which takes the place of the Porkington text's two supper scenes with Gawain and Kay. A lady sits on the Carl's knee, harping and singing of love, and Gawain says aloud, "Well were that man . . . that ere were borne, That might lye with that lady till day att morne." The Carl says, "'That were great shame . . . That thou sholdest doe me such villanye.'" Gawain denies that he said anything, and the Carl replies, "'No, man . . . more thou thought.'" (ll. 217–26)
The bishop, Kay, and Gawain go out in turn to see to their horses, and the first two each drive out the Carl's small horse when they find it beside their own, giving it a clout. The Carl arrives and gives each a return buffet. Gawain, by contrast, brings the Carl's horse in from the rain and covers it with his mantle. The Carl thanks him courteously many times. (ll. 299–354)	
At supper, the Carl's beautiful wife is sitting next to Kay, and Kay thinks it a pity she is married to the ugly Carl. The Carl orders him to sit still and get on with his meal, saying that he thinks more than he dare say. (ll. 355–78)	Supper, without mention of the Carl's wife. (ll. 299–306)
No one has asked Gawain to sit down,	

(continued)

(Continued)

Porkington	Percy
and he remains standing. The Carl orders him to take a spear and hit him straight in the face with it. He assures him that he will not hurt him, and so Gawain gladly obeys, throwing the spear with great passion. The Carl avoids the spear and, saying, "'Gentyll knyȝt, þou hast well doune,'" he takes his hand. (ll. 379–402)	After supper, the Carl orders Gawain to take a spear and aim for the middle of his face. Kay wishes he had been given the order, and the Carl reads his thoughts. Gawain is not told he cannot harm the Carl (as in the Porkington text), but he still gladly obeys the order, doing so with passion ("ire"). The Carl says he was too eager (or hasty), and Gawain replies, "'I did but, Sir, as you me bade.'" The Carl responds that if he had hit him as he had meant, he would have hit him a fierce blow. (ll. 307–30)
Gawain is placed opposite the Carl's wife and he cannot eat or drink for love of her. The Carl reads his thoughts and tells him to drink his wine; sin is sweet, but the lady is his and Gawain cannot have her. (ll. 403–14)	These supper scenes are not in this version.
The Carl's daughter is brought forward, and she harps and sings of love and Arthur's feats of arms. (ll. 415–38)	
Gawain is taken to the Carl's chamber and told to get into bed. Then the Carl bids his wife get into the bed. Gawain is undressed by a squire. The Carl then says, "'Syr Gawene, Go take my wyfe in þi armus tweyne And kys her in my syȝte.'" Gawain replies, "'Syr, þi byddynge schall be doune Sertaynly in dede, Kyll or sley or laye adoune'" [Even if you strike or kill or throw me down]. He gets into bed with great speed and there wishes to complete the sexual act. The Carl stops him: "'Whoo ther. That game I þe forbede.'" (ll. 442–68)	Immediately after the spear-throwing, the Carl takes Gawain by the hand and they go into a bedchamber, where the Carl's wife is in bed. Gawain is ordered to get into bed and kiss the lady three times while the Carl watches: "'Looke thou doe no other villanye.'" Gawain's flesh begins to warm and he wishes to go further. "'Hold!,'" cries the Carl, "'man, stopp thee! Itt were great shame . . . for me That thou sholdest doe me such villanye.'" (ll. 331–46)
Then the Carl says that, since Gawain has done his bidding, he must show	

Porkington	Percy
him some kindness, and he gives him his daughter for the night. Leaving them, he says, "'My blessynge I geyfe yow bouthe to, And play togeydor all þis nyȝt.'" (ll. 469–95)	ll. 349–60
The next day, the Carl tells Gawain that twenty years ago he made a vow that anyone staying with him would be slain unless he did his bidding. Only Gawain has not had to be killed. The Carl shows Gawain the heap of bones, result of all those who disobeyed. He will now forsake his wicked ways and, for love of Gawain, make all guests welcome. (ll. 517–49)	There is no vow in this version. The next day, the Carl gets Gawain out of bed to see his heap of bones, the remains of "1500" dead men. At this point, he is told simply that the Carl and his whelps have slain these men. (ll. 361–72) After dinner, the Carl bids Gawain strike off his head. Gawain says he would rather be dead, and the Carl replies that, if he does not do it, he will strike off Gawain's head. So Gawain says, "'Sir, your bidding shall be done.'" The beheading transforms the Carl into a man, and he explains his enchantment. He had been transformed into a Carl by "nigromance" until a knight of the Round Table delivered him by beheading him. During his forty years as a Carl, ". . . none lodged within this woonn But I and my whelpes driuen them downe. And but if hee did my bidding soone I killed him and drew him downe, Euery one but only thee. Christ grant thee of his mercye. . . ." (ll. 379–418)
The Carl gives Gawain his daughter and a gift of gold. They return home and tell Arthur what wonders they have seen, and Arthur comes to meet the Carl, finally making him a knight of the Round Table. (ll. 565–636)	ll.427–88

Chart 16. The Defense Structures in Eilhart's *Tristrant*

	Opening Defenses		
Preliminary rituals (based on Cornwall) in which the hero becomes loved son of the king and his champion against enemies	Rituals in Ireland through which the hero is declared rightful winner of the lady, with the full acceptance of the lady and the king, and then renounces her in favor of the king		Under the further defense of the potion the hero takes the lady even as he gives her to the king
1. Tristrant arrives at court. Welcomed by King Mark (his uncle). Grows up at court incognito.	1. Tristrant slays the dragon and thus wins the princess (Isalde), promised to the slayer.		1. Isalde's mother gives Brangene a love potion for her daughter and Mark. It will cause great passion for four years and great love for life. Tristrant and Isalde drink it and are unable to eat or drink until they become lovers. With the help of Brangene and Kurneval they do so, to save themselves from death.
2. He defeats an invader who threatens the king's sovereignty (Morolt of Ireland), first declaring his identity to the king. He is armed by the king, in the king's armor and on the king's horse. He refuses Morolt's offer that he share his lands instead of defending the king.	2. He is healed of his burns by Isalde and she recognizes him through fitting the splinter taken from her slain kinsman (Morolt) to Tristrant's sword. Brangene says that, if she reveals this to the king, she will have to marry the steward, who is pretending to be the dragon slayer ("such a thief"). Thus Isalde accepts that Tristrant is to be her husband. She dresses him finely, and he looks so handsome that she kisses him on the lips.		2. On the wedding night, Brangene takes Isalde's place because the potion is her fault. Thus the king does not suspect the love affair.
3. He is poisoned during the conflict and he stinks, so he lives outside the city. He is then healed in Ireland by its princess (Isalde), using disguise, since he is Ireland's enemy. He relieves Ireland's famine.	3. Isalde makes known to the king that she knows the real dragon slayer. She says this dragon slayer deserves the king's favor, and the king says, "whatever he may		3. Isalde arranges for Brangene's murder, fearing she will tell. Brangene pleads, telling her killers her story without revealing the truth. They kill a dog instead. Isalde is glad. The hero's agent
4. King Mark does not wish to marry; he			

wants Tristrant for son and heir. But the kingdom desires his marriage, so Tristrant is sent to find a queen. His ship is blown to Ireland.

5. The king of Ireland orders that the foreigners be beheaded. Tristrant offers to relieve the kingdom's famine, but there is little faith in this strategy. While they wait to hear from the king, they learn of a dragon harming the land.

have done to me will be forgiven because of this." Isalde replies, "Kiss me, father, for the warrior, and make a complete and lasting peace with him," and the king says he fully pardons him from this day.

4. The king and Tristrant gather their people. The steward thinks he is to receive the princess at this gathering. When Isalde leads Tristrant forward, the king asks who he is, but she says he must kiss Tristrant first. The king kisses Tristrant and grants a firm pardon to him and all his family.

5. Then Isalde tells the king who Tristrant is. The king tells Tristrant that, if his deed had not already been pardoned, he would have been scorned. As it is, what he has done against him is fully forgiven.

6. The thief is proved a thief by Tristrant, and eliminated from the situation.

7. Tristrant renounces the lady in favor of his uncle. The king gladly agrees that King Mark should be the one to have her.

8. The king places Isalde in Tristrant's charge, on Tristrant's oath that he will consider her fully with honor ("mit êren wol bedéchte") and bring her to his uncle.

(Brangene) is ritually tested and established as reliable.

(continued)

(Continued)

Defended Adventures	Closing Defenses	
	The defenses to close the plot begin with the sword between the lovers	The hero safely returns the queen to the king through the hermit Ugrim strategy
Any arrangement of amorous adventures can appear in this part of the plot: the defenses have created the conditions in which amorous feelings can be given full play.	The sword between the lovers episode is a trick, in keeping with the defended adventures—the king is tricked from his wedding night onwards—but it is bound up with the hermit's negotiations, in which the king's conviction of the lovers' innocence plays a vital part.	The priest Ugrim is used for the removal of guilt upon the return of the queen: when he yields up Isalde, Ugrim gives him absolution.
These adventures are much concerned with suspicion, and various strategies are used to remove it, but these strategies are not part of a step-by-step move structure; the intent is no more than play.	It is likely that the king's taking back a wife he believes innocent is more acceptable than his taking back a tainted queen: hence his strange gullibility. The hero needs an emblem that can give convincing form to the king's acceptance of his queen's chastity, while it also expresses the opposite—the truth. Such an emblem plays an important role in dealing with the sense of guilt in the plot.	Ugrim is also used as a character with the power to persuade the king to take the queen back. Ugrim is the king's confessor, and he writes to the king, asking him to take back his wife. The letter is given to the king by Tristrant, with the words that Ugrim grants the king God's salvation and imposes the contents of the letter as a penance for all his sins.
The strategies used are distinguished by their impudent trickery.		
In the Eilhart version, the adventures included are the tryst under the tree, the flour on the floor adventure, and the period in the forest. The chief feature is that the lovers can be together.	The king goes through certain rituals: the exchange of swords and the laying of his glove on Isalde.	The king, in response, refers only to the accusations of the councilors, swearing that Tristrant has never had the queen as his woman—he had only been kind to her and too fond of her. However, he disagrees with Ugrim over Tristrant's

return to his favor: he refuses to have Tristrant back at court.

It is probably the case that the hero does not wish to end his story back at court. In another defended narrative, Gawain refuses to return to the Green Knight's castle for a reconciliation with the lady. Where the lady has been finally ritually renounced—as an essential part of the defenses enabling the adventure to take place—the hero's renunciation is best expressed by his departure. However, the hermit's request to the king that Tristrant be taken back into favor plays a role: it establishes a favorable view of the hero. Moreover, with such a safeguard as the queen's being returned safely, there need be no sense that there can never be a return.

Chart 17. The Defense Structures in Beroul's *Tristran*

			Defended Adventures
There are scraps of evidence suggesting that Beroul used the opening defenses found in Eilhart, but there is nothing to indicate the rituals used in Ireland.			
Preliminary rituals (based on Cornwall) in which the hero becomes champion against the king's enemies	Rituals in Ireland through which the hero is declared rightful winner of the lady and then renounces her in favor of the king	Under the further defense of the potion the hero takes the lady even as he gives her	
1. Tristran came to Mark from over the sea (v. 161, Fedrick 50).	1. Tristran killed "the huge crested dragon, for which [Yseut] was given to [him]" (vv. 2558–61, Fedrick 104).	1. "you have heard of the wine they drank which caused them to suffer greatly for so long.... Yseut's mother, who brewed it, made it for three years of love. She made it for Mark and her daughter; [Tristran] tasted it and suffered because of this." The love-drink had power over Tristran and Yseut for three years. (vv. 2133–46, Fedrick 95–96)	Similar to those in Eilhart.
2. For the honor of the king, Tristran armed himself and fought Morholt, driving him away; no one else dared to do so (vv. 136–42, Fedrick 50; vv. 848–55, Fedrick 66). Tristran killed Morholt (vv. 27–28, Fedrick 48).	2. Yseut cured him from the wound the dragon gave him (vv. 483–86, Fedrick 57).		
3. Tristran had to endure great pain from a wound Morholt gave him (vv. 50–53, Fedrick 48; vv. 857–58, Fedrick 66).	The act of giving Yseut to the king is referred to in contexts where it is a defense against accusations. When planning the letter to the king, the hermit says, "You took her from her own land to give to him in marriage. All that was done, he well	We are not told the duration of the potion until it wears off.	

The killing of Morholt is referred to in a context where it is a defense against the condemnation of Tristran, after the flour on the floor episode (vv. 847–59, Fedrick 66), and also in vv. 141–44 ("For the honour of the king I armed myself; I did battle with Morholt and drove him away. My dear uncle ought not to believe the slanders that are told about me," Fedrick 50).

knows. He was married in Lantyan" (vv. 2391–94, Fedrick 101). In the letter itself, Tristran's opening lines say, "Sire, remember well your marriage with the king of Ireland's daughter. I crossed the sea to Ireland and I won her by my prowess. I killed the huge, crested dragon, for which she was given to me. I brought her to your country, sire, where you took her to wife, as all your knights saw" (vv. 2556–64, Fedrick 104). The two contradictory defenses are stated here—that Tristran acknowledged the king's prior right to the queen and that she had rightfully been given to Tristran.

2. Nothing relating to the wedding night has survived in the text.

(continued)

(Continued)

Closing Defenses		Additional Defenses	
The defenses to close the plot begin with the sword between the lovers	The hero safely returns the queen to the king through the hermit Ogrin strategy	Exculpation ritual through Yseut's ambiguous oath	The removal of the three spying accusers
As in Eilhart. The lovers remain dressed and the king takes note of this. The king says he will give them a sign so that they will know for certain that someone found them asleep and took pity on them, and that neither the king nor anyone else in the kingdom is in any way seeking their death. He takes the queen's ring, which he had given her, and also Tristran's sword—calling it the sword that split Morholt's head—putting his own in its place; he shields Yseut from the sun with his gloves, which	As in Eilhart. We are told at this juncture that the potion had had power for only three years, and this power has now passed. This version does not use the detail in Eilhart that the hermit is the king's confessor. The hermit tells the lovers that God will pardon them and advises that he and they will have to think of some suitable falsehoods to remove the shame and cover up the wrong. He advises Tristran to write a letter to the king, using for its persuasive power a challenge to any-	Yseut swears an oath by holy relics, and before a great company including King Arthur, that no man ever came between her thighs except her husband and the leper who helped her cross the mire on her way to this event. The leper is Tristran in disguise. The oath, emphasizing the leper's position between Yseut's legs, is accepted immediately, and King Arthur, as the queen's surety, begs the king never to believe her accusers. Tristran remains hidden "with few worries."	In this fragment, Tristran is engaged in killing the three accusing barons as they spy on his meeting with Yseut in her bedroom.

she brought from Ireland. Beroul's plot invests more power in this part of the defenses than does Eilhart's.	one who accuses him of loving the queen dishonorably; he can give this advice because no knight will dare to take up the challenge. When the letter is read out, the barons say, "King, take back your wife. The men whose accusations of the queen we have just been reminded of acted unwisely." This text makes use throughout of three accusing barons, denounced by the narrator as wicked liars.

The king replies generously that he is willing to forgo all his anger towards Yseut and will gladly take her back. Tristran will not be received back, but may be sent for later. |

Chart 18. The Cambridge Fragment and *Tristrams saga* Compared

Saga Version	Cambridge Fragment
Ok bar þá svá til einn dag, at þau sátu bæði saman í einum eplagarði, ok helt Tristram dróttningu í fangi sér; ok er þau hugðust þar óhætt búa, þá fell þeim leyniligr atburðr til, at konungr kom þar gangandi ok hinn illi dvergr með hánum, ok hugðist hann þá finna þau í syndum bæði; en þau váru sofandi. Sem konungrinn sá þau, þá mælti hann til dvergsins: "Bíð mín, meðan ek geng í kastalann, ok skal ek leiða þangat mestu menn mína, at sjá, með hverjum atburð er vér hǫfum fundit þau bæði saman hér, ok skal ek láta þau á báli brenna, er þau verða fundin bæði saman!" Sem konungrinn mælti þetta, þá vaknaði Tristram ok lét ekki á sér finnast, stóð upp skjótt ok mælti: "Harmr er nú, Ísönd, unnusta mín! Vakna nú, því(at) vélar eru til okkar gørvar ok um okkr legit! Markis konungr hefir nú hér verit ok sét hvat vit hǫfum gørt, ok gekk hann nú eptir mǫnnum sínum í hǫllina, ok ef hann getr fundit okkr bæði samt, þá mun hann láta brenna okkr (at) kǫldum kolum. En nú vil ek, hin fríðasta unnusta mín! á burtu fara, en þú þarft ekki at þínu lífi óttast, því(at) þeir mega øngum sǫnnum sǫkum á þik koma, ef engi maðr finnst hjá nema þú ein. En ek vil burt fara í annat ríki, ok sakir þín mun ek bera harm ok hugsótt alla mína daga. Nú er mér svá mikill angr at okkrum skilnaði, at aldri fæ ek huggun í þessu lífi. Hin sœtasta unnusta! Ek bið þik, at þú gleymir mér aldri, þó(at) ek sé	Entre ses bras Yseut la reïne. Bein cuidoient estre aseor. Sorvient i par estrange eor Li rois, que li nains i amene. Prendre les cuidoit a l'ovraine, Mes, merci Deu, bein i demorerent Quant aus endormis les troverent. Li rois les voit, au naim a dit: "Atendés moi chi un petit; En cel palais la sus irai, De mes barons i amerrai: Verront com les avon trovez; Ardoir les frai, quant ert pruvez." Tristran s'esvella a itant, Voit le roi, mes ne fait senblant: Car el palés va il son pas. Tristram se dreche et dit: "A! las! Amie Yseut, car esvelliez: Par engien somes agaitiez Li rois a veü quanque avon fait, Au palais a ses omes vait; Fra nos, s'il puet, ensenble prendre, Par jugement ardoir en cendre. Je m'en voil aler, bele amie, Vox n'avét garde de la vie, Car ne porez estre provée * * * * * * * * * Fuir deport et querre eschil, Guerpir joie, sievre peril. Tel duel ai por la departie Ja n'avrai hait jor de ma vie. Ma doce dame, je vos pri Ne me metés mie en obli: En loing de vos autant m'amez Comme vos de pres fait avez. Je n'i os, dame, plus atendre;

fjarri: unn þú mér jafnmikit fráveranda sem þú hefir mér nærveranda! Vit, ei má ek lengr hér dveljast, því(at) þeir er hata okkr, koma hér skjótt. Nú kyss mik í þessum skilnaði, ok gæti okkar guð ok varðveiti okkr!" Dvaldist Ísond í lengra lagi; sem hun skildi rœðu Tristrams ok sá hann bera sik illa, þá runnu henni tár ok andvarpaði af ǫllu hjarta ok svarar þá harmsfullum orðum: "Mínn kærasti unnusti!" kvað hun, "at sǫnnu sómir þér þenna dag at muna, at vit skiljum svá hǫrmuliga; svá er mér mikil písl at okkar skilnaði, at aldri vissa ek fyrri svá mjǫk, hvat harmr eðr hugsótt var, angr eðr óró! Eigi mun ek huggun fá, frið né fǫgnuð, ok aldri kvídda ek svá mínu lífi sem nú okkrum skilnaði! Nú ei at síðr skaltu þiggja þetta fingrgull, ok varðveit vel fyrir mínar sakir."
(Kölbing, *Die nordische Version der Tristan Sage* 81, ll. 31–37; 82, ll. 1–24)

Or me baisiés au congié prendre."

De li baisier Yseut demore,
Entent les dis et voit qu'il plore;
Lerment si oil, du cuer sospire,
Tendrement dit: "Amis, bel sire,
Bien vos doit menbrer de cest jor
Que partistes a tel dolor.
Tel paine ai de la desevranche
Ains mais ne sui que fu pesanche.
Ja n'avrai mais, amis, deport,
Quant j'ai perdu vostre confort,
Si grand pitié, ne tel tendrour
Quant doi partir de vostre amor;
Nos cors partir ore convient,
Mais l'amor ne partira nient.
Nequedent cest anel pernés:
Por m'amor, amis, le gardés;
* * *
(Wind 31–33)

(continued)

(Continued)

Translation of Saga	Translation of Fragment
It happened one day that he and Ísönd were sitting together in an orchard, and Tristram held the queen in his arms. And when they thought they were in no danger, an unforeseen event befell them, for the king came into the orchard with the evil dwarf, and he believed that he had caught them in sin, and both were asleep.	* * * the Queen in his arms. They fully imagined they were safe. But, by a strange chance, the King suddenly appeared, led there by the dwarf. He was thinking he would catch them in the deed, but, thank God, they were decently composed when these two found them sleeping. The King sees them and says to the dwarf: "Wait here for me a little. I shall go up to the Palace and fetch some of my barons. They shall see how we have found them. When the fact is proved I shall have them burnt!"
As soon as the king caught sight of them, he said to the dwarf, "Wait for me here while I go to the castle to fetch my most distinguished men so that they can see under what circumstances we have found the two of them here. I shall have them burned at the stake if my men see them together."	Then Tristran awakes. He sees the King, but gives no sign, for the King is making for the Palace. Tristran sits up. "Alas!" says he, "Ysolt, my love, wake up, do! We are being treacherously spied upon! The King has seen what we have been at and he is going to the Palace for his men. He will have us seized together, if he can, and condemned to be burned to ashes! I am going away, fair love! Your life is not in danger, for you cannot be convicted * * *
While the king was saying this, Tristram awoke, but he pretended not to be awake. Then he got up quickly and said, "My dearest Ísönd, wake up, something terrible has happened. We have been tricked and betrayed. King Markis was here and saw what we did, and has gone to his hall for witnesses. If they are able to see us together, he will have us burned to ashes. But now, my most lovely sweetheart, I intend to depart. You need not fear for your life, for no true charges can be brought against you if no one else is found here but you. But I shall go abroad to some other country. For your sake I will endure grief and anguish all the rest of my days. I feel such deep sorrow because of our parting that I shall never find consolation in this life. My sweetest darling, I beg you never to forget me even though I am far away. Love me as much when I am far away from you as you did when I was close to	* * * flee pleasure and seek exile, abandon joy, follow danger! This parting so afflicts me that I shall never be happy again! Sweet lady, I pray you, do not forget me—love me when I am far away as much as you have done while I was near. I dare wait no longer, my lady. Now kiss me at our leavetaking!"
	Ysolt is slow to give her kiss. She hears what he says, and sees that he is weeping. Her eyes fill with tears and she sighs from her heart. "My dear, fair lord," she says tenderly, "you must ever

you. You know that I cannot remain here any longer, for those who hate us will soon be here. Now kiss me farewell, and may God guard and protect us."

Ísönd remained there somewhat longer. When she heard Tristram's words and saw his distress, she wept and sighed from the bottom of her heart and replied with sorrowful words.

"My dearest darling," she said, "it behooves you in truth to remember this day on which we part in such unhappiness. I feel such terrible torment at our parting that I have never fully understood before what grief and concern, and care and distress really are. I shall never again find comfort and consolation, nor peace and joy. Never before did I suffer such apprehension for my life as I do now at our parting. All the same, you are to have this finger ring, and guard it well for my sake." (Schach 104–5)

remember this day when you went away in such grief. This separation gives me such pain that never before have I known what it was to suffer. I shall never be happy again, dear love, since I have lost your consolation; I shall never know such tender pity as now when I must part from your love. Our bodies now must part, but our love will never be sundered. Take this ring, nevertheless. Guard it well, my love, for my sake!" * * *
(Hatto, Appendix 2)

Chart 19. The Defended Narrative in *The Pursuit of Diarmaid and Gráinne*

Opening Defenses
Rituals at Tara through which it is declared right that the hero should take the lady from her husband [in the older tale she is already married to him]; the hero himself declares it wrong and he is overruled
1. *The lady puts the hero in her magical power.* During the betrothal feast at Tara, when Cormac, King of Ireland, gives his daughter Gráinne to the widowed Fionn mac Cumhaill, Gráinne puts almost everyone to sleep by means of a potion and takes a seat between Oisín son of Fionn and Diarmaid ó Duighne. She proposes to Oisín that he take his father's place as her husband; he replies that he will not have anything to do with a woman betrothed to Fionn. Then she proposes to Diarmaid; he replies that it is not right for him to have anything to do with a woman betrothed to Oisín, were she not betrothed to Fionn. Then she puts Diarmaid under bonds (lit. taboos) of strife and destruction, if he does not take her with him out of that house before Fionn and the king wake. "'Wicked are those bonds which you have put on me, woman,'" Diarmaid says, and he asks her why she has done this to him rather than to other worthier men, and she tells him how she fell in love when watching his exploits in a game of hurling: she did not give her love to any other person from that time to this. Diarmaid says it is a wonder that she should give that love to him instead of to Fionn, since there is not in Ireland a man more worthy of a woman than he. He adds that Fionn has the keys to Tara, so they cannot leave. Gráinne says there is an escape door out of her chamber, but Diarmaid replies that it is a taboo of his to go through any escape door whatsoever. Gráinne says he can make a special champion's escape, while she uses the escape door.
2. *The hero's friends give him ritual advice.* Diarmaid asks his friends for advice. Oisín replies, "'You are not guilty of those bonds . . . and I say to you to follow Gráinne and to protect yourself well against the old guile of Fionn mac Cumhaill.'" Osgar replies, "'I say to you to follow Gráinne . . . for he is a doomed man who violates his bonds.'" Caoilte replies, "'I would rather than the wealth of the world that it were to me that she had given that love.'" Diorraing replies, "'I say to you to follow Gráinne . . . and your death will come of it, and I regret it.'" Mac Lughach replies, "'it is not becoming of you to refuse the daughter of the king of Ireland.'" "'Is that the advice of you all to me?'" asks Diarmaid; "'It is,' said Oisín and all the others together" (15). After that Diarmaid rises and, after sadly taking leave, he puts the shafts of his two spears under him and lifts himself with a "wild, light leap," landing firmly on his feet outside Tara. He greets Gráinne with, "'this is a bad journey on which you have come, for it would be better for you to have Fionn mac Cumhaill for a lover than myself, and I do not know where I should take you now.'"

Chart 19

Defended Adventures	Closing Defenses	
1. The couple travel, taking steps to throw off the scent, till they reach the grove Doire Dá Bhaoth. Diarmaid makes a clearing with seven doors, and here the couple lie hidden. Fionn pursues them, and Diarmaid's Otherworld foster-father Aonghus of the Brugh (once a divinity) saves Gráinne, while Diarmaid refuses to be rescued and arranges his own escape. Aonghus leaves the next day, giving advice. When the couple depart, Diarmaid leaves a spit of cooked flesh without a bite taken out of it, as a sign for Fionn that he has not taken Gráinne sexually; another time he leaves a salmon on the bank of the Leanhain cooked likewise. "Wherefore it was that Fionn hastened after him" (33). [17–29]	The taking of the lady is forgiven, justified, and upheld through the use of the magical Aonghus. The peace lasts sixteen years	The hero pays the price for taking the lady, dying with honor
2. Muadhán joins them, fishing for them and keeping watch, while Diarmaid engages in exploits (29–45). The couple continue chaste, but, after Muadhán departs and they arrive in Dubhros, a splash of water springs up beside Gráinne's leg and she says it is more daring than Diarmaid; they become lovers (47). Diarmaid rises early next day and goes to see the giant Searbhán Lochlannach: he makes a bond of contract and agreement with him, getting his permission to hunt, while never touching his berries. [29–47]	Aonghus makes a peace between Diarmaid and Fionn, which lasts sixteen years. Diarmaid keeps Gráinne, with a cantred from the king as her dowry, and he receives the best cantred in Ireland as a gift from the king; he also receives a cantred that belonged to his father, on which Fionn will not be allowed to hunt, and the king will have no right of rent or tribute.	As in tradition, Diarmaid is slain in a fight with the Wild Boar of Ben Gulban, and the present narrative invents a magic healing property for Fionn which he fails to use to save Diarmaid, so that he becomes the cause of his death.
3. While the couple are at Dubhros, there is much additional material in the text, but Fionn again takes up the chase when Diarmaid kills Searbhán and gains possession of the magical quicken tree and its berries. He sends some berries to Fionn who recognizes them and knows who picked them, and that it was he who killed the giant. He goes to see whether he can catch him at the quicken tree. Diarmaid and Gráinne hide in the tree, with Fionn below, and, once again, Aonghus rescues Gráinne while Diarmaid escapes (65–77). [47–77]	Diarmaid and Gráinne live in great prosperity under the protection of Aonghus. [79]	Fionn is unwilling, rather than vengeful, finally bringing his healing drink too late. Diarmaid dies because of Fionn's resentment against him for taking Gráinne. [83–97] Amid the grief of the Fiana, Aonghus comes to mourn for Diarmaid and take his body. [97–101] Only one manuscript has Gráinne return to Fionn, finally. Other texts have her spending the rest of her days in sadness or exhorting her children to vengeance.

Chart 20. Saxo Grammaticus's Hamlet Plot

1

The brothers Orvendil and Fengi are made joint governors of Jutland by the Danish king Rorik. Orvendil devotes himself to piracy, gaining high renown. He defeats the king of Norway and gains favor with Rorik by giving him his choicest plunder. Thus he gains Rorik's daughter Gerutha for his wife. She bears him a son Amleth.

The jealous Fengi kills Orvendil and takes possession of his wife.

Amleth pretends to be an imbecile to save his life and prevent suspicion as he prepares for vengeance. He sits listless and unwashed near his mother's hearth, making wooden hooks and hardening them in the fire; when asked why he does this, he says he is getting these stings sharp to avenge his father.

2

Amleth is laughed at, and yet his skill is noticed, and it is decided to test him to find out whether he is simulating stupidity, the means being to bring him together with a supremely attractive woman who can lure him into sexual entanglement. He is sent to a distant part of the forest on horseback with companions, one of whom is his foster brother, who has no doubt that Amleth will come to grief if he gives any sign of his true sanity, above all if he openly performs the sexual act. Amleth is well aware of this. He gets on his horse backwards and guides it by its tail, thus overcoming his uncle's plot. On the journey, he speaks in ways that skillfully disguise truth with nonsense. On encountering the woman, he is prevented from having his pleasure with her by the silent warning of his foster brother; this warning is a horsefly with a straw inserted beneath its tail. Interpreting this to mean an ambush, he takes the woman to a remote and trackless fen and has intercourse with her there. He earnestly begs for her silence about it and she readily promises it as she is his foster sister,

3

Then one of Fengi's friends suggests to Fengi that Amleth should be shut up alone with his mother in her bedroom after a spy has been planted without either of them knowing. If Amleth were in his right mind he would trust his mother and be ready to speak openly in her hearing. This friend is to be the spy, and Fengi pretends to leave on a long journey.

But Amleth finds and kills the spy before the interview; he chops up and cooks the body and throws it into an open sewer for the pigs.

Then he upbraids his mother, who is weeping over his folly, for her incestuous marriage to her husband's murderer. He tells her he is playing the fool in order to survive and avenge his father. She should be weeping over her own dishonor. He shows her how to set the fires of her previous love before the lures ("illecebris") of the present.

When asked whether he has seen Fengi's friend anywhere, he says he has gone to the

4 Fengi still suspects that Amleth is feigning, and he wants to do away with him, but to do so himself would incur the disfavor of his wife and her royal father. So he sends Amleth to the king of Britain, together with two of his own parasites, bearing a letter engraved on wood requesting that the king slay the young man sent over to him. Before leaving, Amleth secretly asks his mother to hang tapestries around the hall and conduct a pretended funeral for him after a year has gone by—when, he promises, he will return. On the voyage, Amleth steals the letter and alters it so that his companions are to be killed. He also adds a request that the British king should give his daughter to the youth of great judgment sent to him.	(4 continued) On arrival, Amleth spurns the state banquet, and the king finds out why by having a servant overhear Amleth's conversation with his companions. Amleth is overheard saying that the bread was tainted with blood and the drink had the flavor of iron, while the banquet meat was smothered in the odor of a corpse. He is also heard saying that the king has the eyes of a slave and his queen has three mannerisms like those of a maidservant. His companions reply that this is aggressive and disrespectful talk about a famous king and a lady of impeccable conduct. The king investigates Amleth's allegations and finds them all true. The corn for the bread was grown in a field where there had once been a massacre, the	(4 continued) pigs providing the pork had fed on the carcass of a robber, and the water in the drink had come from a spring containing rusted swords (in other versions, Saxo tells us, the bees providing honey for the drink had been bred in the belly of a corpse). The king's mother, meanwhile, confesses that the king is the son of a slave and the queen is found to be the daughter of a female slave. The king worships Amleth's powers and gives him his daughter in marriage. The two companions he hangs the next day.
	and they were brought up together. When they are later jeeringly questioned, Amleth speaks the truth, skillfully making it sound like nonsense, and the girl denies that they made love.	sewer and been devoured by the pigs. This seems senseless to everyone.

(continued)

(Continued)

5

Amleth returns to Jutland and enters the banqueting hall as the fool once more. The guests are frightened at first, but then laugh at the idea of their having held a funeral for someone who, after all, turns up. To amuse them more, Amleth becomes a cupbearer. He often unsheathes his sword and pricks his fingers with the point, so they have the sword and scabbard riveted through with an iron pin. Amleth makes the nobles drunk so that they go to sleep in the hall, and then he pins them down with his mother's tapestries, using the books he has made, and sets fire to the hall. Next, he finds Fengi in his bedchamber, and substitutes his own sword for Fengi's before he wakes him. Fengi cannot draw the sword, and Amleth slays him with Fengi's own sword.

6

Amleth is then afraid, not knowing how his countrymen will react, and he decides to wait in hiding. But the populace is calm, and he makes a speech, explaining that Fengi was a murderer, not a monarch, and it was best that he himself should punish him, without involving the people in the danger. He exhorts the crowd to carry out their own revenge on the body of a man who has been a tyrant, robbing them of their rights, and a fratricide. He refers to his own sorrows and pretence of imbecility, and says that they should now rejoice that the queen's disgrace is at an end.

Then he asks them to grant him the kingdom, if he has earned it. He is the lawful inheritor of the realm and dutiful avenger of fratricide. To him they owe the removal of a tyrant. They are amazed at his abilities, and he is appointed king by prompt and general acclaim.

7

Amleth returns to Britain to see his wife and father-in-law, taking with him a shield he has had made, with pictures painted on it depicting all his exploits so far related, in precise detail.

The British king is hospitable, but, when he learns that Amleth has killed Fengi, he is aghast because he is bound by an old promise to avenge him. In order not to break the laws of hospitality, he chooses to execute the role of avenger by another's hand. He sends Amleth to woo the Scottish queen Herminthrud on his behalf (his own wife has died), and this queen kills all her suitors.

Amleth rests not far from the queen's palace and, while he is asleep, the queen's men steal the shield, which he is using as a pillow, and the British king's letter. The queen studies the shield and learns that its owner has punished his uncle for his father's murder. She alters the letter, having it ask her to

8

The princess of Britain decides that it is beneath her dignity to complain, and she warns Amleth to beware of her father, since he has transferred the profit of his mission to himself and foiled the wishes of the man who sent him.

The king unsuccessfully attacks him and he escapes, sending back to the king Herminthrud's servant, captured when returning the shield and letter. He intends to throw the blame back on the queen, but the king attacks again, killing most of his troops. In order to seem to have more forces, Amleth props up his dead men so that they seem alive and about to join combat. The king's men are terrified, conquered by the corpses. The king is killed.

9

Amleth returns to Jutland with his wives.

Viglek has succeeded Rorik to the Danish throne. He has harassed Amleth's mother with every kind of insolence and deprived her of her royal wealth, and he goes on to charge Amleth of seizing control of Jutland and cheating the Danish king, whose prerogative it is to confer and remove the duties of high office. Amleth gives the king the finest spoils of his victory, but afterwards he seizes a chance of taking vengeance, attacking and subduing him and becoming an open foe.

Viglek challenges Amleth to war, and, fearing death, Amleth wishes to secure a second marriage for Herminthrud. She protests, promising that she will not forsake him even in the field and saying she hates the woman who would be afraid to join her husband at his end.

Viglek kills Amleth, and Herminthrud then marries Viglek.

(7 continued)

marry the bearer. She also makes sure that the letter refers to the adventures on the shield, so that the shield and letter confirm each other. The shield and letter are then returned to Amleth. Amleth has only pretended not to be aware of the thefts, and he grabs the man returning them and has him fettered. The queen warmly commends Amleth's achievements and intelligence, and she pronounces that Fengi has been punished legitimately. She says she is puzzled by his one mistake of marrying the daughter of slaves. However, there is a lady he can take whose rank is equal to his own. The man she honors with her bed, moreover, receives a kingdom together with her caresses. Her scepter and her hand go together.

Their marriage is celebrated.

Chart 21. The Plots of Saxo Grammaticus's Hamlet, *Bevis of Hampton*, and *Meriadoc* Compared

	Saxo	Bevis	Meriadoc
A¹	A ruler (of Jutland) is killed by his brother (Fengi), who takes his kingdom and wife. His son Amleth is a child in danger.	An earl (of South-Hampton) is killed by a usurper who takes his wife and land. His son Bevis is a child in danger	A ruler (of Cambria) is killed by his brother, who takes the kingdom. His son Meriadoc is a child in danger.
	Amleth pretends to be a listless simpleton as he secretly prepares for vengeance.	Bevis is saved from death by his tutor, who hides him in the guise of a shepherd. When he attacks the usurper, he is sold to merchants.	Meriadoc is hanged and rescued by his foster father, who brings him up in a forest for the next five years. He is then transported to those who later assist his revenge.
	He is sent to Britain with a letter requesting his death.		
B	He wins the friendship of the king of Britain and marries his daughter.	He wins the friendship (temporally) of the king of Armenia, and the king's daughter Josian falls in love with him.	
		After Josian is married to a king, Bevis takes her away with him.	
A²	Following the marriage, he avenges his father.	He avenges his father, becomes the earl, and marries Josian, now a queen.	With the help of friendly kings (Arthur and Urien), he avenges his father.

Chart 21 · 209

		Second Part	
A¹	Amleth becomes king and leaves for Britain carrying a shield depicting the major events of his life.	Bevis's horse kills the English king's son, and Bevis goes into exile with Josian, Terri, and the giant Ascopart.	Meriadoc becomes king, but leaves his kingdom in the care of King Urien, as he wishes to be free for knighthood.
			He spends an interim time at Arthur's court and becomes his champion, receiving land from him and bestowing it upon the rightful claimants.
B¹	The British king welcomes him at first, but then sends him to Queen Herminthrud, slayer of suitors, in order to avenge Fengi.	The giant Ascopart abducts Josian after she gives birth to twin sons. Foster parents are found for the babies.	He becomes a knight in the service of the emperor of the Alemanni, in his war with King Gundebald, who has abducted his daughter.
			He enters two castles of fear, with a lady at a table, and is brave enough to take what he wants (food) the second time.
			He defeats Gundebald's brother and takes over his kingdom. The emperor promises him both his gains in land and the princess, if he rescues her.

(continued)

210 · Chart 21

(Continued)

	Saxo	Bevis	Meriadoc
C	Queen Herminthrud in Scotland reads the shield and marries Amleth. She tells him that "whatever man she honoured with her bed was actually king, and received a realm and her caresses together."	Bevis wins the hand of a princess in a tournament, but she allows him seven years' grace to find his wife before consummating the marriage.	At the invitation of the emperor's daughter, he goes to Gundebald's kingdom and rescues her, killing the king. She has been sovereign lady in that kingdom. The people wish him to be king.
B^2		Bevis's former tutor rescues Josian, and, after seven years, they find Bevis.	On his return to the emperor, he is imprisoned. The princess is to be married to the invading king of Gaul, in return for peace.
	The king of Britain makes war on him, and he defeats and kills the king.	Josian's former husband King Yvor makes war on him, and Bevis defeats and kills him, taking over his kingdom.	He joins forces with the king of Gaul, and the emperor is defeated and killed for his treachery.
A^2	The king of Denmark declares him a usurper and kills him. Queen Herminthrud marries the king of Denmark.		Both the princess and his conquered kingdoms are restored to him.

Notes

Questions, Definitions, and Practice

1. Propp, *Morphology of the Folk Tale*. See also Guerin et al., *A Handbook of Critical Approaches to Literature*, 334.
2. See Holland, *The Shakespearian Imagination*; Ernest Jones, *Hamlet and Oedipus*; Russell, *Hamlet and Narcissus*.
3. Murray, "Hamlet and Orestes." See also Guerin et al., 171–75.
4. See Guerin et al., 17, 89; Culler, *Literary Theory*, 83–94; Bal, *Narratology*, 5; Martin, *Recent Theories of Narrative*, 9.
5. I am indebted to John Cummins for these suggestions. They are examples of the sort of multidisciplinary approaches to this material, in particular to its psychological/emotional function, that may prove fruitful in the future.
6. I arrived at these principles with the help of my reading of O'Keefe.
7. See O'Keefe, 320, for various studies of rainmaking.
8. See O'Keefe, 523–70, and Keith Thomas, *Religion and the Decline of Magic*.
9. See O'Keefe, 282, and Mead, *Mind, Self and Society*, chaps. 20–22.
10. See Laplanche and Pontalis, *The Language of Psychoanalysis*, 110, 477, 399, for Anna Freud's list and explanations of "undoing" and "reversal."
11. See Freud, "Inhibitions, Symptoms and Anxiety," 274–75, 294, 326. For magic as a defense against psychic death, see his essay "The Uncanny," where he considers the magical operation of repression. In the essay he also observes that the uncanny is evoked by anything that reactivates "animistic beliefs" present in the mind although "we have *surmounted* these modes of thought." Belief in the omnipotence of thoughts, in the prompt fulfillment of wishes, in secret injurious powers, and in the return of the dead "still exist within us ready to seize upon any confirmation."

> As soon as something *actually happens* in our lives which seems to confirm the old, discarded beliefs we get a feeling of the uncanny; it is as though we were making a judgement something like this: "So, after all, it is *true* that one can kill a person by the mere wish!" or, "So the dead *do* live on and appear on the scene of their former activities!" and so on. (370–71)

12. See O'Keefe, 62–75, 79–110; (myth) 43, 224–25.
13. Róheim, *Magic and Schizophrenia*, suggests that magic defends the indi-

vidual against society (against the superego), and O'Keefe comments that he has found this hypothesis "enormously productive; it helps explain a great deal about the endless dialectic of magic and religion" (263).

14. O'Keefe, 215. See also 224 and, for initiation, 217–24.

15. For the source of the whole of this discussion of Anglo-Saxon charms, see L.M.C. Weston, "The Language of Magic in Two Old English Metrical Charms," 176–86. Weston uses E.V.K. Dobbie's edition of *Wið Færstice*, in *The Anglo-Saxon Minor Poems*, and I take my quotations from the same edition. My translation owes much to that of R. K. Gordon, in his *Anglo-Saxon Poetry*.

16. See Wilson, *The Magical Quest*, 9–10, and, for the full text of the EMIN dream, Wilson, *Traditional Romance and Tale*, 11–12. There is a useful discussion of dreams, reassessing Freud in light of later research, in Richard M. Jones, *The New Psychology of Dreaming*. Martin was a seven-year-old child whose dreams I studied in the early stages of my project (1971–74) and included in my first publication, *Traditional Romance and Tale*. The quotations from the child were taken down as he spoke during that study. He also drew pictures to describe his dreams.

17. See Kirk, *The Nature of Greek Myths*, and Lewis, *An Experiment in Criticism*, 40–49. For an important field study of myth in Ghana, see Goody, *The Myth of the Bagre*. I have published a study of Tolkien's *The Lord of the Rings* in *Magical Thought in Creative Writing*, 70–81; at the time, I was interested in it as a nonmagical text by comparison with magical texts, rather than as a mythic text. While reconsidering *The Lord of the Rings* as possibly mythic, I reconsidered *The Odyssey* (discussed as fantasy in my first book, 1976) and now see it as epic making use of mythic material for Odysseus's account of his sea voyages to the Phaeacians and of folktale and other material elsewhere in the text.

18. Liberman, in his edition of Vladimir Propp's *Theory and History of Folklore*, xxxix–xlii. See also Lévi-Strauss, *The Raw and the Cooked*. Lévi-Strauss admits that his attempts to decipher the symbols of myths are really his own writing of new versions of the myths (see O'Keefe 48).

19. For editions of *King Horn*, see Sands, *Middle English Verse Romances*, 15–54; French and Hale, *Middle English Metrical Romances*, 1:25–70; Hall, *King Horn* (giving us the three texts in parallel); and McKnight's reedition for the Early English Text Society, 1962, which also gives us all three texts in parallel.

20. For Propp, a move is a repetition of the story sequence of leaving home, adventures, victory, return, and recognition, which occurs when a fresh act of villainy creates a new initial lack in the home situation. Propp's work was a liberating experience for me at this stage of my project and an influence, but, since I was working on the thought in the texts, I slowly moved away from this influence. When describing the moves I see, I sometimes use the word *step* because it is clearer in places; a move is more complex than a step.

21. I use Reid's edition, *Yvain (Le Chevalier au Lion)*. There is a good translation by Owen, *Chrétien de Troyes: Arthurian Romances*, 281–373. My study of the romance is in *The Magical Quest*, 53–93.

22. For this study, see *The Magical Quest*, 68–73.

23. Bersani, *A Future for Astyanax*, 189–229. Leo Bersani notes that Emily Brontë tells the same story twice, the replay substituting a tamed Heathcliff in Hareton and reestablishing the family. I am interested in the replay Bersani notes and also in the filtering of the narrative through two layers of narrator, the respectable Lockwood and his informant the upright Nelly Dean. I am also interested in the roles of Joseph and the Jabes Branderham sermon (dreamed by Lockwood), where the punitive, moralizing religion of the period is caricatured and made ridiculous. It is clear that the narrative is defended against moral censure, and I find it conceivable that it might also have been used magically, if a great deal of fear demanded it. The structures seem to be there for an investment of power, creating defenses against a fear that might prevent the reader from entering into an adventure felt forbidden. For my discussion in *The Magical Quest*, see 21, 190–91, 218–19.

24. For this study, see *The Magical Quest*, 189–212.

25. See Thomas, *Eilhart von Oberge's "Tristrant,"* 74: "The king placed her in Tristrant's charge on the latter's oath that he would care for the beautiful maiden well and honorably and bring her to his uncle."

26. For my study of the Apollonius texts, see *The Magical Quest*, 24–49.

Introductory Studies

1. I use the edition of Auchinleck by Schmidt and Jacobs, *Medieval English Romances*, pt. 2, 57–88; see Hales and Furnivall, eds., *Bishop Percy's Folio Manuscript*, 3:16–48.

2. "But mice and rats and such small deer / Have been Tom's food for seven long year" (*King Lear* 3.4.132–33). These lines refer to Bevis's imprisonment in the dungeon, and they appear in the Cambridge text of *Bevis* as "Ratons & myse and soche smale dere, / That was hys mete that VII yere" (Kölbing, *Romance of Sir Beues of Hamtoun*, 74, ll. 85–86).

3. All the texts are edited by Kölbing, *Romance of Sir Beues of Hamtoun*.

4. For the Anglo-Norman version, see Stimming, *Der anglonormannische Boeve de Haumtone*.

5. For Mills's discussion of the King Horn and Bevis texts as demonstrating the exile-and-return narrative structure, see his article "Structure and Meaning in *Guy of Warwick*," 54–68.

6. See Mills, "Structure and Meaning in *Guy of Warwick*."

7. Discussing the history of the various texts of *Bevis*, Kölbing comments on a different reading: "the writer . . . may have altered the original text, thinking that it was an unnecessary and inconceivable act of cruelty on the part of Sir Beves, to deprive Terri of all hope of seeing his cousin again" (*Romance of Sir Beues of Hamtoun*, xli).

8. I use Ewert's edition, *Marie de France: Lais*, 58–74, and the translation of Burgess and Busby, *The Lais of Marie de France*.

9. I use Sands's edition, *Middle English Verse Romances*, 203–32. One of Thomas Chestre's sources, the anonymous Old French *Graelent*, presents an interesting contrast to *Lanval*: similar narrative material is used to create a very different magical text. The plot has four moves. In the first, Graelent refuses the queen's advances, professing his loyalty to the king, and her love turns to hate: by her means, he is reduced to poverty. In the second, he acquires his fairy mistress, whom he must keep secret. In the third, he refuses to join the court in declaring the queen the fairest of all women, saying he knows one fairer. He incurs the king's anger and is imprisoned. In the fourth move, the fairy mistress comes to the court and proves him right about her beauty. Graelent is released and has to pursue the lady in the forest until she relents. The first and third moves are concerned chiefly with separating the queen and the fairy mistress from each other, a magical arrangement made necessary by their essential oneness. Neither the plot itself nor its treatment are of a kind that presents problems: the magic has less to do, and there is no courtly development, creating a separate theme of the boast, such as I find in *Lanval*. Graelent breaks the fairy's injunction to secrecy, and this has the magical function of separating the two women characters. For *Graelent*, see Weingartner's edition and translation, *"Graelent" and "Guingamor": Two Breton Lays*.

10. For full details, see Mildred Leake Day, ed. and trans., *The Story of Meriadoc, King of Cambria*, xxiii–xli. The edition and translation used in my study are those of Mildred Leake Day.

11. A striking example is the Middle English "Fair Unknown" romance *Lybeaus Desconus*. But a better example here may be *The Story of Meriadoc*'s sister text, *The Rise of Gawain*, which uses similar narrative material for a plot in which a magical structure might be suspected, while there is no convincing evidence for it. The Knight of the Surcoat's curious separation from his family and ignorance of his identity, and also the recognition tokens, might seem to offer opportunities for a magical use, the narrative becoming a defended narrative, but there need to be opportunities in the later part of the text, forming closing defenses, for the text to be firmly identified as magical.

12. *Das Blumenkörbchen*. Jacob's words to Marie concerning the violet, lily, and rose, given in the first move of my chart of the plot, appear in von Schmid's original as follows:

> "Das holde Veilchen sei Dir, liebe Marie, ein Bild der Demut, der Eingezogenheit, der Wohlthätigkeit im Stillen. Es kleidet sich in die sanfte Farbe der Bescheidenheit, es blüht am liebsten im Verborgenen, es erfüllt, unter Blättern versteckt, die Luft mit dem lieblichsten Wohlgeruche. Sei auch Du, liebe Marie, ein stilles Veilchen, das einen bunten, prahlerischen Anzug verschmäht, nicht bemerkt sein will und, bis es verblüht ist, im stillen Gutes thut."

> "Die Lilie sei Dir, liebe Tochter, das Bild der Unschuld! Sieh', wie schön, wie hell und rein sie dasteht! Der weißeste Atlas ist nichts gegen ihre Blätter; sie

gleichen dem Schnee. Wohl der Jungfrau, deren Herz so rein von allem Bösen ist! Die reinste aller Farben ist aber auch am schwersten rein zu bewahren. Leicht ist ein Lilienblatt verletzt; man darf es nicht rauh anfassen, oder es bleiben Flecken zurück. So kann auch ein Wort, ein Gedanke, die Unschuld verletzen!" — "Die Rose aber . . . sei Dir, liebe Marie, das Bild der Schamhaftigkeit. Schöner als die Rosenfarbe ist die Farbe der Schamröte. Heil der Jungfrau, die über jeden unanständigen Scherz errötet und sich von der Glut, die sie auf ihren Wangen fühlt, vor Gefahr der Sünde warnen läßt. Wangen, die leicht erröten, bleiben lange schön und rot; Wangen, die nicht mehr erröten können, werden bald bleich und gelb und modern vor der Zeit im Grabe." (10–11)

13. This American adaptation was made in 1833, by a clergyman, Gregory Townsend Bedell, whose source was a French version. He altered and arranged the story so that it conveyed clear evangelical lessons. Many other translations into English, and versions of Bedell, were published in the nineteenth and early twentieth centuries, and I use one of them, *The Basket of Flowers, and Other Tales* (London: Milner, n.d.). See Renier, "Christoph von Schmid's 'The Basket of Flowers'" for details of publication.

14. There were the very popular melodramas *La Pie Voleuse*, in Paris, and *The Maid and the Magpie*, in London (1815). The theme was also the subject of Italian opera, including one by Rossini. See Renier, "Christoph von Schmid's 'The Basket of Flowers.'"

15. I use an edition published by Scott (London, 1900).

16. For my study of *Jane Eyre*, see *Magical Thought in Creative Writing*, 48–61.

17. This information was given by Michael Thornton, in a copyright article in *The Observer*, April 23, 1989. See also Margaret Forster, *Daphne du Maurier*, 137.

18. I published an early study of *Rebecca* in *Signal: Approaches to Children's Books* 36 (September 1981): 147–49 and also brief studies of *The Basket of Flowers* and *The Wide, Wide World* in *Signal* 38 (May 1982): 92–97, 99–100.

I. Emaré, Catskin, and Constance: Princesses in Exile and Accused Queens

1. Archibald, "The Flight from Incest," 259–72; Schlauch, *Chaucer's Constance and Accused Queens* (New York, 1927). There is also an interesting psychoanalytical account of the Accused Queen texts, concentrating on *La Manekine*, in Fenster, "Beaumanoir's *La Manekine*: Kin D(r)ead," 41–58. Fenster argues that the heroine is a representation of the castration anxiety expressed by the text, and as such is a means through which the childish sexual desire for the parent of the opposite sex is lived out and punished.

2. Rickert, *The Romance of Emaré*, xxvi; Mills, *Six Middle English Romances*, xiii–xv.

3. I discuss the Apollonius of Tyre texts in *The Magical Quest*, 24–49.
4. See Suchier's edition of "La Manekine," in *Oeuvres Poétiques de Philippe de Remi, Sire de Beaumanoir*, vol. 1.
5. Suchier, xxiii, xxxi; Suchier surveys the versions, xxv–lxv.
6. *Le Roman en Prose de La Manekine, par Jean Wauquelin*, edited by Suchier in *Oeuvres Poétiques de Philippe de Remi, Sire de Beaumanoir*, 1:300: "*mancus* c'est a dire homme qui n'a que une main et *manca* c'est une femme qui n'a que une main, et pource je vous mech a non *Manca* qui sera a dire en Ronmant Manequine."
7. I have used Sir Richard Burton's translation of *The Pentameron* of Giambattista Basile (1575–1632), which was first published in 1893. "Penta the Handless" is the story for the Second Diversion of the Third Day. Basile's *Lo Cunto Deli Cunti overo Lo Trattenemiento de'Peccerille*, later titled *Il Pentamerone*, first appeared in 1634.
8. For the first edition version of "Das Mädchen ohne Hände," I use the reprint edited by Panzer, *Die Kinder- und Hausmärchen der Brüder Grimm*, where the story is no. 31. For the later version, I use the Reclam edition (Stuttgart, 1980), where the story is also no. 31. The brothers Grimm have left us only a brief summary of the material they removed, in their notes; it is no longer than the translation I give in my text: "ein Vater habe seine eigene Tochter zur Frau begehrt, und als diese sich geweigert, ihre Hände (und Brüste) abschneiden und ein weißes Hemd anthun lassen, darauf sie in die Welt fort gejagt." For a discussion of this removal, see John M. Ellis, *One Fairy Story Too Many*, 77–78.
9. See particularly John M. Ellis, *One Fairy Story Too Many*. Ellis shows how we have ignored firm evidence that belies the Grimm brothers' claim that they have faithfully collected and preserved true folk material.
10. Matthew Paris's *Vita Offae Primi*, contained in *Matthaei Paris Historia Major et Duorum Offarum Merciorum Regum*, edited by William Wats in 1684; for the Accused Queen story, see 965–68. Wats's edition of the story was republished by the Chaucer Society, under the title "King Offa's intercepted letters and banisht Queen," in *Originals and Analogues of Some of Chaucer's Canterbury Tales*, pt. 1, 71–84 (1872).
11. For the relevant passage, see the Chaucer Society republication, 75.
12. For the first edition of the Grimm brothers' "Allerleirauh," see Panzer's reprint, and for the later version the Reclam edition; in both, the story is no. 65.
13. For Perrault's version of *Peau d'Asne* in verse, I use Lang's edition, *Perrault's Popular Tales*, 83–105.
14. For Trivet's "Life of Constance," see Bryan and Dempster, *Sources and Analogues of Chaucer's "Canterbury Tales,"* 165–81, and also Brock's edition and translation for the Chaucer Society, "The Life of Constance from the Anglo-Norman Chronicle of Nicholas Trivet," 1–53. For Gower's version, see his *Confessio Amantis*, edited by Macaulay, in *The English Works of John Gower*, vol. 1, bk. 2, ll. 587–1612. For Chaucer's "Man of Law's Tale," I use Robinson, *The Works of Geoffrey Chaucer*, 2d ed.

2. The King Lear Stories and Cap o' Rushes

1. This text was first published in the *Ipswich Journal*: "Suffolk Notes and Queries," and republished in *Longman's Magazine*, February 1889, 441–45; *Folk-Lore*, September 1890, 295–99; and *English Fairy Tales*, collected by Jacob Jacobs, 51–56. It is of interest here as an English text: surviving texts tend to be Continental, while the King Lear tradition belongs to Britain.

2. For this text, see Sébillot, *Littérature Orale de la Haute-Bretagne*, 45–52.

3. See Perrett, *The Story of King Lear from Geoffrey of Monmouth to Shakespeare*, and Bullough, *Narrative and Dramatic Sources of Shakespeare*, 7:269–420.

4. *The Historia Regum Britanniae of Geoffrey of Monmouth*, c. 1136, edited by Acton Griscom, 263–64. The sources of the corresponding passages are as follows: Laʒamon's *Brut*, late twelfth century, edited in *Laʒamon: "Brut"* by Brook and Leslie, 1:78 (when quoting from this edition, I have given the word "and" in full); the fifteenth-century Welsh *MS. LXI, Jesus College, Oxford*, translated by Robert Ellis Jones and published in Griscom's edition of Geoffrey of Monmouth, 263–64 (this chronicle represents much older traditional Welsh history); MS Addit. 9066, late thirteenth century, published in Sydney J. H. Herrtage, ed., *The Early English Versions of the "Gesta Romanorum,"* 49; part of the 1587 edition of Holinshed, published in Bullough, 7:317; *The True Chronicle Historie of King Leir and his three daughters* (Anon., 1605, but of earlier date), published in Bullough, 7:339–45; *King Lear*, edited by Hunter, 64; Aaron Thompson's early-eighteenth-century translation of Geoffrey of Monmouth, published in Bullough, 7:312.

5. See Dundes, "'To Love My Father All': A Psychoanalytic Study of the Folktale Source of *King Lear*," 229–44. Dundes gives full references for other such studies.

6. See Perrett, 13. There is, however, a remarkable version of the Cap o' Rushes tale from Corsica, where, in the King Lear judgment, the daughter does not give the loving-like salt reply but the Cordelia one: "'Moi, mon père, je vous aime comme une fille soumise et dévouée doit aimer un père comme vous.'" Then, at the end of the "Peau d'Ane" events that follow, when the heroine wishes her father to acknowledge his error and come to her wedding, she learns that he has been dethroned by her siblings and put in an impenetrable dungeon. He is now mad. The heroine says she will not marry her prince until her father has been restored to his throne and can attend the wedding, well in body and spirit. The parents of the young prince declare war on the ungrateful children and the king is restored to his throne, but only after a year of devotion from the daughter is he restored to his reason, so that the marriage can take place. (See Ortoli, *Les Contes Populaires de l'Ile de Corse*, 48–56.) Perhaps the best explanation for this (magical) Cap o' Rushes tale, evidently influenced by the King Lear story, is the same one that A. H. Krappe has argued for the Gascon village Hamlet tale discovered by J. F. Bladé in the nineteenth century: that the tale developed from memories of

a French translation of Shakespeare's play, made in the eighteenth or nineteenth century. (See Bullough's discussion of the sources of *Hamlet*, 7:9–10.)

3. Cinderella and Other Sovereignty Tales

1. For the old play of King Leir, see the previous chapter and note 4 for that chapter.

2. See Cox, *Cinderella*, and Dundes, "To Love My Father All."

3. For "Rashin Coatie," see *Revue Celtique* 3 (1876–78): 365–67; and *Folk-Lore*, September 1890, 289–91. I use the version in *Revue Celtique*, together with its spelling and punctuation. The informant was Margaret Craig of Darliston, Elgin (A. Lang).

4. For Perrault's "Cendrillon ou la Petite Pantoufle de Verre," I use Lang, *Perrault's Popular Tales*, 41–48. There is a translation in Lang, *The Blue Fairy Book*, 96–104.

5. See Cook, *The Ordinary and the Fabulous*, 105–7, for a consideration of the trial (initiation), recognition, and judgment themes in Perrault's version.

6. For "Roswall and Lillian," see Laing's edition, *Early Popular Poetry of Scotland and the Northern Border*, revised by W. Carew Hazlitt, 2:239–67. Lillian H. Hornstein refers to the "male Cinderella" motif in *A Manual of the Writings in Middle English*, edited by Severs, 1:153. For "The Goose-Girl" I have used Panzer's edition, 355–61, apart from altering the description of the heroine's hair from "eitel Silber" to "eitel Gold," the description of the later versions. My translation of the verse owes some debt to James Stern's revision of Margaret Hunt's translation. In Panzer's edition, the verse is as follows:

o du Falada, da du hangest. . . .

o du Jungfer Königin, da du gangest,
wenn das deine Mutter wüßte,
ihr Herz thät ihr zerspringen!

weh'! weh'! Windchen,
nimm Kürdchen sein Hütchen,
und laß'n sich mit jagen,
bis ich mich geflochten und geschnatzt
und wieder aufgesatzt.

"Die Gänsemagd" is usually given the standard number 89. I have published an earlier analysis of the story in my introduction to *Magical Thought in Creative Writing*.

7. I have used H. C. Andersen, *Eventyr og Historier*, i udvalg ved Hans Brix (Copenhagen, 1953), 205–14. I discuss this story in *Magical Thought in Creative Writing*, 62–66, where my grasp of magic was still too uncertain for a study with which I can still agree.

4. Cúroí's Castle and Its Tests

1. See, for example, Kittredge, *A Study of "Gawain and the Green Knight"*; Buchanan, "The Irish Framework of *Sir Gawain and the Green Knight*"; R. S. Loomis, "The Visit to the Perilous Castle: a study of the Arthurian modifications of an Irish theme"; Kurvinen, "*Sir Gawain and the Carl of Carlisle* in Two Versions"; and Owen, "Parallel Readings with *Sir Gawain and the Green Knight*."

2. *Syre Gawene and the Carle of Carelyle* is also edited by Sands, in *Middle English Verse Romances*, 348–98; and *Carle off Carlile* is edited by Hales and Furnivall, *Bishop Percy's Folio Manuscript*, 3:277–94.

3. See Kurvinen, 90. Kurvinen includes the "whelps" and daughter because it is possible they were thought of as tests.

4. I find a similar use of a horse in Chrétien's *Yvain* and related texts; see *The Magical Quest*, 80–83.

5. I find a similar attribute in the giant herdsman of Chrétien's *Yvain*; see *The Magical Quest*, 71.

6. For the text in the Book of the Dun Cow, see Best and Bergin, *Lebor na Huidre: Book of the Dun Cow*, which distinguishes the hands of the scribes in the print, and Henderson's edition and translation, *Fled Bricrend*. The second scribe is the thirteenth-century interpolator, known as H, who sought to turn M's text into the longer form found in later manuscripts. He encountered technical difficulties that prevented him from inserting the additions in the right places, so the Dun Cow text does not represent the longer form as well as do the later manuscripts. Nevertheless, it is this defective longer form that is best known as the story of *Bricriu's Feast*. Fortunately, it is still possible to establish the original text of M. The problems of the Dun Cow text are discussed by Slotkin, in "The structure of *Fled Bricrenn* before and after the *Lebor na hUidre* interpolations." Slotkin's method of analysis is mainly a careful reconstruction of the purposes, problems, and stratagems of the interpolator. He establishes that H only wished to add material (the material of the later versions), not to change anything that was there, and that the necessity of inserting new pages for these additions prevented his placing the additions in the correct parts of the narrative. This necessity also presented him with problems over arranging matter in the space available. One adventure—that involving the beheading bargain with Úath—is thought by Slotkin to be H's own invention, to replace the lost beheading bargain in M's text (five pages were lost from the Book of the Dun Cow at that point). H must have wished to replace it in some way, and did so by using different material, since he regarded M's core text as sacrosanct (both that part of it preserved in the book and that part of it missing). Thus, he invented his own beheading story (it shows unusual features) and inserted it where he could—a long way from a suitable place, because he could not disturb the important material relating to Cúroí's castle in that place. A good translation of the Dun Cow text, in its interpolated state, is available in Gantz, *Early Irish Myths and Sagas*, 221–55.

7. The Edinburgh fragment, which contains only the beheading bargain, is

edited and translated by Meyer in "The Edinburgh Version of the *Cennach ind Rúanado.*"

8. I have used the translation of Gantz, *Early Irish Myths and Sagas*, negotiating the interpolations (see note 6), and occasionally quote from it.

9. *Le Chevalier à l'Épée* is edited by Johnston and Owen, in *Two Old English Gauvain Romances*, 30–60. There is a translation by Elisabeth Brewer, in *From Cuchulainn to Gawain: Sources and Analogues of "Sir Gawain and the Green Knight,"* 59–74.

5. The Tristan Verse Romances and *The Pursuit of Diarmaid and Gráinne*

1. There is a helpful discussion of the Eilhart material in the introduction to J. W. Thomas's translation, *Eilhart von Oberge's "Tristrant,"* 1–4, 32–41. I use Thomas's translation for this chapter.

2. See Gallais, *Genèse du Roman Occidental*, 45. Gallais's answer to this excellent question is that it would not be a good thing to have a potion lasting a long time for a married couple: it would be neither necessary nor wise for the couple to be foolishly in love for more than three or four years.

3. I use Ewert's edition, *The Romance of Tristran by Beroul*, and Fedrick's translation, *The Romance of Tristan by Beroul*. The material I describe as Additional Defenses is known as "Beroul 2" and held by many scholars to be by another author; it is regarded by Joseph Bédier as among those "végétations parasites qui se sont développées autour de l'*estoire*" (2.265).

4. I use Pfaff's edition of the chapbook, *"Tristrant und Isalde": Prosaroman des Fünfzehnten Jahrhunderts.*

5. See Closs's edition, *Tristan und Isolt*, xxxii, and J. W. Thomas, 34–37.

6. I use Ganz's edition of Gottfried's *Tristan*.

7. I use Kölbing's edition, *Die nordische Version der Tristan Sage*.

8. I use Schach's translation, *The Saga of Tristram and Ísönd*.

9. For the Cambridge fragment, see Wind, *Les Fragments du Roman de Tristan*, 31–33, and Hatto's translation in *Tristan*, appendix 2.

10. For Gottfried's narrative corresponding with the Cambridge fragment, see ll. 18163–362 (pp. 280–82 in Hatto's translation).

11. See Gertrude Schoepperle Loomis, 108–11, 445, 472. See also the comments of Winfrey in "Kaherdin and Camille: The Sources of Eilhart's *Tristrant.*"

12. The early fragments of Eilhart are available in Bußmann's edition, *Eilhart von Oberge: "Tristrant."*

13. See Shéaghdha's edition, *Tóruigheacht Dhiarmada agus Ghráinne.*

6. The Hamlet Stories

1. The Danish History of Saxo Grammaticus is available in Fisher's translation, in *Saxo Grammaticus: The History of the Danes*, edited by Davidson. The

Amleth material from the Danish history is available in Elton's translation, in *Narrative and Dramatic Sources of Shakespeare*, edited by Bullough, 7:60–79; and, with Latin and translation in parallel texts, in *The Sources of Hamlet*, edited by Gollancz, 93–163. There is a translation also in Hansen, *Saxo Grammaticus and the Life of Hamlet*. The date of the work is c. 1200.

2. For *Ambales Saga* see Gollancz, *Hamlet in Iceland*, 1–191; the Icelandic and translation appear in parallel texts. The Hamlet material is interwoven with Tamburlaine material, and the narrative is a tale of vengeance for a father's death, ending happily with Ambales as king. This late-sixteenth- or seventeenth-century work probably used native Icelandic sources rather than Saxo's account of Amleth (see Hansen 13). For *Brjáms-Saga* see Gollancz, *Hamlet in Iceland*, 247–49 (Icelandic) and *The Sources of Hamlet*, 73–79 (translation). *Brjáms-Saga* is a folktale about vengeance for a father's death, ending with Brjám becoming king. It was collected in Iceland from an old woman, Hildur Arngrímsdóttir, in 1707.

3. Mills's study of Saxo's narrative was part of a paper given at an Aberystwyth/Swansea colloquium, and not published. His exile-and-return approach is published in "Structure and Meaning in *Guy of Warwick*," where the Anglo-Norman *Romance of Horn*, *King Horn*, and *Beues of Hamtoun* are also discussed.

4. Kölbing, *Romance of Sir Beues of Hamtoun*, 14. The text quoted here is the Manchester text.

5. Dr. Davidson told me this personally.

6. See Davidson, *Saxo Grammaticus*, 91–92. The shield of Aeneas appears at the end of book 8, *The Aeneid*.

7. See Davidson, "Loki and Saxo's Hamlet."

8. See Davidson, *Saxo Grammaticus*, 1:68. Hansen, 129–30, asks why, if Fengi only needs an attractive girl for his trap, he chooses one who will owe loyalty to Amleth. He also points out that Saxo the moralist makes no comment on the sexual encounter involving foster siblings.

9. Fisher's translation in Davidson, *Saxo Grammaticus*, 1:84.

10. For Belleforest's version see Gollancz, *Sources of Hamlet*, 166–310 (in parallel edition with *The Hystorie of Hamblet*). The quotation is from page 200.

11. Saxo's book was known in Shakespeare's England, but there is no evidence that Shakespeare, or the author of the lost Hamlet play—his probable chief source—consulted Saxo. They are more likely to have read Belleforest. (See Hansen 67, 177.) The earlier dramatist (Thomas Kyd?) will have made some of the alterations transforming the Saxo/Belleforest material into a play. (See Hansen 66–91, for a discussion of this transformation.)

12. For my full discussion of Shakespeare's play, see *Magical Thought in Creative Writing*, 115–24. While my methods of analysis and discussion have altered greatly since that publication, my view of the play has not radically changed.

Bibliography

Adams, Alison, and T. D. Hemming. "Le Fin du *Tristan* de Béroul." *Le Moyen Age* 79 (1973): 449–68.
Archibald, Elizabeth. "The Flight from Incest: Two Late Classical Precursors of the Constance Theme." *The Chaucer Review* 20, no. 4 (1986): 259–72.
Bal, Mieke. *Narratology: Introduction to the Theory of Narrative*. Trans. Christine van Boheemen. 2d rev. ed. Toronto: University of Toronto Press, 1985.
Bédier. Joseph. *Le Roman de Tristan par Thomas*. 2 vols. Société des Anciens Textes Français. Paris: Librarie de Firmin Didot et cie., 1902, 1905.
Bersani, Leo. *A Future for Astyanax*. Boston: Little, Brown, 1978; London: Boyars, 1978.
Best, R. I., and Osborn Bergin. *Lebor na Huidre: Book of the Dun Cow*. Dublin: Published for the Royal Irish Academy, 1929.
Bouchard, Constance B. "The Possible Nonexistence of Thomas, Author of *Tristan and Isolde*." *Modern Philology* 79 (August 1981): 66–72.
Bratton, J. S. *The Impact of Victorian Children's Fiction*. London: Croom Helm, 1981.
Brewer, Derek. *Symbolic Stories: Traditional Narratives of the Family Drama in English Literature*. Cambridge: D. S. Brewer, 1980. Reprint, London, 1988.
Brewer, Elisabeth. *From Cuchulainn to Gawain: Sources and Analogues of "Sir Gawain and the Green Knight."* Cambridge: D. S. Brewer, 1973.
Brock, Edmund, ed. "The Life of Constance from the Anglo-Norman Chronicle of Nicholas Trivet." In *Originals and Analogues of some of Chaucer's Canterbury Tales*, pt. 1. London: Published for the Chaucer Society by N. Trübner, 1872.
Brook, G. L., and R. F. Leslie. *Laʒamon: "Brut."* Early English Text Society. London: Oxford University Press, 1963.
Bruce, J. D. *The Evolution of the Arthurian Romance from the Beginning Down to the Year 1300*. 2 vols. Baltimore, 1928. Reprint, Gloucester, Mass.: Peter Smith, 1958.
Bryan, W. F., and Germaine Dempster. *Sources and Analogues of Chaucer's "Canterbury Tales."* Chicago: University of Chicago Press, 1941.

Buchanan, Alice. "The Irish Framework of *Sir Gawain and the Green Knight.*" *PMLA* 47 (1932): 315–38.
Bullough, Geoffrey. *Narrative and Dramatic Sources of Shakespeare*. Vol. 7. London: Routledge and Kegan Paul, 1973; New York: Columbia University Press, 1973.
Burgess, Glyn S., and Keith Busby, trans. *The Lais of Marie de France*. Harmondsworth, Eng.: Penguin Books, 1986.
Burton, Julie. "Folktale, Romance and Shakespeare." In *Studies in Medieval English Romances: Some New Approaches*, edited by Derek Brewer. Cambridge: D. S. Brewer, 1988.
Burton, Sir Richard, trans. *Il Pentamerone, or the Tale of Tales, a Translation from Giovanni Batiste Basile*. 1893. New York: Boni and Liveright, 1927.
Bußmann, Hadumod. *Eilhart von Oberge: "Tristrant."* Synoptischer Druck der ergänzten Fragmente mit der gesamten Parallelüberlieferung, vol. 1. Tübingen: Niemeyer, 1969.
Carney, James. *Studies in Irish Literature and History*. Dublin: Dublin Institute of Advanced Studies, 1955.
Chaucer Society. "King Offa's intercepted letters and banisht Queen." In *Originals and Analogues of Some of Chaucer's Canterbury Tales*, pt. 1. London: N. Trübner, 1872.
Chickering, Howell. "The Literary Magic of 'Wið Færstice.'" *Viator* 2 (1971): 83–104.
Closs, A., ed. *Tristan und Isolt*. Oxford: Basil Blackwell, 1958.
Commelin, Jerome. "Galfredi Monumetensis: Historiæ Regum Britanniæ." In *Rerum Britannicarum, id est Angliæ, Scotiæ, vicinarumque insularum ac regionum Scriptores Vetustiores ac Præcipvi*. Heidelberg, 1587.
Cook, Elizabeth. *The Ordinary and the Fabulous*. Cambridge: Cambridge University Press, 1969.
Cox, Marian Roalfe. *Cinderella: Three Hundred and Forty-five Variants of Cinderella, Catskin and Cap o' Rushes, Abstracted and Tabulated*, with a discussion of medieval analogues and notes. London: David Nutt for the Folklore Society, 1893. Reprint, Nendeln, Liechtenstein, Kraus Reprint Ltd., 1967.
Culler, Jonathan. *Literary Theory*. Oxford: Oxford University Press, 1997.
Davidson, Hilda Ellis. "Enter Fairy Godmother." *Signal: Approaches to Children's Books* 66 (September 1991): 171–78.
———. "Loki and Saxo's Hamlet." In *The Fool and the Trickster*, edited by Paul V. A. Williams, 3–17. Cambridge: D. S. Brewer, 1979.
Davidson, Hilda Ellis, ed. *Saxo Grammaticus: The History of the Danes*. 2 vols. Cambridge: D. S. Brewer, 1979.
Delarue, Paul, and Marie-Louise Tenèze. *Le Conte Populaire Français*. Vol. 2. Paris: Editions G.-P. Maisonneuve et Larose, 1963.
Dobbie, E.V.K., ed. *The Anglo-Saxon Minor Poems*. Anglo-Saxon Poetic Records, vol. 6. New York: Columbia University Press, 1942.
Donovan, Mortimer J. "Breton Lays." In *A Manual of the Writings in Middle English, 1050–1500*, edited by J. Burke Severs, 133–43. New Haven: The Connecticut Academy of Arts and Sciences, 1967.

Dundes, Alan. "'To Love My Father All': A Psychoanalytic Study of the Folktale Source of *King Lear*." In *Cinderella: A Casebook*, edited by Alan Dundes. New York: Garland Publishing, 1982. Reprint, Madison: University of Wisconsin Press, 1988.

Dunn, Charles W. "Romances Derived from English Legends." In *A Manual of the Writings in Middle English, 1050–1500*, edited by J. Burke Severs, 17–37. New Haven: The Connecticut Academy of Arts and Sciences, 1967.

Ellis, John M. *One Fairy Story Too Many: The Brothers Grimm and Their Tales*. Chicago: University of Chicago Press, 1983.

Evans-Pritchard, E. E. *Witchcraft, Oracles and Magic among the Azande*. Oxford: Clarendon Press, 1937.

Ewert, Alfred, ed. *Marie de France: Lais*. Oxford: Basil Blackwell, 1965.

———. *The Romance of Tristran by Beroul*. Oxford: Basil Blackwell, 1953.

Fedrick, Alan S. *The Romance of Tristan by Beroul*. Harmondsworth, Eng.: Penguin Books, 1970.

Fenster, Thelma S. "Beaumanoir's *La Manekine*: Kin D(r)ead: Incest, Doubling, and Death." *American Imago* 39 (1982): 41–58.

Folk-Lore. A Quarterly Review of Myth, Tradition, Institution, and Custom. Vol. 1. London: David Nutt, 1890.

Forster, Margaret. *Daphne du Maurier*. London: Chatto and Windus, 1993.

French, W. H., and C. B. Hale, eds. *Middle English Metrical Romances*. New York: Russell and Russell, 1930; reissued 1964.

Frétigny, Roger, and André Virel. *L'Imagerie Mentale*. Geneva: Ed. du Mont-Blanc, 1968.

Freud, Sigmund. "Inhibitions, Symptoms and Anxiety." The Pelican Freud Library, vol. 10, 237–333. Harmondsworth, Eng.: Pelican Books, 1979.

———. "The Uncanny." The Pelican Freud Library, vol. 14, 339–76. Harmondsworth, Eng.: Pelican Books, 1985.

Gallais, Pierre. *Genèse du Roman Occidental: Essais sur Tristan et Iseut et son Modèle Persan*. Paris: Éditions Tête de Feuilles et Éditions du Sirac, 1974.

Gantz, Jeffrey. *Early Irish Myths and Sagas*. Harmondsworth, Eng.: Penguin Books, 1981.

Ganz, Peter, ed. *Gottfried von Straßburg: "Tristan."* Wiesbaden: F. A. Brockhaus, 1978.

Gollancz, Israel, ed. *Hamlet in Iceland*. London: David Nutt, 1898.

———. *The Sources of "Hamlet."* London: Humphrey Milford and Oxford University Press, 1926.

Goody, Jack. *The Myth of the Bagre*. Oxford: Clarendon Press, 1972.

Gordon, R. K. *Anglo-Saxon Poetry*. London: J. M. Dent, 1926.

Griscom, Acton, ed. *The Historia Regum Britanniae of Geoffrey of Monmouth*. London: Longmans, 1929.

Guerin, Wilfred L., et al. *A Handbook of Critical Approaches to Literature*. 4th ed. Oxford: Oxford University Press, 1999.

Hales, John W., and Frederick J. Furnivall, eds. *Bishop Percy's Folio Manuscript*. 3 vols. London: N. Trübner, 1868.

Hall, Joseph, ed. *King Horn*. Oxford: Oxford University Press, 1901.
Hansen, William F. *Saxo Grammaticus and the Life of Hamlet*. Lincoln: University of Nebraska Press, 1983.
Hatto, A. T., trans. *Gottfried von Strassburg: Tristan*. With the surviving fragments of the Tristran of Thomas. Harmondsworth, Eng.: Penguin Books, 1960.
Henderson, George, ed. and trans. *Fled Bricrend: Bricriu's Feast*. Dublin: Irish Texts Society, 1899.
Herrtage, Sydney J. H., ed. *The Early English Versions of the "Gesta Romanorum."* Early English Text Society. London: N. Trübner, 1879.
Holland, Norman N. *The Shakespearian Imagination*. Bloomington: Indiana University Press, 1968.
Hunter, G. K., ed. *King Lear*. Harmondsworth, Eng.: New Penguin Shakespeare, 1972.
Jacobs, Joseph. *English Fairy Tales*. London: David Nutt, 1890.
Johnston, R. C., and D.D.R. Owen, eds. *Two Old French Gauvain Romances*. Edinburgh: Scottish Academic Press, 1972.
Jones, Ernest. *Hamlet and Oedipus*. Garden City, N.Y.: Doubleday Anchor, 1949.
Jones, Richard M. *The New Psychology of Dreaming*. 1970. Reprint, Harmondsworth, Eng.: Penguin Books, 1978.
Jones, Robert Ellis, trans. *Welsh Manuscript No. LXI of Jesus College, Oxford*. In *The Historia Regum Britanniae of Geoffrey of Monmouth*, edited by Acton Griscom. London: Longmans, 1929.
Kirk, G. S. *The Nature of Greek Myths*. Harmondsworth, Eng.: Penguin Books, 1974.
Kittredge, G. L. *A Study of "Gawain and the Green Knight."* Cambridge, Mass.: Harvard University Press, 1916. Reprint, Gloucester, Mass.: Peter Smith, 1960.
Kölbing, Eugen, ed. *Die nordische Version der Tristan Sage: Tristrams Saga ok Ísöndar*. 1878. Reprint, Hildesheim: Georg Olms Verlag, 1978.
———. *The Romance of Sir Beues of Hamtoun*. Edited from six manuscripts and the old printed copy, Early English Text Society Extra Series 46, 48, 65. London: Kegan Paul, Trench, Trübner, 1885, 1886, 1894.
Kurvinen, Auvo. "Sir Gawain and the Carl of Carlisle in Two Versions." *Annales Academiae Scientiarum Fennicae*. Ser. B, no. 71, 80–104. Helsinki, 1951.
Laing, David, ed. *Early Popular Poetry of Scotland and the Northern Border*. 1822, 1826. Revised by W. Carew Hazlett, London: Reeves and Turner, 1895.
Lang, Andrew, ed. *The Blue Fairy Book*. London: Longmans, 1889. New ed., New York: Longmans, 1948.
———. *Perrault's Popular Tales*. Oxford: Clarendon Press, 1888.
Laplanche, J., and J. B. Pontalis. *The Language of Psychoanalysis*. London: Karnac Books and the Institute of Psychoanalysis, 1988.
Leake Day, Mildred, ed. and trans. *The Rise of Gawain, Nephew of Arthur (De ortu Waluuanii nepotis Arturi)*. New York: Garland Library of Medieval Literature, 1984.

———. *The Story of Meriadoc, King of Cambria (Historia Meriadoci Regis Cambrie)*. New York: Garland Library of Medieval Literature, 1988.
Lévi-Strauss, Claude. *The Raw and the Cooked (Mythologiques 1: Le cru et le cuit)*. Paris: Librairie Plon, 1964. Translation by John and Doreen Weightman. London: Jonathan Cape, 1970; Harmondsworth, Eng.: Penguin Books, 1986.
Lewis, C. S. *An Experiment in Criticism*. Cambridge: Cambridge University Press, 1961.
Liberman, Anatoly, ed. *Vladimir Propp: Theory and History of Folklore*. Minneapolis: University of Minnesota Press, 1984; Manchester, Eng.: Manchester University Press, 1984.
Lichtenstein, Franz, ed. *Eilhart von Oberge*. Strassburg: Karl J. Trübner, 1877.
Loomis, Gertrude Schoepperle. *Tristan and Isolt*. 1913. 2d ed., New York: Burt Franklin, 1970.
Loomis, R. S. "The Visit to the Perilous Castle: A Study of the Arthurian Modifications of an Irish Theme." *PMLA* 48 (1933): 1000–1035.
Macaulay, G. C., ed. *The English Works of John Gower*. 2 vols. Early English Text Society Extra Series, nos. 81–82. London: Kegan Paul, Trench, Trübner, 1900–1901.
Martin, Wallace. *Recent Theories of Narrative*. Ithaca: Cornell University Press, 1986.
McKnight, George H., ed. *King Horn, Floris and Blauncheflur, The Assumption of our Lady*. Early English Text Society. London: Trübner, 1866. 2d ed., Oxford University Press, 1962.
Mead, George Herbert. *Mind, Self and Society: From the Standpoint of a Social Behaviorist*. Chicago: University of Chicago Press, 1934.
Meyer, Kuno. "The Edinburgh Version of the *Cennach ind Rúanado*." *Revue Celtique* 14 (1893): 450–59.
Mills, Maldwyn, ed. *Six Middle English Romances*. London: J. M. Dent, 1973.
———. "Structure and Meaning in *Guy of Warwick*." In *From Medieval to Medievalism,* edited by John Simons (Insights). Basingstoke, Hants., U.K.: Macmillan, 1992.
Murray, Gilbert. "Hamlet and Orestes." In *The Classical Tradition in Poetry*, by Gilbert Murray. Cambridge, Mass.: Harvard University Press, 1927.
O'Keefe, Daniel Lawrence. *Stolen Lightning: The Social Theory of Magic*. Oxford: Martin Robertson, 1982.
Ortoli, J. B. Frederic. *Les Contes Populaires de l'Ile de Corse*. Paris: Maisonneuve et cie., 1883.
Owen, D.D.R. *Chrétien de Troyes: Arthurian Romances*. London: J. M. Dent, 1987.
———. "Parallel Readings with *Sir Gawain and the Green Knight*." In *Two Old French Gauvain Romances,* edited by R. C. Johnston and D.D.R. Owen, 159–208. Edinburgh: Scottish Academic Press, 1972.

Panzer, Friedrich, ed. *Die Kinder- und Hausmärchen der Brüder Grimm; Vollständige Ausgabe in der Urfassung.* Wiesbaden: Emil Vollmer Verlag, 1953.
Paris, Matthew. *Vita Offae Primi.* In *Matthaei Paris Historia Major et Duorum Offarum Merciorum Regum,* edited by William Wats. London, 1684.
Pearsall, Derek. "The Development of Middle English Romance." In *Studies in Medieval English Romances: Some New Approaches,* edited by Derek Brewer. Cambridge: D. S. Brewer, 1988.
Perrett, Wilfred. *The Story of King Lear from Geoffrey of Monmouth to Shakespeare.* Palaestra 35. Berlin: Mayer and Müller, 1904.
Pfaff, Fridrich. *"Tristrant und Isalde": Prosaroman des Fünfzehnten Jahrhunderts. Bibliothek des Litterarischen Vereins in Stuttgart,* no. 152, 1–236. Tübingen: Gedruckt auf Kosten des Litterarischen Vereins, 1881.
Propp, Vladimir. *Morphology of the Folktale.* 2d ed. Austin: University of Texas Press, 1968.
Ramsey, Lee C. *Chivalric Romances: Popular Literature in Medieval England.* Bloomington: Indiana University Press, 1983.
Reclam. *Brüder Grimm: Kinder- und Hausmärchen.* 3 vols. Stuttgart: Philipp Reclam jun., 1980.
Reid, T.B.W., ed. *Yvain (Le Chevalier au Lion).* Manchester, Eng.: Manchester University Press, 1942.
Religious Tract Society. *Our Sister May or Number One.* London: The Religious Tract Society, n.d.
Renier, Anne. "Christoph von Schmid's 'The Basket of Flowers.'" *Signal: Approaches to Children's Books,* 7 (January 1972): Supplement 1.
Review Celtique. Publiée avec le concours de principaux savants des Iles Britanniques et du continent, et dirigée par H. Gaidoz. Vol. 3. London: Trübner, 1876–78.
Rickert, Edith, ed. *The Romance of Emaré.* Early English Text Society Extra Series 99. London: Kegan Paul, Trench, Trübner, 1908.
Robinson, F. N., ed. *The Works of Geoffrey Chaucer.* 2d ed. London: Oxford University Press, 1957.
Róheim, Géza. *Magic and Schizophrenia.* Posthumously ed. by Warner Muensterberger. New York: International Universities Press, 1955. Reprint, Bloomington: Indiana University Press, 1962.
Rougemont, D. de. *L'Amour et l'Occident.* Paris: Librairie Plan, 1972.
Russell, John. *Hamlet and Narcissus.* London: Associated University Press, 1995.
Sands, Donald B. *Middle English Verse Romances.* Exeter: University of Exeter, 1986.
Schach, Paul. *The Saga of Tristram and Ísönd.* Lincoln: University of Nebraska Press, 1973.
Schlauch, Margaret. *Chaucer's Constance and Accused Queens.* New York: New York University Press, 1927.
Schmid, Christoph von. *Das Blumenkörbchen.* In Christoph von Schmid, *Gesammelte Schriften,* Bd. 6, Regensburg: G. J. Manz, n.d.

Schmidt, A.V.C., and Nicolas Jacobs, eds. *Medieval English Romances*. London: Hodder and Stoughton, 1980.
Sébillot, Paul. *Littérature Orale de la Haute-Bretagne*. Paris: Maisonneuve et cie., 1881.
Severs, J. Burke, ed. *A Manual of the Writings in Middle English, 1050–1500*. New Haven: The Connecticut Academy of Arts and Sciences, 1967.
Shéaghdha, Nessa Ní, ed. *Tóruigheacht Dhiarmada agus Ghráinne: The Pursuit of Diarmaid and Gráinne*. Dublin: Irish Texts Society, 1967.
Slotkin, Edgar M. "The structure of *Fled Bricrenn* before and after the *Lebor na hUidre* interpolations." *Ériu* 29 (1978): 64–77.
Stimming, Albert, ed. *Der anglonormannische Boeve de Haumtone*. Halle: Biblioteca Normannica 7, 1899.
Suchier, Hermann, ed. "La Manekine." In *Oeuvres Poétiques de Philippe de Remi, Sire de Beaumanoir*, vol. 1. Société des Anciens Textes Français. Paris: Librairie de Firmin Didot et cie., 1884.
Thomas, J. W., trans. *Eilhart von Oberge's "Tristrant."* Lincoln: University of Nebraska Press, 1978.
Thomas, Keith. *Religion and the Decline of Magic*. London: Weidenfeld and Nicolson, 1971. Reprint, Harmondsworth, Eng.: Penguin Books, 1973.
Weingartner, Russell, ed. and trans. *"Graelent" and "Guingamor": Two Breton Lays*. New York: Garland Library of Medieval Literature, 1985.
Weston, Jessie L. *From Ritual to Romance*. 1920. Reprint, New York: Doubleday Anchor, 1957.
Weston, L.M.C. "The Language of Magic in Two Old English Metrical Charms." *Neuphilologische Mitteilungen* (Bulletin of the Modern Language Society of Helsinki), no. 86, 1985.
Wetherell, Elizabeth (Susan Warner). *The Wide, Wide World*. 1850, 3 vols. London: Scott, 1900.
Whitteridge, Gweneth. "The *Tristan* of Béroul." In *Medieval Miscellany Presented to Eugène Vinaver*. Manchester, Eng.: Manchester University Press, 1965.
Wilson, Anne. *The Magical Quest*. Manchester: Manchester University Press, 1988.
———. *Magical Thought in Creative Writing*. Stroud, Eng.: The Thimble Press, 1983.
———. *Traditional Romance and Tale*. Ipswich, Eng.: D. S. Brewer, 1976.
Wind, Bartina H. *Les Fragments du Roman de Tristan*. Geneva: Librairie Droz, 1960.
Winfrey, Lewis Edgar. "Kaherdin and Camille: The Sources of Eilhart's *Tristrant*." *Modern Philology* 25 (1928): 257–67.
Wright, Neil, ed. *Bern, Burgerbibliothek, MS. 568. The Historia Regum Britannie of Geoffrey of Monmouth*. Vol. 1. Cambridge: D. S. Brewer, 1984.

Index of Texts

Allerleirauh, 80–81
Ambales Saga, 142, 145, 147, 221n.2
Apollonius of Tyre texts, xiv, 23, 24, 31, 46, 72, 75, 78, 79

Basket of Flowers, The, 30, 58–61, 214–15n.12; chart 7 (165–67)
Belleforest's translation of Saxo Grammaticus, 147. See also *Hystorie of Hamblet*
Beroul's *Tristran,* 9, 117, 119–24, 135, 137–38, 139, 141; chart 17 (194–97)
Bevis of Hampton, xiv–xv, 42–47, 142–44, 150; chart 4 (156–58). See also chart 21 (208–10)
Bricriu's Feast, 107, 109, 112–15, 219n.6
Brjáms-Saga, 142, 145, 147, 221n.2

Cambridge fragment, *Tristran,* 135–37; chart 18 (198–201)
Cap o'Rushes stories, xiv, 71, 83–96, 97, 100; Corsican version influenced by Shakespeare, 217–18n.6. See also *Pouilleuse, La*
Carle off Carlile, xiv, 107–12, 116; chart 15 (186–89)
Catskin stories, 70, 71, 80–81, 83, 97. See also *Allerleirauh; Peau d'Anon, La;* Perrault's *Peau d'Ane*
Cendrouse, La, 102–3
Chapbook *Tristrant,* 124, 128–30, 133
Chevalier à l'Epée, Le, 107, 115–16
Chrétien de Troyes's *Yvain,* 19, 21, 23, 24, 30, 219nn.4, 5. For Chrétien, see also *Lancelot; Perceval*
Cinderella stories, 30, 71, 97–103, 106. See also *Cendrouse, La;* Perrault's version; *Rashin Coatie*
Commelin's edition of Geoffrey of Monmouth, 91–92
Constance, Life of (Trivet), 81–82, 83

Diarmaid and Gráinne, The Pursuit of, 117, 138–41; chart 19 (202–3)

Eilhart von Oberge's *Tristrant,* 9, 26–28, 29, 117–31, 133, 135–38, 139; chart 16 (190–93)
Emaré, 34, 70–75, 76, 78, 80; chart 8 (168–69)

Geoffrey of Monmouth's King Lear story, 83–84, 90–96, 142; chart 13 (178)
Gesta Romanorum King Lear story, 90, 92, 95; chart 13 (181)
Gilla decair, In, 22–23
Goose-Girl, The, 71, 103–5, 218n.6; chart 14 (184–85)
Gottfried von Strassburg's *Tristan,* 9, 25–26, 31, 117, 124, 130–33, 135–37
Graelent, 214n.9
Guy of Warwick, 46

Hartmann von Aue's *Iwein,* 21, 24
Holinshed's King Lear story, 90, 92, 95; chart 13 (181)

Hystorie of Hamblet (1608 translation of Belleforest), 147

Jane Eyre, 65, 69

King Horn, 17–19, 24, 38, 42–43, 44–45, 50, 56
King Lear stories, xiv, 71, 83–84, 90–96. See also Geoffrey of Monmouth; *Gesta Romanorum;* Holinshed; *King Leir* (the old play); Laȝamon; Shakespeare's play; Welsh chronicle version
King Leir (the old play), 90–91, 92, 93–94, 97; chart 13 (180)

Lady of the Fountain (Ywain), 19–21, 22–23, 24, 38, 50. See also Chrétien de Troyes's *Yvain;* Hartmann von Aue's *Iwein*
Lancelot of Chrétien de Troyes, 115
Lanval, 30, 47–50; chart 5 (159–60)
Laȝamon's King Lear story, 90, 92; chart 13 (179)

Manekine, La, 70, 75–76, 77, 78; chart 9 (170–71)
Mädchen ohne Hände, Das, 76, 77–78, 216n.8
Man of Law's Tale, xiv, 70, 71, 81–82
Martin's dreams, 13–15, 17
Meriadoc, The Story of, xiv–xv, 29, 30, 31, 50–58, 106, 142–44, 150; chart 6 (161–64). See also chart 21 (208–10)

Offa I, Life of, 70, 78–79; chart 11 (174–75)

Peau d'Anon, La, 71, 80–81, 83; chart 12 (176–77)
Penta the Handless, 70, 76–77; chart 10 (172–73)
Perceval (Le Conte du Graal) of Chrétien de Troyes, 23, 24, 115, 117

Perrault's *Peau d'Ane*, 80–81
Perrault's version of Cinderella, 100, 101
Pouilleuse, La, 88–90

Rashin Coatie, 71, 97–101, 106
Rebecca, 30, 65–69
Rise of Gawain, The, 50, 214n.11
Roswall and Lillian, 71, 103–5; chart 14 (182–83)

Saxo Grammaticus's Amleth story, xiv–xv, 4, 30, 42, 142–50; chart 20 (204–7). See also chart 21 (208–10); chart 22 (149)
Shakespeare's *Hamlet*, xiv–xv, 4, 142, 150
Shakespeare's *King Lear*, 42, 91, 92–93, 94–95, 97, 213n.2; chart 13 (181)
Sir Degarré, 34–41, 56; chart 3 (152–55)
Sir Degree (Percy's Folio Manuscript), 34–41; chart 3 (152–55)
Sir Gawain and the Green Knight, xiii, xiv, 23, 24, 25, 29, 107, 111, 117, 139, 193
Sir Launfal, 47, 49; chart 5 (159–60)
Syre Gawene and the Carle of Carelyle, xiv, 107–12, 116; chart 15 (186–89)

Thompson's translation of Geoffrey of Monmouth, 91, 92; chart 13 (178)
Tristan, Tristran, Tristrant. See Beroul; Cambridge fragment; Chapbook *Tristrant;* Eilhart von Oberge; Gottfried von Strassburg
Tristrams saga ok Ísöndar, 9, 25–26, 117, 133–37; chart 18 (198–201)

Ugly Duckling, The, 71, 105–6

Welsh chronicle King Lear story, 90, 92; chart 13 (179)
Wide, Wide World, The, 30, 61–65
Wið Færstice, 11–13, 15
Wuthering Heights, 24, 213n.23

Ywain. See Lady of the Fountain

Index of the Methodology

Characters, inexplicable behavior of, 2, 25, 27, 30–31, 46–47, 50–55, 66, 76, 79, 80–81, 148
Conflicting themes, 1–2, 21, 25, 28–30, 47–50, 62–64, 145–48
Contradiction, 2, 27–28, 29, 51–55; moral contradiction, 2, 25, 30, 62–64

Defended narrative, xiv, 24–28, 56–57, 108, 110–12, 118–19, 128, 140–41; charts 16 (190–93), 17 (194–97), 19 (202–3)
Disguise, 50, 112
Dream, 5, 13–15, 17

Exile and return approach, 42–46, 142–44; chart 21 (208–10)
Exorcism, 18–21, 22, 24, 31, 64–65, 103, 105

Family drama criticism, 35–37
Freud, Anna, 7
Freud, Sigmund, 8, 211n.11. *See also* Psychoanalysis

Hero, heroine, the single point of view, 4–5, 9, 17, 22, 39, 61, 64, 70, 75, 78, 101

Incongruity, 2, 27–28, 46–47, 143
Indications of a magical plot, initial signs, 28–32, 33–34, 37–38, 46–47, 49–50, 55, 58–59, 64–65, 66–67, 101, 108, 110–11, 118–19, 145–48

Irrational (nonrational), xi, 1–3, 3–4, 24–25, 28–29, 31–32, 37, 38, 65, 106

Logical problems in texts, xi, 1–2, 28–31, 37–38; impenetrable illogicality, 2, 29, 51–52, 108, 145–46. *See also* Characters, inexplicable behaviour of; Conflicting themes; Contradiction; Incongruity; Indications of a magical plot

Magic, as an investment of power, xii, 9–11, 13, 33, 101, 102, 112; as a system of thought, xii, 4, 9–11, 13–15, 23, 31–32, 33, 45–46, 61, 105–6, 148–50
Magic, general theory, 5–8
Magical plot, magical narrative, 8–10, 23–25, 29–30, 64, 66, 78, 79, 105. *See also* Defended narrative; Purification plot; Sovereignty plot
Magical text, xii, 8–10, 11–13, 23–24, 28–32, 101
Magic formula, 22–23
Model, working with models, 17–19, 21–22, 23–25, 38, 42, 49–50, 110–11, 117, 118–19, 150
Moral contradiction. *See under* Contradiction
Moral themes, xi, 2, 10, 21, 29, 30. *See also* Moral contradiction
Move, 17–21, 39–41, 45–46, 49–50, 60–61, 64–65
Myth, 4, 15–16

234 · Index of the Methodology

Narratology, 4
New criticism, 4
Nonrational *See* Irrational

Overlay (superstructure, additional level of thought), xi, xiv, xv, 1–2, 4, 10, 21, 29–30, 47–50, 55, 61–65, 66, 144–48, 150

Propp, Vladimir, 3, 16, 19, 43, 46, 143, 212n.20
Psychoanalysis, psychoanalytic criticism, xii–xiii, 3–4, 7–8, 37
Purification plot, xiv, 24, 58–60, 70, 72–74, 75–78, 78–79, 80–81, 150; chart 22 (149); charts 7–12 (165–77)

Rationalization: author's, 2, 21, 29, 31, 52, 55, 64, 121, 133; critic's, 2, 26–27, 29, 37, 38, 107–8; translator's, 29
Ritual punishment, 22, 24, 45–46, 47, 60, 75–76, 78, 79, 80, 104
Ritual reversal, 19, 20, 44–45, 46, 150
Ritual separation, 31, 39–40, 45–46, 47, 64, 72, 75, 76, 78–79, 80

Sovereignty plot, xiv, 17–21, 24, 38, 45–46, 56, 103; charts 1 (18), 2 (20), 3–6 (152–64)
Superstructure. *See* Overlay

Talisman, 59, 74–75, 81

Anne Wilson is Honorary Fellow in the Institute for Advanced Research in Arts and Social Sciences at the University of Birmingham, U.K. An independent scholar, she has engaged in cross-disciplinary research into European medieval literature, spending more than twenty years in hitherto unexplored areas significant for literature well beyond the medieval.